HITLER'S ELITE

HITLER'S
ELITE

THE SS 1939–45

EDITED BY
CHRIS McNAB

First published in Great Britain in 2013 by Osprey Publishing,
PO Box 883, Oxford, OX1 9PL, UK
PO Box 3985, New York, NY 10185-3985, USA

E-mail: info@ospreypublishing.com

Osprey Publishing is part of the Osprey Group

A CIP catalogue record for this book is available from the British Library

ISBN: 978 1 78200 088 4
E-pub ISBN: 978 1 47280 645 1
PDF ISBN: 978 1 47280 644 4

Page design by Myriam Bell Design, UK
Index by Alan Thatcher
Typeset in Bembo and Conduit ITC
Originated by PDQ Digital Media Solutions, Sufolk
Printed in China through Worldprint

13 14 15 16 17 18   10 9 8 7 6 5 4 3 2 1

Osprey Publishing is supporting the Woodland Trust, the UK's leading woodland conservation charity, by funding the dedication of trees.

www.ospreypublishing.com

EDITOR'S NOTE:

This work is a compilation of several Osprey books, in particular the mini-series on the Waffen-SS written by Gordon Williamson for Osprey's Men-at-Arms series, Men-at-Arms 266 *The Allgemeine-SS* by Robin Lumsden and Warrior 2 *Waffen-SS Soldier* by Bruce Quarrie. All Osprey books used in the compilation are listed below:

CAM 159 *Stalingrad 1942*, Peter Antil
ELI 11 *Ardennes 1944: Peiper & Skorzeny*, Jean-Paul Pallud
ELI 157 *The German Home Front 1939–45*, Brian Davis
ELI 177 *German Special Forces of World War II*, Gordon Williamson
MAA 34 *The Waffen-SS*, Martin Windrow
MAA 124 *German Commanders of World War II*, Anthony Kemp
MAA 220 *The SA 1921–45: Hitler's Stormtroopers*, David Littlejohn
MAA 266 *The Allgemeine-SS*, Robin Lumsden
MAA 363 *Germany's Eastern Front Allies (2): Baltic Forces*, Carlos Caballero Jurado and Nigel Thomas
MAA 401 *The Waffen-SS (1): 1. to 5. Divisions*, Gordon Williamson
MAA 404 *The Waffen-SS (2): 6. to 10. Divisions*, Gordon Williamson
MAA 415 *The Waffen-SS (3): 11. to 23. Divisions*, Gordon Williamson
MAA 420 *The Waffen-SS (4): 24. to 38. Divisions, & Volunteer Legions*, Gordon Williamson
MAA 434 *World War II German Police Units*, Gordon Williamson
RAID 9 *Rescuing Mussolini: Gran Sasso 1943*, Robert Forczyk
WAR 2 *Waffen-SS Soldier*, Bruce Quarrie
WAR 46 *Panzer Crewman 1939–45*, Gordon Williamson
WAR 61 *German Security and Police Soldier 1939–45*, Gordon Williamson
WAR 93 *German Infantryman (3): Eastern Front 1943–45*, David Westwood
WAR 102 *The Hitler Youth 1933–45*, Alan Dearn

IMAGE RIGHTS:

Front cover: The Nazi death head.
Back cover: 'Sepp' Dietrich inspects SS troops in France 1940. (Cody Images)
Unless otherwise stated, all the images in this book are courtesy of Cody Images

CONTENTS

OCT 2013

INTRODUCTION: ORIGINS AND EVOLUTION OF THE SS

LEFT: Hitler and Röhm march side by side at a rally in 1931, surrounded by men of the Sturmabteilung (SA). The SA would become something of an embarrassment and threat to Hitler, resulting in the 1934 'Blood Purge'.

IN 1919, ADOLF HITLER JOINED THE TINY GERMAN DEUTSCHE ARBEITERPARTEI (DAP; German Workers Party) in Munich, becoming its leader the following year and adding 'National Socialist' to its title. It was an infamous moment in 20th-century history, as the Nationalsozialistische Deutsche Arbeiterpartei (NSDAP), popularly known as the Nazi Party, was born.

Hitler's fiery brand of politics had found an opportune moment to flower. After four years of appalling slaughter, Germany had been defeated decisively in 1918. Kaiser Wilhelm II abdicated just days before the Armistice was signed and a left-wing government took over the country. This new government was obliged to sign what many Germans, at least, perceived to be an unfair *Diktat* masquerading as a peace settlement. The Treaty of Versailles that formally brought the war to an end was a controversial settlement, and a catalyst for future conflict. The treaty laid the blame for starting the war squarely upon Germany, saddled it with enormous reparations payments and also took away large areas of German territory, in many cases creating new states.

All of these considerations would have a bearing on the later outbreak of World War II, although in all probability the failure to implement the treaty adequately was as serious a factor as its provisions. Of particular significance also was the fact that the government that signed the humiliating treaty found itself being blamed for doing so, when in reality it had little choice. The Social Democrats were also criticized for the German capitulation – many right-wingers and particularly the army considered that the German people had not been defeated, but rather had been 'stabbed in the back' by the government. This myth gained widespread credence in Germany during the inter-war years, and Hitler more than capitalized upon the grievance.

In the early years after the war, Germany suffered along with most of the continent and political extremism was rife. The new German republic was established in the small town of Weimar, later to become famous for its proximity to the Buchenwald concentration camp. Hence this period of German history, the first ever of genuine German democracy, is known as the Weimar Republic. Weimar was chosen in preference to Berlin as the site of the new government because of Berlin's associations with Prussian militarism.

Berlin itself was a testing place to be in the early years after World War I, and politics was a thuggish affair. The Weimar government was assailed from both sides of the political spectrum. Extremists fought in many large German cities and occasional attempts were made by left and right to overthrow the government; the insurrection led by Wolfgang Kapp (known as the 'Kapp Putsch') in March 1920 was one of the most serious. The constitutional system that underpinned the Weimar government also complicated matters. The system was so representative of political opinion that it produced only minority governments or fragile coalitions that had little opportunity to achieve anything. Meanwhile, international tensions rose when Germany suspended its reparations payments, as a result of which the French, eager to draw every pfennig from the Germans, occupied the Ruhr region in 1923. These international concerns were exacerbated by soaring inflation, with the German mark being traded at 10,000 million to the pound.

Amidst all this social, economic and political turbulence, one radical among many was making a name for himself. Adolf Hitler, an Austrian by birth, had served in the German Army throughout World War I. In 1923 Hitler, who had become leader of the NSDAP by virtue of his personal dynamism and skills of oratory, organized his first clumsy attempt to seize power. However, the Munich Putsch, on 9 November 1923, was a failure and earned him five years in Landsberg prison.

Despite the sentence, Hitler served only nine months in rather plush conditions. The authorities, many of whom had some sympathy for Hitler's position, were persuaded to release him early, after Hitler temporarily resigned the leadership of the Nazi Party and agreed to refrain from addressing public meetings on political issues. However, Hitler neatly circumvented these restrictions by moving his meetings into the private homes of his wealthier supporters.

While Hitler was in jail, dictating his memoirs and thoughts, later to be published as *Mein Kampf*, the situation in Germany improved considerably. A new scheme, the Dawes Plan, was accepted to reschedule Germany's repayments, which now reflected more closely Germany's ability to pay. It also allowed Germany to borrow substantially, mainly from the United States, and fuelled a brief flurry of credit-induced economic prosperity. Germany later ratified a more comprehensive restructuring of the payments in the Young Plan, which further improved her economic situation.

Similarly, the efforts of a new Chancellor, Gustav Stresemann, led to Germany entering the League of Nations in 1926 and signing the Treaty of Locarno with Britain and France, which helped to thaw the international situation. This treaty confirmed the existing borders of the participating states of Western Europe. The prevailing feeling of reconciliation appeared to usher in a more constructive period of international relations. Importantly, however, Locarno failed to guarantee the frontiers of Germany in the east, suggesting to many in Germany that the Western powers would not be as concerned if Germany were to attempt to reclaim lost territory there. Unfortunately, the improvements in Germany's position by 1929 were undone totally by an unforeseen event that would have tremendous ramifications for the world at large. On 29 October 1929 came the Wall Street crash. The immediate effect was that all the American loans that had been artificially buoying up the world economy were recalled. The broader effects on the global economy were dramatic enough, but Germany, whose tenuous economic recovery had been sustained by extensive borrowing from the United States,

was among the hardest hit. This new round of economic hardship gave Hitler another opportunity to make political capital, and he seized it with both hands.

Political violence on the streets of German cities characterized the years between 1929 and 1933 as Nazi fought communist and Germany's economy laboured under the pressures of worldwide recession and reparations. It was Hitler and the Nazis who promised a brighter future for Germany, and on 29 January 1933, the President of the German Republic, Paul von Beneckendorff und von Hindenburg, appointed Adolf Hitler as Chancellor of Germany. In the elections of the following March, the Nazi Party received 44 per cent of all votes cast. Even in the overly representational system of the Weimar Republic, this was still sufficient to give the Nazis 288 out of the 647 seats in the Reichstag. Hitler made ample use of his position, passing various 'Enabling Laws' to make himself effectively a legal dictator.

Once Hitler took power, he began immediately to destroy the old structures of society and rebuild them in the mode of National Socialism. All political parties other than the Nazi Party were banned. Progressively, Jews were excluded from society and publicly shunned, culminating in the anti-Jewish pogrom of *Kristallnacht* in 1938 when Jewish property was vandalized. Concentration camps were also opened for 'undesirables' where hard labour was the order of the day – the extermination role of these camps was as yet in the future. Hitler attempted to get Germans back to work with an ambitious programme of public works, the planning and construction of the *Autobahnen* being the most famous. Hitler also presided over a massive rearmament effort, creating a Wehrmacht (armed forces) that was one of the most professional and well equipped in the world, and ready for war.

During Hitler's ascent to power, all political parties had strong-arm squads to protect their meetings from disruption by rivals, and the NSDAP was no exception. In August 1921, ex-naval Lieutenant Hans Ulrich Klintzsch took command of the NSDAP's 'Defence and Propaganda Troop' which, the following month, was renamed the Sturmabteilung (SA; Storm Detachment). The SA was essentially a uniformed political thuggery, and that November it had its 'baptism of fire' when the communists attempted to break up a Nazi meeting in the Hofbrauhaus in Munich; although outnumbered, the SA gave their adversaries a bloody nose.

LEFT: Early National Socialist paramilitaries. Here we see, from left to right, a Freikorps trooper, a squad leader from the Stosstrupp *Adolf Hitler* and an SS-Mann, c. 1925. The central figure depicts Karl Fiehler, one of the founder members of the Stosstrupp *Adolf Hitler*, carrying the Imperial War Flag as he appeared at the 'German Day' rally in Bayreuth on 2 September 1923. His uniform is basically Reichswehr in character, but features an early hand-made *Kampfbinde* of the NSDAP on the left sleeve, and a Prussian-style *Totenkopf* and national cockade on the Austrian army-pattern cap. By the end of 1925, SS men were wearing the recently adopted plain brownshirt uniform of the SA, but with several distinctive accoutrements. The SS was now set apart not only by the *Totenkopf* but also by black képis, black ties, black borders to the swastika armband and, more gradually, black breeches. The truncheon was frequently used against political opponents in the street battles of the time. (Osprey Publishing © Paul Hannon)

Adolf Hitler

DEUTSCHLAND

ERWACHE

Expansion brought new levels of organization. In 1922 the NSDAP created a youth section (Jugendbund) for males between the ages of 14 and 18 years. It was sub-divided into two age groups, the elder of which, for 16- to 18-year-olds and titled Jungsturm *Adolf Hitler* (Youth Assault Force Adolf Hitler), was in effect a junior SA. Its successor, the Hitlerjugend (Hitler Youth), remained under SA command until May 1932.

Originally confined to Munich, the SA made its first important sally outside that city when, on 14–15 October 1922, it took part in a 'German Day' at Coburg, which resulted in a pitched battle with the communists who held sway there. The 'Battle of Coburg' succeeded in breaking the hold of the Red Front in the city, and the press coverage which this incident achieved served to make Hitler's name known to a wider public.

The first 'national' rally of the NSDAP was held on 28 January 1923 when some 6,000 SA men paraded before Hitler, who presented *Standarten* (standards) to four recently formed SA units: München, München II, Nürnberg and Landshut. A *Sturmfahne* ('battle flag') was, at the same time, conferred upon an SA company from Zwickau – the first SA unit to be formed outside Bavaria. On 1 March 1923, SA Regiment München was formed. In the same month, command of the SA passed to Hermann Göring after Klintzsch, a member of Korvettenkapitän Hermann Ehrhardt's Freikorps (Free Corps), was recalled by his chief following a quarrel between Ehrhardt and Hitler over their differing reactions to French occupation of the Ruhr. Göring brought with him the prestige of a hero of World War I, but was, by nature, indolent and self-indulgent. The true moving force behind the SA was Ernst Röhm, a staff officer at army headquarters in Munich. It was Röhm who persuaded the military to supply the SA with arms, thus transforming it into one among several *Wehrverbände* (officially tolerated 'armed groups' who were without exception anti-communist).

In September 1923 Hitler succeeded in creating a *Kampfbund* (fighting union) of some 70,000 men, mainly SA but also Bund *Oberland* (a Freikorps unit) and Reichs-Kriegsflagge (an armed formation commanded by Röhm). On 9 November 1923, as noted above, Hitler attempted to use this force to overthrow the Munich government. The badly planned, badly executed operation ended in humiliating defeat. The police opened fire on the demonstrators, killing 16 and wounding many more. Hitler was arrested; Göring, wounded, escaped to Austria. The SA was banned; those of its leaders who managed to avoid arrest fled to other German states where Bavarian law could not touch them. Hitler was given a five-year prison sentence but was released under an amnesty in December 1924. Röhm, protected by his army masters, received nothing worse than a 'severe reprimand'.

The failure of the putsch, far from destroying the SA, served rather to spread it to other German regions. Refugees from Munich set up clandestine SA units under the name Frontbann. Hitler did not fail to draw the correct conclusions from this disaster.

Symbols of new power. A standard bearer of the *Leibstandarte Adolf Hitler* carries a *Feldzeichen* standard, topped with a metal eagle and wreathed swastika. Note the gorget and bandolier of the standard bearer.

Armed insurrection against a government that commands the loyalty of the police and army is foredoomed. Henceforth he would employ only legal methods.

When the SA was re-activated in February 1925, Hitler categorically forbade it to bear arms or function as any form of private army. The days of the SA as a *Wehrverband* were over. Its purpose was to clear the streets of his political enemies. Hitler's view of the SA's role was hotly contested by Röhm, who envisaged it as a citizens' army, part of Germany's secret re-armament. The disagreement between the two became so bitter that Röhm resigned from the Party in April and in 1928 quit Germany for a military adviser's post in Bolivia. The SA remained without an overall command (its various units each being accountable to their area Gauleiter (regional party leader) until November 1926, when Hitler named himself Oberste SA Führer (Supreme SA Leader). The actual executive leadership was vested in the Chef des Stabes (Chief of Staff). This post was entrusted to a prominent Freikorps leader, Franz Felix Pfeffer von Salomon, who set about organizing the SA along military lines. It was now formed into:

Gruppen (the smallest units)
Standarten (regiments)
Trupps (roughly platoons)
Brigaden (brigades)
Stürme (roughly companies)
Gaustürme (roughly divisions)
A Gausturm corresponded exactly to an NSDAP Gau (region).

In August 1927, the SA numbered some 30,000 men. Two years later that strength had doubled. In 1930 a Motor SA was established to give greater mobility and allow a quick mustering of strength. Despite his success in expanding the SA and increasing its efficiency, Pfeffer ceased to enjoy Hitler's confidence. It became apparent that Pfeffer's concept of the SA differed little from that of Röhm. Hitler discovered that Pfeffer had been secretly attempting to involve the army in the paramilitary training of the SA. In August 1930 Hitler dismissed Pfeffer and telegraphed Röhm in Bolivia asking him to return and take charge of the SA. Röhm was back in Germany before Christmas and officially assumed duty as Chef des Stabes on 5 January 1931. He revised the structure of the SA, now dividing it into:

RIGHT: Pre-war black service uniforms. 1: SS-Schütze, *Leibstandarte SS Adolf Hitler*, 1934. A private in pre-war parade and guard dress. 2: SS-Oberscharführer, SS-Standarte *Deutschland*, 1934. He wears the black service dress with Gothic script 'Deutschland' cuffband, and the Standarte identifying number '1' alongside the runes on his right collar patch. 3: SS-Hauptsturmführer, SS-Totenkopf Standarte *Oberbayern*, 1936. This captain's officer-quality black service dress tunic has the collar and collar patches edged with silver twist cord. (Osprey Publishing © Stephen Andrew)

Scharen (the former Gruppen)

Trupps

Stürme

Sturmbanne

Standarten

Untergruppen (the former Gaustürme)

Gruppen

Under Pfeffer the highest SA formation, the Gausturm, had been subordinate to the Party leadership; but the new Gruppe had no NSDAP counterpart as it extended over several *Gaue,* and its leader (Gruppenführer) was thus answerable only to Röhm or, of course, to Hitler himself.

On 17/18 October 1931 a 'token mobilization' of the Nazis' forces took place in the town of Brunswick, with around 104,000 uniformed participants. It was an impressive display of strength, but its very success alarmed the Weimar authorities. In December they imposed a ban on the wearing of *all* political uniforms. This proscription remained in force until the following June, by which time it had been demonstrated to have had little practical effect. The Nazis simply adopted a civilian 'uniform' of white shirt and black tie, and carried on as before.

In July 1932 Röhm created a yet larger SA agglomerate – the Obergruppe – of which there were, at this stage, five. The SA now dominated the streets, disrupting the meetings of its rivals, and terrorizing its opponents. Without actually challenging the government to a head-on confrontation, Hitler was able to blackmail and intimidate it with the size and discipline of his brown-shirted army.

On 30 January 1933, as a result of a combination of victory at the polls and backstairs intrigues, Hitler was appointed Chancellor (Prime Minister) of Germany. The burning of the Reichstag building the following month was blamed on the communists and used as the pretext for pushing through an enabling law which gave Hitler virtually dictatorial powers. Göring, Minister of the Interior for Prussia, authorized the SA to act as a police auxiliary and to sweep all 'enemies of the state' into concentration camps.

At the Party Day of Victory at Nuremberg that September, some 120,000 uniformed men participated. Röhm was made a member of the Reichs cabinet as Minister without Portfolio. The number of SA Obergruppen had increased to ten by January 1934. But time was running out for the SA's most celebrated Chief of Staff. Röhm made no attempt to conceal his differences with Hitler over the role of the SA: an advocate of 'the second revolution', he wished to transform it into an armed force to supplement, even replace, the regular army.

Hitler, on the contrary, felt that the SA had already fulfilled its task of crushing its political opponents and now, with its rowdy behaviour, was becoming something of an embarrassment. He already looked ahead to a future war of conquest for which a fully professional army was essential. The army, for its part, regarded the SA with undisguised contempt as 'brown scum', and was eager to co-operate with Hitler in expansion and re-armament. Recklessly foolhardy, or naive to an incredible degree, Röhm continued publicly to voice his criticisms of his leader and to back them with scarcely veiled threats. The SA was now set to clash with another paramilitary body that had emerged from the roots of the NSDAP.

HITLER'S BODYGUARD

By the time it paraded before Hitler at the first national rally of the NSDAP in January 1923 the SA numbered 6,000 men in four regiments, and there were sufficient recruits during the next month alone to form a fifth. Frustrated by Röhm's continued ambition and independence despite Göring's leadership, which were upheld by the former leaders of the Freikorps, Hitler was compelled to set up a small troop of men from outside the SA which would be entirely devoted to him alone. Thus the SS was born.

In March 1923 Hitler ordered the formation of the Munich-based bodyguard known as the Stabswache, whose members swore an oath of loyalty to him personally. Two months later, to avoid confusion with an SA unit of the same name which protected Röhm and Göring, the Stabswache was renamed the Stosstrupp *Adolf Hitler* and, like the German Army shock troops of World War I, it adopted the death's head as its distinctive emblem. The Stosstrupp *Adolf Hitler* was led by Julius Schreck and Josef Berchtold, and its membership included Josef 'Sepp' Dietrich, Rudolf Hess, Julius Schaub, Ulrich Graf and Karl Fiehler. The 30-man squad participated in the ill-fated Munich Putsch on 9 November 1923 – during the episode Graf saved the Führer's life, so fulfilling the primary duty of the Stosstrupp. He was later rewarded with the title 'des

Heinrich Himmler, although a physically weak and militarily uncertain man, combined driving ambition with administrative acumen. Himmler was arguably the true architect of the Holocaust, putting in place the entire system of extermination and concentration camps.

Führers alter Begleiter', or 'The Führer's Senior Bodyguard', and his bravery that day left a lasting impression on Hitler.

On his release from prison in December 1924, Hitler began to rebuild his party, and to continue his attempts to reign in the SA. In April 1925, therefore, Hitler formed a new bodyguard commanded by Schaub, Schreck and his other Stosstrupp favourites. The guard, which still came under the auspices of the SA High Command, was known first as the Schutzkommando (Protection Command), then as the Sturmstaffel (Assault Squadron), but on 9 November it adopted the title of Schutzstaffel or Protection Squad, soon commonly abbreviated to SS.

From the start it was laid down that the SS, unlike the SA, should never become a mass organization. Groups of Ten, or Zehnerstaffeln, were set up across Germany so that the Führer could have access to a local SS bodyguard wherever he went during his political campaigning. Applicants had to be between 25 and 35 years of age, have two sponsors, be registered with the police as residents of five years' standing, and be sober, disciplined, strong and healthy. The seeds of elitism were sown. Yet despite the gradual extension of its numbers and prestige, the SS remained a limited organization subordinated to the SA. The latter kept a jealous eye on SS expansion, and local SA commanders consistently used the SS under their control for the most demeaning tasks such as distributing propaganda leaflets and recruiting subscribers to the party newspaper, the *Völkischer Beobachter*. By the end of 1928 morale in the SS was at an all-time low.

The watershed in the development of the SS can be traced to a single date – 6 January 1929. On that fateful day Heinrich Himmler took command of the organization at a time when the SA was becoming increasingly rebellious. From then on, SS progress became bound up with the career of Himmler, who obtained one important post after another; indeed, by 1945 he had concentrated more power in his hands than any other man except Hitler. In April 1929 Himmler received approval for a recruiting plan designed to create a truly elite

LEFT: A Hauptsturmführer of the *Leibstandarte Adolf Hitler*, Röhm Purge, 30 June 1934. Typifying the Hollywood stereotype of an SS officer, this captain clasping a 9mm P 08 Luger is dressed in the all-black uniform which would later be reserved for ceremonial duties, and was shared (with different insignia) by members of the Allgemeine-SS. For headgear he wears the smart service dress cap (*Tellermütze*) with SS-pattern eagle and the *Totenkopf* device that was shared with personnel of the army Panzertruppen. (Osprey Publishing © Jeffrey Burn)

A soldier of the LSSAH stands in a Czech town in 1939. Civilian populations in occupied territories quickly learned to fear the SS, an organization with an ideological as well as military agenda.

body out of the SS; and by 1930 it had grown to a force of 2,000 men. When the SA in northern Germany rebelled against the bourgeois NSDAP hierarchy in 1931, only the SS remained loyal to Hitler. The revolt collapsed, and Himmler was rewarded with his appointment as security chief of the NSDAP headquarters in Munich. In effect, he was made head of the party police.

Less than a month after Hitler became Chancellor the Reichstag building was burned to the ground, and the blame put on the communists. Hitler immediately gave police powers to 25,000 SA but also 15,000 SS men, who began to arrest left-wing opponents of the new regime in large numbers and herd them into makeshift prisons and camps. While the SS was consolidating its position and controlling its membership and recruitment by a constant purging process, the SA began to throw its weight about noisily. Now Hitler decided to act.

Matters came to a head in the spring of 1934, when Hitler learned that Röhm was secretly arming his Staff Guards, something he had expressly forbidden. During June the SA was ordered to take a month's leave. On 30 June Hitler cut down its entire leadership in a single decisive blow, using the SS as the tool of destruction. Dozens of SA men (and others) were shot dead by SS squads working from death lists prepared by Hitler and Göring. Röhm was arrested and, in prison, offered the chance to shoot himself. When he refused, he was shot through the window of his cell by his SS guard.

Hitler now declared the 200,000-strong SS an independent formation of the NSDAP and removed it completely from SA control. Its ascendancy was now assured; and it entered a period of consolidation during which it developed a new command structure and organization under Himmler, whose rank as Reichsführer-SS for the first time actually meant what it implied and made him directly subordinate to Hitler. From the middle of 1934 the traditional non-military SS, the backbone of the organisation, began to be known as the Allgemeine-SS (General SS) to distinguish it from the newly developing armed branches.

Although the SS was now clearly in the ascendancy, the SA continued to exist. In Röhm's place Hitler appointed a loyal but colourless SA Obergruppenführer, Viktor Lutze, like all previous incumbents of the post a former army officer. Lutze had to preside over the emasculation of the SA. On 20 July 1934 the SS, until this time subordinate to the SA Supreme Command, was granted its independence. The Motor SA was hived off and amalgamated with its 'junior partner' the Nationalsozialistisches Kraftfahrkorps (NSKK; National Socialist Motor Corps) to become a separate body. The Flieger SA (Airborne SA) was integrated into the Deutscher Luftsportverband (German Air Sport Association), while the SA Feldjägerkorps was incorporated into the Prussian Police. The ten SA Obergruppen were abolished (although the rank Obergruppenführer was retained), the largest SA formation now being the Gruppe.

Despite these amputations and revisions, the numerical strength of the SA continued to grow. Thirty-six new Standarten were created in 1935, a further 25 in 1936, 30 in 1937 and 42 in 1938. Although membership was, as before, voluntary, there can be little doubt that many joined out of opportunism, since job prospects or advancement often depended on evidence of Nazi affiliation. What now was to be the function of the SA? The leadership had no clear answer. The most favoured solution was that it should act as a sort of paramilitary sports club providing both physical and martial training although without, in the case of the latter, the actual use of arms. The SA might practise throwing grenades – but only wooden dummies. A secondary task was to assist in the dissemination of Nazi propaganda and to furnish – as it did dramatically each year at Nuremberg – a physical manifestation of the power and authority of the state. The role of the SA as a preparatory school for the

SA troopers on parade at Nuremberg in 1934. The 'Blood Purge' of 1934, in which the SS beheaded the SA leadership, secured an already growing enmity between the two organizations.

armed forces was established only in January 1939 with the creation of the SA Wehrmannschaften (SA Military Units).

In May 1943 Lutze was killed in a motor accident and was succeeded by Wilhelm Schepmann. When the Volkssturm was formed in October 1944 Schepmann was appointed its Director of Rifle Training, while Franz Pfeffer re-emerged from obscurity to take command of a Volkssturm brigade on the quiet Swiss border.

ROLE OF THE SS

The period 1934–39 saw the expanding SS take over responsibility for political police work, and it extended its tentacles into many other areas of Party and government function. By the outbreak of war it would have been impossible to define exactly the role within the German state of this huge organization. Apart from direct powers, the SS employed a system of granting SS rank to functionaries in many governmental and semi-governmental bureaux and institutions, extending *de facto* SS influence over areas in which the organization had no powers *de jure*. For the purposes of this book the armed SS troops – initially SS-Verfügungstruppen (SS-VT; SS Dispositional Troops) and from 1940 Waffen-SS (explored in greater depth in later chapters) – may be treated as a distinct part of the Reichsführer's complex empire. Readers new to this subject may find it helpful to remember that during World War II the black-uniformed SS men beloved of Hollywood drama were in fact simply the Allgemeine-SS, whose function was mainly political and bureaucratic rather than executive. The 'teeth' arms of the NSDAP were the grey-uniformed Sicherheitsdienst (SD; Security Service) security police, the plain clothes Gestapo secret police, and the grey-uniformed military units of the Waffen-SS.

The first and foremost duty of the SS was the protection of Adolf Hitler. After the advent of the *Leibstandarte* (see below), however, whose members worked full-time to a rota and accompanied Hitler on his journeys through the Reich, the part-time SS men who had originally been recruited on a local basis to protect the Führer during his trips around Germany found that aspect of their work taken from them. Consequently, it was decided that as of 1934 the main day-to-day function of these highly disciplined Allgemeine-SS volunteers would be to support the police in maintaining public order.

The SS rapidly expanded with the formation of many new Allgemeine-SS Standarten, trained and equipped to combat any internal uprising or counter-revolution. In such an event the SS would take over the operation of the post office, national radio network, public utilities and public transport, as well as acting as police reinforcements. The anticipated civil unrest never came about, and so the police duties of the Allgemeine-SS before the outbreak of war in 1939 were generally restricted to overseeing crowd control at party rallies and other celebrations, including national holidays and state visits of foreign dignitaries.

During World War II members of the Allgemeine-SS who had not been called up for military service took an active role in the war effort at home. In many cities special SS Wachkompanien (guard companies) and Alarmstürme (air raid alarm units) were

detailed to protect factories, bridges, roads and other strategic points, and to assist the Luftschutzwarndienst (LSW; Air Protection Warning Service or 'Luftschutz') during air raids. On the Reich's borders, SS men worked as Auxiliary Frontier Personnel in conjunction with the Customs Service. Others helped with the harvest, supervised foreign labourers, and engaged upon welfare work. During 1944–45 the cadres of the Allgemeine-SS throughout Germany were trained to co-ordinate the short-lived guerrilla fighting which took place against Allied troops.

Conditions of service in the SS highlighted the elite nature of the formation. Recruiting was tightly controlled, most young SS men after 1934 coming directly from the ranks of the Hitlerjugend. Out of every 100 applicants, only 10 to 15 were finally admitted. Selection was based on racial purity, good health and disciplined character. Training was carried out over a three-year period, with statutory breaks for obligatory service in the armed forces and in the Reichsarbeitsdienst (RAD; Reich Labour Service). The confirmed SS man remained in the active Allgemeine-SS until he was 35 years old, after which he could transfer to one of the SS reserve units. Promotion

April 1938, and SS-VT soldiers of the SS-Standarte 1/VT Deutschland stand watch over crowds on the streets of Innsbrück, Austria. The SS-VT gained some limited operational experience in Sudetenland, Austria and Czechoslovakia before World War II.

was awarded on merit, and a strict SS Legal Code and Discipline Code governed the behaviour of every SS member. Ultimately, SS men were answerable only to special SS and police courts for any crimes or offences they committed, and were, in effect, put above the normal jurisdiction of the civil courts.

Under Himmler, the SS came to regard itself not merely as a temporary political organization but as a 'Sippe', i.e. a tribe or clan. The same racial qualities looked for in the SS man were therefore also required of his wife. A special Marriage Order, dating from 1931, dictated that SS men had to seek permission to marry, and that the prospective wives had to undergo close scrutiny into their health, background and fertility. Christian weddings were replaced by neopagan rites for the Allgemeine-SS, and couples were expected to raise at least four children, either naturally or by adoption. A network of maternity homes administered by the SS Lebensborn Society was set up to assist in that goal.

THE SS IN GERMANY

The SS had a wide-ranging effect on all aspects of life in Nazi Germany. The racial policies of the Third Reich were put into operation through SS agencies, primarily the Reichskommissariat für die Festigung des deutschen Volkstums (RKFDV; The Reich Commission for the Consolidation of Germanism), which organized the resettlement of racial Germans in the occupied eastern territories. Another SS group, the Hauptamt Volksdeutsche Mittelstelle (VoMi; Main Welfare Office for Ethnic Germans), played a significant part in infiltrating racial German communities in Austria and Czechoslovakia during the late 1930s, ultimately paving the way for the Nazi occupation of these states. In an effort to prove the racial hypotheses of National Socialism by scientific means, Himmler also set up the Ahnenerbe, a body for the research of ancestral heritage. The SS duly carried out spurious archaeological excavations throughout Europe in the search for the origins of the Nordic race – an apparently innocent obsession which ultimately resulted in human experimentation using concentration camp inmates.

The concentration camp system also gave the SS access to an unlimited supply of cheap, expendable labour, which led to a thriving SS economy. Various manufacturing enterprises were set up in the camps, and workers leased out to private firms on subcontract. The acquisition of large fertile territories during the war greatly enlarged the scope of these activities. Farming and stockbreeding in Poland, and forestry, mining and fishing in Russia all entered the field of SS economics, and between 1941 and 1944 the SS exploited the wealth, resources and population of the conquered east on a massive scale. Himmler eventually controlled over 500 factories, producing, for example, 75 per cent of Germany's soft drinks and 95 per cent of the country's furniture. Most of the uniforms and equipment used by the Allgemeine-SS, Waffen-SS and police were manufactured in the concentration camps, alongside military armaments and leather goods. The SS ran quarries, brickworks, cement factories, bakeries, food research establishments and processing plants, a publishing house, a sword smithy and even a porcelain works. The sums which flowed into SS coffers as a result were vast, and helped to strengthen the Reichsführer's position and maintain the financial autonomy of his organization.

Through its industrial connections, the SS cultivated and recruited hundreds of company directors, businessmen and landowners. Many of these influential men became members of the Circle of Friends of the Reichsführer-SS, or SS Patron Members, and made regular donations to SS funds. In return, they secured the protection and favour of the Black Corps. By means of a conscious policy of infiltration, the SS thoroughly permeated every branch of official and semi-official German life. By May 1944 no fewer than 25 per cent of the leading personalities in Germany were members of the SS, some being regulars and others so-called 'Ehrenführer' or Honorary Officers. They included almost all of Hitler's immediate entourage, men in key party and government posts, top

A Waffen-SS squad on parade. Apart from the SS insignia, they are dressed little differently from regular army troops. Note the M1911 cartridge pouches on the waist; each pouch carried a clip of 7.92mm ammunition.

ABOVE: Officers of the early Waffen-SS, 1939–40. 1: SS-Sturmbannführer, SS-VT, seen wearing service dress in 1939. 2: SS-Brigadeführer und Generalmajor der Waffen-SS, late 1940. 3: SS-Hauptsturmführer of artillery, SS-Verfügungs Division, summer 1940. (Osprey Publishing © Jeffrey Burn)

civil servants, the leaders of local government, members of the military aristocracy, doctors, scientists and those prominent in the fields of culture and charitable works. After the failed plot to assassinate Hitler in July 1944, the SS finally overcame the last bastion of the old traditional Germany, the army; SS generals took over the Volkssturm (Home Army) and military administration, as well as the secret weapons programme. With its eyes clearly set on the future, the SS set out to control the education system at an early stage and with considerable success. The NPEA (Nationalpolitische Erziehungsanstalten – National Political Institutes of Education) schools, which existed to train the future elite of the party, fell under SS direction, as did the Nationalsozialistischer Deutscher Studentenbund (National Socialist Students' League) and the Nationalsozialistische Lehrerbund (National Socialist Teachers' Association). Above all, the Hitler Youth worked hand-in-glove with the SS so that their racial and political thinking could be transmitted to the young. Many of the uniform accoutrements and rituals of the Hitler Youth were copied directly from those of the SS.

A poster encouraging Waffen-SS recruitment. The double Sig-Rune 'lightning flashes' were introduced into the SS in 1933, and became the universal symbol of the SS organization as a whole.

WAFFEN-SS

Away from the commercial and racial interests of the Allgemeine-SS, at the outbreak of war the Waffen-SS was an insignificant force. Hitler's experience with the SA had taught him to be wary of private armies; and at this stage he was careful not to provoke the Wehrmacht leadership, who were jealous holders of their rights as 'sole bearers of arms' in the Reich. Waffen-SS participation in Poland in 1939 and the West in 1940 may be seen partly as a propaganda exercise mounted by Himmler to enhance the prestige of his corner of the Nazi state; the upper levels of the Third Reich were always to be characterized by viciously pursued personal and departmental rivalries. The failed chicken-farmer who now enjoyed awesome powers as Reichsführer-SS and national police overlord entertained hazy dreams of turning his hand-picked legion of racially and politically pure Aryan manhood into a sort of latter-day Order of the Teutonic Knights. Hitler saw the role of the SS as an elite and totally loyal political gendarmerie to control the Reich and the occupied territories. Both ambitions

WAFFEN-⚡⚡

EINTRITT NACH VOLLENDETEM 17. LEBENSJAHR

demanded that the Waffen-SS be given a chance to participate visibly in the Wehrmacht's victories. They were not expected to achieve much, but by 1939 they had been trained to a standard that made combat feasible. The ex-army general who served as Inspector of SS-Verfügungstruppen (SS-VT) from 1936 to 1939, Paul Hausser, had in fact achieved a great deal, and the military capabilities of the Waffen-SS probably owed more to him than to any other individual. A combination of rigid physical selection, extremely tough military training, ideological indoctrination and parade-ground spit-and-polish had produced, by summer 1939, the following units:

Leibstandarte Adolf Hitler (LSSAH) – A motorized infantry regiment of three battalions with integral light artillery, anti-tank and reconnaissance units. This premier Waffen-SS unit was commanded by Josef 'Sepp' Dietrich, Hitler's old comrade from the gutter-fighting days. 'LSSAH' provided a battalion for the Austrian *Anschluss* in 1938.

SS-Standarte 1 *Deutschland* – Similar composition but with four battalions. Took part in Sudetenland occupation of 1938.

SS-Standarte 2 *Germania* – Similar to LSSAH; took part in Austrian and Sudetenland occupations.

SS-Standarte 3 *Der Führer* – Composition and experience as *Germania*. (Note that officially these regiments dropped their numbers when awarded their honour titles; I have quoted both, for clarity.)

In addition to these SS–VT units, Himmler had at his disposal five regiments of Totenkopfwachsturmbanne (Death's Head Guard Units). These poor-quality units were internal security police and concentration camp guards, commanded by the head of the KL (Konzentrationslager – Concentration Camp) service, Theodor Eicke.

LSSAH and *Germania* fought in Poland in 1939 under 10. Armee and 14. Armee respectively, and *Deutschland* formed part of the so-called Panzerverband Ostpreussen (Armoured Unit East Prussia) or Panzer-Division *Kempf. Der Führer* was sent to defensive positions on the Westwall. All were pulled back for reorganization after the ceasefire. LSSAH remained an autonomous motorized regiment, but received generous allocations of new equipment. The other three regiments were gathered in October 1939 into a formation named by spring 1940 'SS-Verfügungs Division' (SS-V-Div), incorporating artillery and other supporting services.

The most interesting decision concerned the *Totenkopf* security units. The regiments served as occupation troops in Poland, but were then recalled; numbers of their personnel were assembled with other *Totenkopf* units, some SS-VT troops and Allgemeine-SS reservists into a field division – SS-*Totenkopf* Division (SS-T-Div) – under Eicke's command. This blurring of the distinction between SS combat troops and security police thus stemmed from the tight restriction on Waffen-SS recruiting: neither the Wehrmacht nor Hitler, for their own reasons, wanted Himmler creaming off too many good potential soldiers. As police overlord Himmler was able to recruit 'security personnel' without these restrictions, and by transferring *Totenkopf* men to the combat units and then replacing them by direct recruitment he had a neat back-door method of expanding his fighting units. Ten new *Totenkopf* regiments were put in hand in 1939–40.

The part played by the Waffen-SS in the West in 1940 was much photographed but of little military significance – they represented, after all, only two divisions and a regimental group, out of 89 divisions employed. The LSSAH and SS-V-Div fought well; the markedly inferior qualities of the SS-T-Div were underlined by heavy casualties. (The Le Paradis massacre of 97 British prisoners on 27 May 1940 was instigated by a *Totenkopf* officer hysterical over the losses suffered by his ill-trained men when taking the position.)

Both LSSAH and the SS-V-Div (now named *Das Reich*) used their excellent motorized elements to good effect in the lightning campaign in the Balkans in spring

Soldiers of the *Wiking* Division engage Red Army troops in southern Russia, 1941. At this point in its history, *Wiking* was a motorized division; the transport here is an SdKpz 232 radio command vehicle.

1941, and by the invasion of Russia in spring 1941 the former had been awarded divisional status in name, if not yet in physical fact. LSSAH served on the Leningrad Front in the far north. All served strictly under army tactical command – there was no question of anything approaching an 'SS Corps'. Hitler still regarded Himmler's military pretensions as slightly comical, but had no objection to his potential elite security forces being hardened in combat and adding some prestigious medals to their tunics. He had also allowed Himmler to expand the Waffen-SS slightly, although not at the cost of recruiting manpower better employed in the army: and the method he used was to prove highly significant.

He had scrambled together one more hand-dog formation of *Totenkopf* guards, grandiosely entitled SS-Division *Nord*, just before Operation *Barbarossa*. He retained under his ultimate control as police overlord another low-priority formation of former policemen, the *Polizei* Division, who saw some fighting in France and occupation duty in Poland, but who were neither nominally nor 'spritually' part of the Waffen-SS at this date – although the SS eagle they wore on their sleeves pointed the way. Far more important than either of these divisions was a new formation with the ringing title of SS-Division *Wiking*, which was to march into Russia under Heeresgruppe Süd (Army Group South): for about half its strength was composed not of SS men, nor even Germans, but of volunteer recruits from the occupied nations of Europe.

That recruits were forthcoming was hardly surprising. Overrun with bewildering speed only months before, the Western nations had yet to feel the full weight of Nazi brutality. It was too soon for significant resistance activities to provide a focus for patriotism. These countries already nourished genuinely populist anti-communist political movements, which provided recruiters with a good first harvest and a natural conduit for their fine rhetoric about the 'anti-Bolshevik crusade'. Large numbers of volunteers were found in 1940–41. Despite their emotive titles, however, it should be recalled that they always contained significant numbers of Germans, and as the war drew on they were used as repositories for all kinds of odd foreign renegades. Their courage won their occupied homelands no hint of political concession: their privileges were limited to dying as German cannon-fodder. Alongside the *Wiking* Division smaller volunteer 'legions' were raised for service in Russia, mostly with the army but some with the Waffen-SS from the outset.

The three classic Waffen-SS divisions and the new *Wiking* fought hard in Russia, earning an altogether more respectable reputation among their army comrades for

LEFT: The German conquest of Western Europe brought a new wave of recruits into the Allgemeine-SS. Here (from left to right) are Norwegian, Flemish and Dutch members of the SS. Note how the Germanic-SS in Norway evolved a very distinctive uniform with mountain cap, ski trousers and ankle boots. (Osprey Publishing © Paul Hannon)

steadiness in the face of grim conditions and high casualties; this reputation was not seriously impeded by the relatively poor showing of the *Polizei* Division and the disgrace of *Nord*. In spring 1942 the *Polizei* Division was taken into the Waffen-SS proper. At the same time another essentially foreign division was formed. The SS-Freiwilligen Division *Prinz Eugen* (SS-Volunteer Division *Prinz Eugen*) was recruited from 'ethnic Germans' in the old Austrian Empire, and was sent into action against the Yugoslav partisans in autumn 1942. That summer an eighth division appeared on the SS order of battle with the uprating to divisional status of the SS-Kavallerie Brigade – later, the 8. SS-Kavallerie Division *Florian Geyer*. This was originally one of three *Totenkopf* brigades (the other two being motorized infantry) which operated behind the Russian frontlines on security duty; these were under Himmler's control, being attached at need to the forces of local SS and police leaders. In time their regiments were gradually dribbled away as replacements for Waffen-SS field formations decimated in the campaigns of 1941–42.

Heinrich Himmler observes a Latvian SS formation conducting an exercise. Although Himmler made appearances amongst frontline combat units, he was ill-suited to actual tactical leadership.

In 1943 the picture changed dramatically. The army was discredited by defeat in Russia and Africa, and Hitler had been seduced at last by the appeal of Himmler's growing army of iron-hard SS formations. Hitler needed generals and divisions who won battles, and Paul Hausser's recapture of Kharkov with the SS armoured divisions had just given him his first victory for a long time. The Waffen-SS now underwent a rapid and enormous expansion, in which certain distinct elements may be traced. There were to be three new *Reichsdeutsche* (German citizens) armoured divisions to join the 'classic' divisions, whose armoured status was a fact long before their titles were officially changed to recognize their actual establishment. They would be joined by new formations of foreigners, formed around existing volunteer legions already serving in army or Waffen-SS uniform. Troops would be freed for the main fronts by passing anti-partisan duties to ever more bizarre foreign SS formations, such as the Muslim *Handschar* Division, which marked the total abandonment of the original racial limitations.

The proliferation and enlargement – on paper, at least – of foreign formations would continue until the end of the war. Between early 1943 and early 1945 the ostensible

A Latvian soldier undergoes training as an SS sniper. By June 1944, the expansion of the Waffen-SS had brought into being two Latvian divisions.

ARDENNES, 1944

This le. SPW SdKfz 250/7, manned by SS troopers during the Ardennes Offensive of winter 1944, was a mortar carrier subtype which mounted an 8cm GrW34 tube; it was issued to the fourth platoon of some PanzerAufklärungs Kompanie, to support the other platoons in action with fire from its mortar. (Osprey Publishing © D. Parker/ R. Volstad)

order of battle of the Waffen-SS rose to 38 divisions. Many of these were purely fictitious, in the sense that orders for their formation and deployment seldom reflect their actual available strength or combat readiness. Several nominal 'divisions' fielded no more than a few hundred ill-equipped men scrambled together from *Volksdeutsche* (ethnic Germans living outside Germany's borders), bewildered foreigners, Luftwaffe or Kriegsmarine personnel for whom there were no longer any aircraft, fuel or ships, and marginal categories of police or Allgemeine-SS reservists, perhaps stiffened by members of a Waffen-SS training school. Bizarre as some of these formations were, however, it must be remembered that the elite SS-Panzer and Panzergrenadier divisions represented

Waffen-SS Rank Insignia

Rank	Collar	Shoulder		Arm Combat dress
Reichsführer-SS (Heinrich Himmler)				
SS-Oberstgruppenführer (Colonel-General) 1942–5			SS-Obst. Gruf. to SS-Brigaf., shoulder strap cords gold & silver on silver-grey underlay; silver pips. Arm patches gold on black, silver pips.	
SS-Obergruppenführer (General) Until 1942				
SS-Obergruppenführer (General) 1942–5				
SS-Gruppenführer (Lieutenant-General) Until 1941				
SS-Gruppenführer (Lieutenant-General) 1942–5				
SS-Brigadeführer (Major-General) Until 1941				
SS-Brigadeführer (Major-General) 1942–5				
SS-Oberführer (Brigadier-General) Until 1941			SS-Oberf., silver cords on Waffenfarbe/black underlay, gold pips –'41, silver pips '42–'45. Arm patches green on black, all ranks from SS-Oberf. down.	
SS-Oberführer (Brigadier-General) 1942–5				
SS-Standartenführer (Colonel)			SS-Staf. to SS-Stubaf., shoulder strap cords silver on Waffenfarbe/black underlay, gold pips –'41, silver '42–'45.	
SS-Obersturmbannführer (Lieutenant-Colonel)				

Germany's most effective troops in the last stages of the war, setting a standard unsurpassed and seldom equalled among the forces of any other nation.

Exact figures will never be known, but the best estimates indicate that some 180,000 Waffen-SS soldiers were killed in action during the war, approximately 400,000 were wounded and probably another 40,000 or more were listed 'missing'. The entire establishment of the classic division – LSSAH, *Das Reich* and *Totenkopf* – were casualties several times over, so to speak, and the teenagers of the 12. Division *Hitlerjugend* were still full of aggressive spirit after suffering losses of 20 per cent dead and 40 per cent wounded in four weeks' continuous fighting in Normandy in the final stages of the war.

By the autumn of 1944, the SS had seized almost total political, military and economic control of Germany. At the beginning of 1945, however, Himmler failed in his post as military commander of two army groups on the Rhine and Vistula fronts, and even sought to negotiate a peace treaty with the Western Allies. Hitler dismissed him, replacing him as Reichsführer-SS by Karl Hanke. With the Führer's suicide on

SS soldiers stand to attention on parade, Munich 1935. In terms of their rise to power, the visual impact of the SS cannot be underestimated, as it separated them from the Wehrmacht.

30 April the Third Reich rapidly collapsed; and all factions of the Nazi regime were only too happy to heap the blame for their atrocities on the shoulders of the SS. The entire organization was declared criminal by the victors, and its members hunted down. Himmler and several of his generals took their own lives rather than face the ordeal of a trial and a certain death sentence. Lesser SS officers, COs and men simply melted into the background of post-war Germany, or fled abroad with the assistance of the secret ODESSA organization. Some used part of the estimated £900,000,000 worth of money and assets held by the SS in 1945 to establish commercial companies throughout the world, many of which are still in existence to this day.

Adolf Eichmann, a key architect of the Holocaust, fled to Argentina following the war. Here we see the Red Cross identity document he used to enter Argentina under the fake name Ricardo Klement in 1950. (Wiki commons)

THE ALLGEMEINE-SS AND THE NAZI POLICE STATE

LEFT: Reinhard Heydrich and Heinrich Himmler inspect an SS guard outside Prague castle in 1941. Heydrich acted as the chair at the Wannsee Conference of January 1942, during which the 'Final Solution to the Jewish Question' was implemented.

As the previous chapter outlined, the SS was really an organization of two halves. On one side was the Waffen-SS, a military wing that became a major component of Germany's land forces. On the other side was the Allgemeine-SS, a sprawling organization whose interests, as we have seen, pushed into many different areas of the German economy and society. In this chapter we will burrow a little deeper into the Allgemeine-SS, revealing its labyrinthine structure and some of its rites and symbolism. Most importantly, we will examine the SS as a police and security body. The fact was that the shadow of the Allgemeine-SS was long, dark and cold, and its reach fell well beyond the confines of Germany itself.

ORGANIZATION

The command structure of the Allgemeine-SS continually grew and developed during the 1930s. By 1942, subject to Himmler's controlling authority and that of his high command – the Reichsführung-SS – the day-to-day work of directing and administering the SS was carried out by eight main departments, or Hauptämter, as listed below.

HAUPTAMT PERSÖNLICHER STAB RFSS (PERS. STAB RFSS)

This was Himmler's personal staff and comprised the heads of the SS Hauptämter, certain specialist officials, and advisory or honorary officers. Its administrative work was processed through the Kommandostab RfSS (Command Staff RfSS), which operated during the war under the title Feldkommandostelle RfSS (Field Headquarters of the Reichsführer-SS). It was then organized like a military HQ, with a signals section, escort battalion and flak detachment, and accompanied Himmler on his tours of the occupied territories.

SS HAUPTAMT (SS-HA)

The SS Central Office was mainly responsible for recruitment and the maintenance of records on non-commissioned personnel.

SS FÜHRUNGSHAUPTAMT (SS-FHA)

The SS Operational Headquarters included as one of its main departments the Kommandoamt der Allgemeinen-SS (Allgemeine-SS HQ), and coordinated training, the payment of wages, the supply of equipment, arms, ammunition and vehicles and the maintenance and repair of stocks. It was also responsible for the transport of the SS and police, SS mail censorship, geology, war archives and dental and medical services.

REICHSSICHERHEITSHAUPTAMT (RSHA OR RSI-H)

The Reich Central Security Office was one of the most powerful bodies of the Third Reich. It controlled the security agencies of the Third Reich, including the Kripo, the Gestapo and the SD (see below). It was responsible for both foreign and domestic intelligence operations, espionage and counter-espionage, combating political and common law crime, and sounding out public opinion on the Nazi regime.

SS WIRTSCHAFTS- UND VERWALTUNGSHAUPTAMT (SSWVHA)

The SS Economic and Administrative Department controlled a large number of SS industrial and agricultural undertakings, carried out housing and construction programmes, administered the finances of the SS and ran the concentration camps.

RASSE- UND SIEDLUNGSHAUPTAMT (RUSHA)

The Race and Settlement Department looked after the racial purity of all SS members, issued lineage certificates, and was responsible for settling SS men, especially ex-servicemen, in the conquered eastern territories.

Bergen-Belsen concentration camp personnel stand trial in front of a British Military Tribunal in September 1945. In total, it is estimated that some 50,000 people – mostly Soviet POWs – died in the camp between 1941 and 1945.

HAUPTAMT SS-GERICHT (HA SS-GERICHT)

The SS Legal Department administered the disciplinary side of the special code of laws to which members of the SS and police were subject. It controlled the SS and police courts, and the penal camps to which convicted SS and police offenders were sent.

SS PERSONALHAUPTAMT (PERS.HA)

The SS Personnel Department dealt with personnel matters and kept records on SS officers.

On a level immediately below the SS Hauptämter were the Oberabschnitte (Oa.) or regions, the bases of the Allgemeine-SS territorial organization. Initially there were five Oberabschnitte, formed in 1932 from the existing SS Gruppen. By 1944 their number had risen to 17 within Germany proper, and each corresponded almost exactly to a Wehrkreis or military district (see below for a more detailed explanation of the Wehrkreis system). The SS regions were generally known by geographical names, but it was also customary to refer to them by the Roman numeral allocated to the corresponding Wehrkreis. In addition, six foreign Oberabschnitte evolved during the war in the occupied territories.

Each Oberabschnitt was commanded by an SS-Obergruppenführer, Gruppenführer or Brigadeführer designated Führer des Oberabschnittes (F.Oa.). He was usually also Himmler's representative at the military HQ of the local Wehrkreis and, in addition, held the post of Höhere SS- und Polizeiführer or HSSPf, the Higher SS & Police Leader in the Region. The Regional SS Headquarters was staffed by full-time officers, assisted by a number of voluntary part-time officials.

Every SS Oberabschnitt in turn comprised an average of three Abschnitte or districts, again distinguished by Roman numerals. They were also referred to by the name of the area they covered, or by the location of their headquarters. The Abschnitt commander, or Führer des Abschnittes (F.Ab.) was generally an officer of the rank of SS-Oberführer or Standartenführer. By 1944 there were 45 Abschnitte, with some large towns and cities being split between two of them.

The organization of the Allgemeine-SS below the level of the Abschnitt was on a unit rather than territorial basis to increase flexibility, although each unit was related to, or recruited from, a particular area. The typical Abschnitt controlled an average of three

LEFT: SA troops, 1928–33. 1: Gruppenführer, 1928 – a man of this rank had bright red collar patches with twin silver oak leaves. 2: Scharführer, Untergruppe *Hamburg*, 1932. A government ban on political uniform was imposed in December 1931, and rescinded six months later on condition that more respectable dress was adopted, seen here. 3: Oberscharführer, Gruppe *Nordmark*, 1933. In 1933 shoulder straps, worn on the right only, were introduced, and side panels in the Gruppe colour added to the képi. (Osprey Publishing © Ron Volstad)

Rather more resplendent than the original 'Stosstruppe', the 120-strong 'Stabwache' on the steps of Munich's Braunehause in 1930. They still wear brown shirts but uniformly black caps, ties, trousers and boots. Josef 'Sepp' Dietrich is third from the left, front row.

SS-Fuss-Standarten, the equivalent of foot or infantry regiments. As the name suggests, the Standarte was the standard unit of the Allgemeine-SS and had been firmly established as such by 1929, long before the SS regional system fully evolved. Prior to the war the average Fuss-Standarte comprised around 2,000 men, but numbers fell to around 1,600 in 1941, and as low as 400 in 1944, due to Allgemeine-SS members being drafted into the Wehrmacht and Waffen-SS. Each regiment was commanded by a Führer des Standartes (F.Sta.) who was assisted by a small staff and part-time HQ unit. Depending on unit size, the regimental commander could be an SS-Standartenführer, Obersturmbannführer or Sturmbannführer. By 1943 it was common for two of the smaller adjacent Standarten to be placed together under a single acting commander. Standarten were numbered consecutively from 1 to 126. A select few also bore the names of celebrated SS men who had died or been killed, and such honour titles were similarly extended to a number of Stürme within certain Standarten.

As well as the Fuss-Standarten, there were 22 Allgemeine-SS cavalry units of regimental size, the Reiterstandarten. Each comprised from five to eight Reiterstürme (cavalry companies), a Sanitätsreiterstaffel (cavalry medical squad) and a Trompeterkorps (trumpet corps). The Reiterstandarten were never concentrated in their HQ city, the component companies usually being dispersed amongst smaller towns of the Abschnitte. They were always essentially ceremonial in function, and were seldom if ever used to assist the Fuss-Standarten and police in domestic crowd control. The SS-Reiterstandarten were numbered from 1 to 22, each number being prefixed by the letter 'R' to distinguish them from the foot regiments. Many of their headquarters were sited in former garrison towns of imperial cavalry units, with excellent equestrian facilities.

After the outbreak of war in 1939, the majority of members of the Reiterstandarten were conscripted into army cavalry units, or into the hastily mustered SS-Totenkopfreiterstandarten for frontline service. In 1941 the latter amalgamated to form the Waffen-SS Kavallerie Brigade which by 1942 had expanded to become the SS-Kavallerie Division, named *Florian Geyer* in 1944 (see Chapter 4).

Each SS-Standarte was composed of three active Sturmbanne or battalions, one Reserve-Sturmbann for men between the ages of 35 and 45, and a Musikzug or

Men of the Stosstrupp *Adolf Hitler*, the seed of the future SS, seen here riding through the streets of Munich in the 1920s.

marching band. A Sturmbann was usually commanded by an SS-Sturmbannführer, assisted by an adjutant. The full peacetime strength of a Sturmbann ranged from 500 to 800 men and, since it was considered the basic tactical unit of the Allgemeine-SS, it was planned that the SS-Sturmbann would be able to operate as an independent entity in time of strife or revolt. The three active Sturmbanne of a Standarte were numbered in Roman numerals from I to III; e.g. the 3rd Sturmbann of the 41st Standarte was abbreviated 'III/41'. The Reserve-Sturmbann was distinguished by the prefix 'Res.', in this case 'Res./41'.

Each active Sturmbann was in turn composed of four Stürme or companies, a Sanitätsstaffel (medical squad) and a Spielmannzug (fife-and-drum corps). The full peacetime strength of a Sturm was 120 to 180 men, under an SS-Hauptsturmführer, Obersturmführer or Untersturmführer. During wartime one of the four Stürme served locally as a Wachkompanie or guard company protecting strategic points. Another stood by as a civil defence Alarmsturm for use during air raids, and the remaining two were assigned to general patrol duties. A Reserve-Sturmbann generally comprised two Reserve-Stürme, numbered 'Res.1' and 'Res.2', and a Reserve-Sanitätsstaffel.

Hitler and Ernst Röhm talk earnestly at a rally in the early 1930s. After Röhm's death, the SA would continue to exist and function, but in an emasculated version of its former self.

The burning of the Reichstag in 1933 – whatever the cause – gave Hitler the excuse to implement 'emergency' powers that made him the undisputed dictator of Germany. There remains some evidence that the SS were personally involved in the fire.

Within each Standarte, the four Stürme of Sturmbann I were numbered 1, 2, 3 and 4. Those of Sturmbann II were numbered 5, 6, 7 and 8 and those of Sturmbann III were numbered 9, 10, 11 and 12. Thus the 1st Sturm of the 2nd Sturmbann of the 3rd Standarte, i.e. the 5th Sturm in the 3rd Standarte, would be referred to within the Standarte as '5/11' and outside the Standarte as '5/3'. Every Sturm was divided into three or four Truppen (platoons), each composed of three Scharen (sections). A Schar generally numbered 10 to 15 men, and was used to patrol blocks of houses within cities and guard official buildings. The Schar itself comprised two or three Rotten (files), the smallest units of the Allgemeine-SS, numbering about five men. Depending on their size, Truppen and Scharen were commanded by NCOs of the ranks between SS-Hauptscharführer and Unterscharführer, while Rotten were led by experienced enlisted men known as Rottenführer.

SPECIALIST FORMATIONS

As we are already beginning to understand, the SS was a labyrinthine organization of many parts, and the Allgemeine-SS' organizational structure was dispersed further by various specialist formations. Each SS Oberabschnitt was assigned one Nachrichtensturmbann or signals battalion, responsible for SS communications in the region. These signals battalions were numbered from 1 to 19, in Arabic rather than Roman numerals, prefixed by the letters 'Na.'. Pioniersturmbanne or engineer battalions were again organic components of the Oberabschnitte, and were equipped to carry out emergency construction work such as road and bridge repairs, and maintenance of public utilities, including gas, electricity and water supplies. Each Pioniersturmbann was numbered consecutively from 1 to 16, prefixed by the letters 'Pi.'.

Health was a key ingredient of SS ideology, hence the Röntgensturmbann SS-HA, or SS Hauptamt X-Ray Battalion, was composed of 350 full-time SS men, and toured all the Allgemeine-SS Oberabschnitte carrying out routine health checks on SS personnel. It utilized portable X-ray equipment, and was primarily employed to detect pulmonary diseases among factory workers who were part-time SS members. The only unit of its kind, its services could be summoned in times of epidemic by any of the SDAP Gauleiters, and it also cooperated with local officials of the German Labour Front. During the war, the Röntgensturmbann was absorbed into the medical branch of the Waffen-SS.

In addition to the Sanitätsstaffel attached to every Sturmbann, each Abschnitt contained at least one Sanitätssturm or medical company. A group of several such Stürme, or a single large Sturm, was often termed a Sanitätsabteilung (medical detachment). These units were referred to by the Roman numeral of the Abschnitt in which they were located.

The SS-Fliegersturm (SS Flying Company) was formed in November 1931 at Munich and remained active until absorbed by the DLV, the forerunner of the Luftwaffe, in 1933. By that time there were several SS-Fliegerstaffeln. They were responsible for flying Hitler and other senior Nazis around Germany, during the formative period of the Third Reich.

What amounted to a military police force for the Allgemeine-SS was brought into being in 1935 with the creation of the SS-Streifendienst or patrol service. Its functions were policing the SS contingents at party rallies, checking SS documentation at transit points and the like, and rooting out any petty criminal elements in the organization. Streifendienst units were fairly small and mobile, and their members were specially selected from amongst the most reliable SS men. Whilst on duty they wore a gorget bearing the legend 'SS Streifendienst'.

OTHER SS FORMATIONS

In addition to the regular and specialist SS units, and the first-line reserve of those between the ages of 35 and 45, each Oberabschnitt also contained an independent Stammabteilung (Supplementary Reserve Detachment) composed partly of unfit or older men over the age of 45, and partly of younger men whose duties to the state or Party debarred them from taking an active part in the SS. For example, it was customary for full-time regular police officers to be assigned to a Stammabteilung upon receiving their SS membership. The Stammabteilung carried the name of the corresponding Oberabschnitt and was divided into Bezirke or sub-districts, each Bezirk working in conjunction with a Standarte and bearing the Arabic numeral of the latter. As their title indicated, these additional second-line reservists supplemented the rest of the Allgemeine-SS in the various functions where normal duty personnel and first-line reserves might be overstretched, as in the case of large national parades or celebrations. They were readily distinguishable by the reverse colour scheme employed on their uniform insignia, i.e. a light-grey background to collar patches and cuff titles with black or silver numbers and script. For a short time, members of the Stammabteilungen also wore light-grey rather than black borders on their armbands.

During the war SS-Helferinnen, or female SS auxiliaries, were recruited to replace male SS personnel who were more urgently needed at the front. Enrolment was on a voluntary basis, and applicants had to undergo a thorough medical examination and background investigation. Helferinnen were trained as teleprinter operators, telephonists and wireless operators, and were assigned to various SS headquarters in Germany and the occupied territories.

Not all who desired to do so could become members of the SS, but those who wished to stand well with the new elite and who could afford to pay for the privilege were allowed to become Fordernde Mitglieder (FM), or Patron Members. All 'Aryan' Germans were eligible for FM membership, and those accepted bound themselves to pay a monthly contribution to SS funds. In return they received a badge, a paybook and the goodwill of Himmler's men. In effect, the FM organization became a sort of 'Old Boys Network' through which members could secure business deals, promotion or employment, and in the Third Reich it virtually replaced the outlawed Society of Freemasons. Membership peaked at 1,000,000 in 1943.

German police harass a political opponent of the National Socialists, 1933. The police became a particularly useful tool through which Hitler and Himmler could control Germany's political evolution.

THE SS AND THE POLICE

On 17 June 1936, Heinrich Himmler became the chief of the German police, even presiding over the Gestapo. The centralization of police functions under SS leadership was to have a profound impact on the German state, and was ultimately a key ingredient in the implementation of the Holocaust both in Germany and in the German-occupied territories. Although not all of police personnel, nor organizations, were direct SS creations, a detailed profile of the German police is essential to understanding the Allgemeine-SS and the reach of its power.

The police had always had a respected status in German society. This may in part have been due to the fact that German policemen had traditionally been recruited fairly

LEFT: The figure in the centre here is SS-Gruppenführer Julius Schaub. Schaub was Hitler's chief personal adjutant during the war and was never far from his side. He is depicted here as he appeared at the signing of the French armistice in June 1940. The field cap is standard army issue, with an SS-*Totenkopf* pinned over the national cockade. The grey version of the black Allgemeine-SS service tunic, designed to be more military looking, has two shoulder boards instead of one, and a sleeve eagle to replace the armband. The figure on the right is Dr Hans Lammers, a wily civil service lawyer who had solved many legal tangles for the Nazis during their formative years. He was subsequently rewarded by Himmler with honorary SS rank, and rose to Obergruppenführer on 20 April 1940. The final figure here is the aristocratic Hyazinth Graf Strachwitz von Gross Zauche und Camminetz, a Standartenführer attached to the staff of Oberabschnitt Südost, and the first SS member to win the Knight's Cross of the Iron Cross with Oakleaves, Swords and Diamonds. (Osprey Publishing © Paul Hannon)

heavily from among former soldiers, and even before the advent of the Nazis were a paramilitary rather than a purely civilian force.

After World War I, the Treaty of Versailles had limited Germany to an army of 100,000 men, which resulted in huge numbers of wartime soldiers being thrown into unemployment. There were no such restrictions on the size of the police forces, however,

A Schutzpolizei officer (left) walks alongside an SS-Sturmführer conducting auxiliary police duties during March elections in Berlin, 1933. Some 15,000 SS men were given full police powers during this period.

and considerable numbers of former soldiers simply moved from one uniformed service to another. Under the precarious conditions of the Weimar Republic, when the greatest threat to the authority and integrity of the state was perceived as coming from the communist movement, the government was quite happy to see the police strengthened by an influx of such men, who tended to hold authoritarian views about society's overriding need for 'order'. The military also saw the benefit of keeping large numbers of trained and disciplined men within the control of an organ of the state, providing a cadre who might at some future date be transferred back to the authority of the armed forces.

Inevitably, when the Nazis came to power at the end of January 1933, they were happy to continue with this expansion and militarization of the police. For years they had been quietly infiltrating the police forces of the various German *Länder* (states), and many SS and Nazi Party members were already in senior positions. Now these officers were empowered to begin combing out policemen whom they felt to be politically unreliable, and any with known democratic sympathies were ousted. Many first-class professional officers were thrown out of the police, only to be replaced with dependable party members who had little or no useful experience, so many who had been ousted subsequently found themselves re-employed. Almost immediately after the Nazis came to power, members of the police were seen wearing the Party's swastika armband on their uniforms. It is also known that police officers who were already members of the party were pressurised to apply for membership of the Allgemeine-SS. Virtually all police officers and many senior NCOs held dual rank in both the police and SS. Those whose loyalty to the state was even remotely in doubt were carefully monitored.

The police structure at this point was still organized on a state-by-state basis. In Hitler's first cabinet, Hermann Göring was appointed as chief ('President') of the Prussian Police, thus gaining control of the largest and most influential of such forces. Within weeks, Department IA of the Prussian Landespolizei had been completely

Julius Schreck was an important figure in the early SS. Having played a role in establishing the SA, he then rose to become the first leader of the SS, a position he held from 1925 to 1926.

purged of any suspect elements, and its Amt III was retitled as the Geheime Staatspolizei – the Secret State Police or Gestapo.

The numbers of police available to the government in Berlin were quickly doubled by Göring's creation of the Prussian Hilfspolizei or police auxiliaries to assist the force in maintaining order. These were generally members of the SA with a smaller number of members of the Allgemeine-SS, and others recruited from war veterans' associations, who could be trusted to support the new and still not fully established regime. Similar Hilfspolizei units were created throughout the other German *Länder* within a matter of days; they wore the uniforms of their parent organizations, if any, with a white 'Hilfspolizei' armband. These auxiliaries were disbanded in August 1933, partly due to foreign protests that they contravened the terms of the Versailles Treaty, but also because Hitler was already becoming uneasy over his ability to control the SA, which provided the greater part of the Hilfspolizei.

Adolf Hitler drives through jubilant Viennese crowds following the *Anschluss* with Austria. The Austrian SS was actually formed covertly in 1934, with a similar structure to the Allgemeine-SS in Germany, and it was used to influence the move to unification with Germany.

LEFT: Unified national police, 1937–43. 1: Oberstleutnant, Schutzpolizei, c. 1938 (Paradeanzug). 2: Leutnant standard-bearer, Schutzpolizei; Berlin, 1937 (Paradeanzug). 3: Generalleutnant der Ordnungspolizei, c. 1940 (Meldeanzug). (Osprey Publishing © Gerry Embleton)

Although short-lived, the Hilfspolizei had served their purpose in helping to ensure the survival of the Nazi government in the first shaky days of its existence, when it was still battling things out in the streets against strong communist and socialist movements. In January 1934, by now more confident, the regime began to unify the Landespolizei forces by transferring police powers to the national – Reichs – level. The post of Chef der Deutschen Polizei im Reichsministerium des Innern (Chief of the German Police in the Ministry of the Interior) was created, and with Heinrich Himmler's appointment to this post in April 1934 the blurring of lines between the police and the SS began. Himmler would ensure that the majority of senior and middle-level police posts were filled by men who were also members of the SS and thus owed obedience to him. The new national police apparatus that he controlled was divided into two major elements: the Ordnungspolizei (Order Police, Orpo) and the Sicherheitspolizei (Security Police, Sipo – into which the Gestapo was absorbed).

When Germany's rearmament and the formation of the new Wehrmacht were openly declared in March 1935, many thousands of policemen were transferred to the army, including those still serving who were perceived as lacking in enthusiasm for the Nazi regime. Senior ranks who remained in the police and who were not already members of the SS were pressured into joining; membership became a prerequisite for a successful police career. (It is interesting to note, however, that at the outbreak of war in September 1939 only some 15 per cent of the membership of the Gestapo were actually members of the SS.)

On the outbreak of war, the manpower needs of the armed forces led to the conscription of many younger, fitter policemen; consequently, numbers of older men not considered fit for military service were taken into the police as reservists 'for the duration' – and some of these were the very men who had been purged for perceived political unreliability between 1933 and 1935. Although the 'Nazification' of the police may have thus been somewhat diluted, it is unlikely that these men had much influence; their reputation for limited political loyalty would certainly have remained on their records, and they would continue to be regarded as suspect.

From 1942, dual police and SS ranks were adopted by police generals, who from then on would wear SS-pattern rank insignia, albeit in police colours. Police personnel were also issued with pay books (Soldbücher) bearing the SS runes rather than the police eagle on the cover.

As time passed, the police, rather than providing the army with manpower as originally envisaged, began to field its own rifle regiments and even light armoured units, to serve behind the military frontlines in the occupied territories. Although many of these units were engaged in actions against heavily armed partisans, others were attached to SS/SD Einsatzgruppen (task forces) and used in sweeps through the civilian

New arrivals at Auschwitz-Birkenau, 1944. The commander of Auschwitz, Rudolf Höss, remembered at his trial in 1945: 'In the summer of 1941 I was summoned to Berlin by Reichsführer-SS Himmler to receive personal orders. He told me something to the effect – I do not remember the exact words – that the Führer had given the order for a final solution of the Jewish question. We, the SS, must carry out that order.'

populations, rounding up Jews and other 'undesirables' (see Chapter 3). It has now been well documented that the German police – although still maintaining tens of thousands of personnel on regular, traditional duties in Germany – became deeply involved in some of the worse excesses of the Nazi regime.

At the end of the war, the need for the overstretched Allied armies to maintain law and order in the chaotic situation which prevailed in Germany meant that in most cases only a cursory review of the conduct of individual police personnel during the Third Reich was made, in order to weed out the worst offenders. Many police officers were simply allowed to go back on duty without any meaningful scrutiny of their wartime records.

Few organizations during the period of the Third Reich came close to the levels of complexity of the German police, and that complexity has resulted in a dearth of available reference material in any manageable form.

A full list of the different functions in the various German *Länder* totals 34, including everything from Forestry and Foodstuffs Police to Lodging and Pathways Police. While this may seem wildly excessive, it should be recalled that many of these functions also existed in most other countries. The principal difference was that whereas in Germany they were performed by the police, elsewhere they tended to be carried out by regulatory officials of various municipal authorities, since many related simply to administrative and licensing functions. Nevertheless, it is unsurprising that when the Nazis came to power they wished to rationalize and unify the numerous policing functions throughout the various Länder. Despite Germany possessing such a huge range of police functions, it is

Another instrument of terror. The Volksgerichtshof (People's Court) excelled at trying and convicting 'enemies of the state', often with much public fanfare and frequently ending in the death sentence. Here we see the trial of Erwin von Witzleben, a German field marshall and conspirator in the July bomb plot.

worth pointing out that the total number of policemen in the country at that time was under 150,000 – significantly less than in Great Britain or France.

To cover the entire German police apparatus would require a significant multi-volume work. In lieu of this project, this chapter will give some insight into the structure, responsibilities and uniform distinctions of the German Order Police.

Ordnungspolizei (Orpo)

Schutzpolizei des Reiches (National Protection Police)

Schutzpolizei der Gemeinden (Municipal Protection Police)

Gendarmerie (Rural Police)

Verwaltungspolizei (Administrative Police)

Kolonialpolizei (Colonial Police)

Wasserschutzpolizei (Water Protection Police)

Feuerschutzpolizei (Fire Protection Police)

Feuerwehren (Fire Brigades, Auxiliary Fire Protection Police)

Luftschutzpolizei (Air Protection Police)

Technische Nothilfe (Technical Emergency Service)

Polizei Fliegerstaffeln (Police Flying Units – liaison and transport)

ABOVE: 1: Oberleutnant, Verwaltungspolizei, c. 1941–43 (Ausgehanzug). The officer's walking-out dress is worn by this first lieutenant of the Administrative Police. 2: Major, Schutzpolizei, c. 1941–43 (Dienstanzug). The officer's service dress differed in including unpiped breeches and riding boots, grey kid gloves and a pistol holstered on the belt. 3: Meister, Wasserschutzpolizei, 1939 (Ausgehanzug). This senior NCO wears the naval-cut reefer jacket and straight trousers of his service. (Osprey Publishing © Gerry Embleton)

Sonderpolizei – Special Police units not directly under control of Hauptamt Orpo, including:

Bahnschutzpolizei (Railway Protection Police)

Reichsbahnfahndungsdienst (Railway Criminal Investigation Department)

Postschutz (Postal Protection)

Funkschutz (Broadcast Protection)

Bergpolizei (Mines Police)

Deichpolizei (Dyke & Dams Police)

Hilfspolizei (Auxiliary Police)

COMMAND STRUCTURE: HAUPTAMT ORPO

The national command office for the Ordnungspolizei ('Orpo') was in Berlin. The position of Chef der Ordnungspolizei was originally held by SS-Oberstgruppenführer und Generaloberst der Polizei Kurt Daluege, replaced in 1943 by SS-Obergruppenführer und General der Polizei Alfred Wünnenberg. Although Daluege remained the senior officer, to all intents and purposes operational control of the Orpo after this date passed to Wünnenberg. The Order Police Main Office was divided into numerous senior and subordinate departments or Ämter:

Amt I – Kommandoamt (Command Department). Headed by SS-Brigadeführer und Generalmajor der Polizei Anton Diermann until late 1944, when Diermann was replaced by SS-Brigadeführer und Generalmajor der Polizei Hans Flade. This command department was further subdivided into three subordinate Amtsgruppen:

Amtsgruppe I comprised sub-offices covering aspects such as finance, clothing, training, ordnance, equipment, etc.

Amtsgruppe II was responsible for personnel matters as well as ideological training.

Amtsgruppe III was the police medical department.

Amt II – Verwaltung und Recht (Administrative and Rights). Headed by SS-Gruppenführer und General der Polizei Ministerialdirektor Dr Werner Bracht, this department was also divided into three Amtsgruppen:

Amtsgruppe I was responsible for pay and allowances, pensions, budgeting, the police legal code and other administrative matters.

Amtsgruppe II covered registration and control of the population, theatres, cinemas and places of entertainment, trades and handicrafts and traffic control.

Amtsgruppe III dealt with police billeting and accommodation.

Amt III – Wirtschaftsverwaltungsamt (Economic Department). Headed by SS-Obergruppenführer und Generalleutnant der Waffen-SS und Polizei August

Frank, this department was subdivided into:

Four Amtsgruppen dealing with clothing and rations, finance and pay, quartering and billeting and pensions and allowances. A fifth subsection also dealt with personnel matters.

Amt IV – Technische Nothilfe (Technical Emergency Service). Headed by SS-Gruppenführer und Generalleutnant der Polizei Willy Schmelcher, this branch was effectively the engineering branch of the SS and the police.

Amt V – Feuerwehren (Fire Brigades Bureau). Headed by Generalmajor der Polizei Schnell.

Amt VI – Kolonialpolizei (Colonial Police). Headed by SS-Obergruppenführer und General der Waffen-SS und Polizei Karl von Pfeffer-Wildenbruch.

Amt VII – Technische SS- und Polizeiakademie (The SS and Police Technical Training Academy). Headed by SS-Brigadeführer und Generalmajor der Polizei Prof Dr Hellmuth Gerloff.

As well as these main administrative offices, Hauptamt Orpo also included various inspectorates, and supervised many training schools.

Since 1919, Germany's national territory had been divided into 'military districts' or Wehrkreise, numbered in Roman numerals – e.g. Wehrkreis III, with headquarters in Berlin, covered the Altmark, Neumark and Brandenburg regions. Their primary purpose had been as army divisional recruitment and training commands, but with the creation of a unified state police service its territorial structure was grafted on to this existing organization. In each Wehrkreis, a Befehlshaber der Ordnungspolizei (BdO; Senior

POLICE RANKS

Police rank	Military equivalent where appropriate
Polizei Anwärter	Private soldiers
Unterwachtmeister	Unteroffizier
Wachtmeister	Unterfeldwebel
Oberwachtmeister	Feldwebel
Revierwachtmeister	–
Hauptwachtmeister	Oberfeldwebel
Meister	–
Obermeister	–

The officer rank titles, from Leutnant up to Generaloberst der Polizei, mirrored those of the army and air force.

Order Police Commander) was appointed as the representative of the Hauptamt Orpo and of the regional Höhere SS- und Polizeiführer (Higher SS & Police Leader). Amongst the staff allocated to the BdO was the Polizei Schulungsleiter; this individual equated roughly to the Soviet political commissar, with the task of ensuring that police personnel were fully indoctrinated in the tenets of Nazism. Below the BdO in the organizational structure were a number of Kommandeure der Orpo, who answered to the BdO for the control of various sub-units of the Ordnungspolizei within a district or region.

Units within the Ordnungspolizei fell into two basic categories, the normal uniformed police (Polizeivollzugsbeamten) and the administrative service of the police (Polizeiverwaltungsbeamten), often comprised of non-uniformed civilian clerical workers. It is the units within the first group that will hold our primary focus here.

RECRUITMENT AND TRAINING

The processes of recruitment and training in the German police reflected the political and militaristic nature of German society after World War I. As the police force expanded it was filled largely with militarily experienced men who in the main had predominantly right- rather than left-wing leanings and could be considered trustworthy in a period when communism was proving a serious threat in Germany.

Great emphasis was placed on weapons training, not merely with small arms, but also with automatic weapons, heavy machine guns, and even armoured vehicles. Needless to say, when the Nazis came to power in 1933, they felt no need to alter the status quo. The careful recruitment of those considered politically reliable after 1933 only served to increase the generally right-wing bias of the police. It has been estimated that when the Wehrmacht was formed in 1935, as many as 60,000 fully trained policemen of high calibre were transferred into the military.

The Schutzpolizei was the nearest equivalent within the German police organization to the British 'bobby' or the American 'cop'. It was divided into two basic components. The Reviere Polizei, or Precinct Police, comprised static units of up to 40 police officers patrolling a specific area. Five or more such Reviere constituted a Polizei Abschnitte or sector, and three to five sectors (but only in the largest cities such as Berlin and Vienna) formed a Polizei Gruppe. The Kasernierte Polizei (Barracked Police) were far more militarized, had received infantry training and were, as their name suggests, based in military barracks. They were available to the Kommandeur der Schutzpolizei for specific

LEFT: SS police officers, 1943–44. Here we see (from left to right) a major in the Luftschutzpolizei, a senior NCO in the security police and a Oberwachtmeister in the SS-Polizei Regiment. From 1943, German police formations serving as security troops in the occupied territories were known as 'SS-Police' Regiments, to distinguish them from the recently raised native auxiliary 'Police Rifle' units. (Osprey Publishing © Paul Hannon)

Nazi police parade in front of Hitler in 1937. One of the greatest extensions of SS power came when all of Germany's police forces were placed under ultimate SS control in 1936.

tasks such as providing additional armed security at large civic events, dealing with internal unrest, maintaining order after enemy air raids and the prevention of looting in such circumstances and also the control of traffic after major disasters. It was principally from the Kasernierte Polizei that most of the principal Polizei battalions were formed.

A number of training schools existed to provide training for those destined to serve in one of the numerous militarized police battalions. As with military units, much of a police serviceman's training was given at a reserve or depot battalion. These training establishments included Polizei-Waffenschulen, I, II, III and IV at Dresden-Hellerau, Dresden-Moritzberg, Den Haag, and Maastricht; Polizei-Kraftfahrschule (Police Driving School), Vienna; Polizei-Schule für Technik und Verkehr (Technical and Traffic School), Berlin; Polizei-Sanitäts Ersatz Abteilung (Medical Depot), Berlin; Polizei-

Nachrichten Ersatz Kompanie (Signals Reserve Coy), Krakau; Polizei-Reiter Ersatz Schwadron (Mounted Replacement Unit), Posen.

On the outbreak of war, some 21 police battalions, each of some 500 men, had been formed, of which 13 were attached to the German armies on the invasion of Poland. Their duties were to round up Polish prisoners, remove weapons and abandoned

POLICE 'AKTION'

A considerable number of the police and security actions carried out in the occupied territories were undertaken by units of the German Civil Police, the Schutzpolizei or Schupo. The police personnel shown here are typical of the appearance of Polizei troops on the Eastern Front. Many troops wore the standard civil police uniform, identifiable from its contrasting brown cuffs and collar, although ultimately a police-pattern field blouse in plain field-grey very similar to that worn by army and Waffen-SS troops was introduced. This inset shows a typical police encirclement tactic. (Osprey Publishing © Velimir Vuksic)

military equipment, and generally secure the areas behind the frontline. By mid-1940, over 100 such police battalions had been formed.

Generally, most police battalions were staffed by slight men in their 30s and 40s unsuitable for frontline service in the Wehrmacht. However, police battalions in the number range 251 to 256 and 301 to 325 were formed around an allocation of younger volunteers to the Ordnungspolizei. These younger men were often far more fanatical in their loyalty to the National Socialist regime than many of the older policemen. On the invasion of the Soviet Union in 1941, 500 members of the Ordnungspolizei were attached to the Einsatzgruppen killing squads and a further 11 battalions (some 5,500 men) allocated to the various regions controlled by the Höhere SS- und Polizeiführer in occupied Russia.

There were two distinct chains of command. The regular police chain began with the head of the Ordnungspolizei, Kurt Daluege, through the Befehlshaber der Ordnungspolizei at regional level, to the district Kommandeur der Polizei and on to the battalions. On the other hand, orders direct from the Reichsführer-SS und Chef der deutschen Polizei, Heinrich Himmler, could be passed down via the Höhere SS- und Polizeiführer to the district SS- und Polizeiführer and on to the battalion. The latter chain was most often used for orders regarding actions by composite forces of both the Ordnungspolizei and Sicherheitspolizei.

A typical police battalion would be made up as follows:

HQ Element	4 officers, 12 men
Medic Detachment	1 officer, 6 men
Signals Platoon	1 officer, 18 men
Police Company (×3)	5 officers, 140–150 men
M/T Section	5 officers, 92 men

In addition, the following elements could be made available from regimental strength:

Motorcycle Platoon	1 officer, 34 men
Armoured Car Platoon	2 officers, 15 men
Anti-Tank Section	1 officer, 25 men
Light Infantry Howitzer Section	1 officer, 25 men

POLICE BATTALION ACTIVE SERVICE

Following the invasion of the Soviet Union in 1941, the original 84 Polizei Bataillonen were formed into 28 Polizei regiments, each of three battalions; the original numbering was then lost and the battalions designated simply as I, II or III Bataillon of a regiment. Subsequently, a number of other regiments were formed, designated as Polizei-Schützen

Regimenter. Finally, in March 1943, all police regiments were re-designated as SS-Polizei Schützen Regimenter. Eventually, a grand total of 38 SS-Polizei Schützen Regimenter were formed.

In addition there were two distinct regiments identified by a name rather than a number: SS-Polizei Regiment *Bozen* and SS-Polizei Regiment *Alpenvorland*, both based in Italy. Police serving in these units were issued with an SS pay book of a special police design, slightly different to that issued to field units of the Waffen-SS. The personnel of these units also continued to wear standard police field dress with police insignia. From the beginning of the actions against the Jews and other 'undesirables' such as the Polish intelligentsia, Ordnungspolizei were used to provide armed escorts for the trains removing these unfortunates to their fates in one of the many concentration camps. Squads consisting of one officer and 15 NCOs and men were generally used, and as they escorted the trains right into the camps themselves, they could hardly have been unaware of what awaited the victims.

Jews boarding a deportation train, destined to take them to a terrible fate. The SS were put in sole charge of the administration of the concentration camp system from December 1934, although some services were subcontracted out to civilian agencies.

A liberated Russian slave labourer points out a particularly brutal guard. Many camp personnel were killed during the first hours of liberation, while dozens of others went to trial and execution, or simply managed to evade capture.

Schutzpolizei were widely used to clear villages of those considered undesirable by the Nazis, often on the pretext that they were 'partisans' or had supported the partisans. While part of the unit entered the town or village, a security cordon would be thrown around the outskirts to prevent any escapes. After the victims had been ordered to assemble, those too old or infirm to move fast enough were usually killed on the spot. The cordon would close in and sweep through the village, searching out those who had sought to conceal themselves. They, too, were usually summarily shot. In some cases, those captured were loaded onto trains to be shipped off to their fate. Often, however, they would simply be marched off to some wood or quarry or similar 'suitable' spot on the outskirts of the town or village and executed.

Police sweeps were also carried out through areas which had already been 'cleared', with the intention of surprising those who thought they had escaped the initial round-up. Many thousands were caught up in these subsequent sweeps.

LEFT: Armed police, 1943–45. 1: Wachtmeister, Schutzpolizei, c. 1943. This Schupo NCO wears the much plainer army-style *Feldbluse* tunic introduced in 1943. 2: Meister, Schutzpolizei armoured troops, 1944. The crews of police light armoured vehicles – usually captured foreign types – were authorized the army-style black 'special uniform for armour crews'. 3: Oberwachtmeister, Schutzpolizei, 1945. This NCO wears the police version of the Waffen-SS so-called 'pea-pattern' non-reversible four-pocket combat uniform. (Osprey Publishing © Gerry Embleton)

Dead Jews scattered around the rubble of the Warsaw ghetto, after its destruction in 1943. The photo was used as evidence against key SS figures at the Nuremberg trial after the war.

Even in cases where civilians had been allowed to remain and put to work in some business or factory contributing to the German war effort, they were often arbitrarily snatched by Ordnungspolizei or Sicherheitspolizei search squads. This annoyed those industrial managers who thought they had found an excellent source of free labour.

The Ordnungspolizei also made great use of Polish informers, rewarding those, often former neighbours, who were only too quick to betray Jews hiding from the Germans. They dealt out swift and usually lethal punishment to any found to be aiding the unfortunate Jews. Given that the men in these police units were predominantly ordinary Germans rather than Nazi fanatics, it is interesting to note that in general there seems to have been no problem in finding volunteers to take part in such punitive actions and the murder of defenceless civilians. Indeed, from surviving documents and testimony, it seems that many of these elderly police reservists were considerably more cruel and bloodthirsty than some of their younger colleagues who were actually SS members.

It has often been claimed that these policemen may have obeyed their gruesome orders through fear that disobedience would lead to court-martial and execution.

While such fears under the totalitarian Nazi regime might sound logical, there is evidence to show that several policemen did refuse to obey such repugnant orders and that they suffered no punishment. Indeed, some were subsequently promoted showing that neither their lives nor their careers were threatened. Certainly if it was clear that no ill befell those who refused similar orders, there can be little or no excuse for those who did obey and took part in the massacre of innocent civilians. The only problem, in fact, was that those who held out suffered abuse and scorn from colleagues who considered them 'weak'.

Policemen also took part in some of the largest, organized mass killings of the war, such as the notorious 'Erntefest' massacre around Lublin. In this incident, the victims were led to believe they were digging anti-tank ditches, a ruse made successful by arranging the ditches in zig-zag fashion. Once the ditches were complete, however, more than 42,000 civilians were driven at gunpoint by the policemen to the ditches, where they were shot by members of the Sicherheitspolizei. One single police battalion is recorded as having directly executed 38,000 civilians and taken part in the murder of 83,000. Few of even the most appalling of Nazi Germany's military units could come close to the levels of murder carried out by these 'ordinary' German policemen. Few were ever punished and indeed most of those who actually survived the war simply went back to their careers in the civil police.

Most battlefield atrocities are carried out by frontline units fired up by the heat of battle, or those desperate for revenge after the death of their comrades. In general, frontline troops are younger, fitter men, probably less temperate than older, more mature men. Yet, here were some of the worst atrocities of the war, carried out by these same mature family men who might have been expected to exercise a calming influence on their younger colleagues. They were men who, by definition, came from a body dedicated to maintaining law and order and protecting civilians from murder, rape and other such crimes. (A more detailed examination of the activities of the Einsatzgruppen in particular is given in Chapter 3.)

SS AND SECURITY POLICE

THE RSHA (REICHSSICHERHEITSHAUPTAMT)

As previously stated, the police resource was divided between the Ordnungspolizei under Kurt Daluege and the Sicherheitspolizei under the command of Reinhard Heydrich. The SiPo itself was part of the RSHA, the Reichssicherheitshauptamt or State Security Main Office formed in 1938. It was organized into seven distinct departments as follows.

Amt I Personnel Department
Amt II Administration Department
Amt III Sicherheitsdienst (SD)
Amt IV Geheime Staatspolizei (GeStaPo)
Amt V Kriminal Polizei (KriPo)
Amt VI SD (Ausland) – SD overseas section
Amt VII Ideology
It is with Amt III, Amt IV and Amt V that this chapter is concerned.

Potential recruits into the RSHA were expected to be of a very high academic standard with a law degree at least. Recruits embarked on four months of intensive training with the Kriminalpolizei, learning the forensic and scientific aspects of police work. This was followed by three months' attachment to the SD for training in intelligence work, and finally, three months with the Gestapo. At the end of this period, the recruit would be posted to whichever branch of the RSHA most suited his skills.

Himmler and Heydrich became two of the Third Reich's most powerful SS men. While Himmler rose to head of the SS overall and the German police, Heydrich was chief of the RSHA. Hitler called Heydrich the 'man with the iron heart'.

SICHERHEITSDIENST

Established in 1931, the Sicherheitsdienst, or SD, was recruited from those with a high level of academic ability – only well-educated candidates from good backgrounds were accepted. Despite the image history has left of this organization, most of its true members were involved in intelligence and counter-intelligence work at which they were, in fact, rather successful. It may be considered as approximately the equivalent of Britain's MI5 and was a direct competitor to the army's intelligence service, the Abwehr, over which it ultimately gained control.

LEFT: The central figure here is, of course, the Reichsführer der SS, Heinrich Himmler, seen in 1932. In this year Himmler held the rank of SS-Gruppenführer, and although he was titular Reichsführer der SS he was still very much subordinate to the SA Stabschef, Ernst Röhm. Here he wears the collar patches of his rank, the SS officer's belt buckle created in 1931, and the newly introduced cuff title for departmental heads. The badge on the left breast pocket commemorates his participation in the Fourth Party Rally held at Nuremberg on 1–4 August 1929. Note also the small NSDAP eagle, introduced In 1929 to replace the national cockade on the kepi. The other figures are (left) Staffelführer Ritter von Schleich, SS-Fliegerstaffel Süd, and an SS-Sturmführer conducting auxiliary police duties. (Osprey Publishing © Paul Hannon)

The SD was the only one of the three branches that was regularly uniformed, the Kripo and Gestapo being predominantly plain-clothed organizations. However, it was decreed that all members of the security police organizations serving outside the borders of the Reich were to wear uniform, specifically that of the SD. Thus, in many wartime photographs showing what appear to be SD personnel, many will in fact be members of other police organizations. Only minor differences in insignia worn on the uniforms will indicate the wearer's true status.

It has been estimated that as little as 3 per cent of those who made up the strength of the SD Einsatzgruppen were in fact actual SD personnel. Nevertheless, the SD must bear its share of responsibility for those deeds carried out by personnel wearing its uniform and under its theoretical control.

THE KRIMINAL POLIZEI

The Kripo was that branch of the civil police apparatus that closely paralleled the plain-clothed criminal investigations departments of other police forces throughout the world. Their main duties were in the investigation of robbery, murder, rape, arson and other statutory, rather than political, crimes.

As we have seen, when the Nazis came to power they lost no time in retiring any policeman considered to have anything but right-wing leanings. Any with suspected socialist tendencies were removed from post and their places filled with younger, politically 'correct' recruits, often members of the SA. This haemorrhage of experienced manpower was a mistake, however, and many experienced policemen were re-employed, although a close eye was kept on any considered to be anything less than completely politically reliable. The Kripo was therefore comprised of a mixture of professional old-style policemen, often apolitical, and younger, fanatically loyal, Nazis.

Kripo personnel carried a bronze oval disc on a chain attached to a leather fob to allow it to be buttoned to the wearer's waistband. On the obverse was the national emblem of an eagle and swastika, and on the reverse the inscription 'Staatliche Kriminal Polizei' over the bearer's personal ID number. This so-called 'warrant-disc' was the policeman's badge of authority, and the only insignia carried other than the *Ausweiss* or ID card.

THE GEHEIME STAATSPOLIZEI

Similar to the Kripo in many respects, the Gestapo was formed in 1933 by Hermann Göring around a core of politically reliable recruits from the Kripo. Its main duties were in combating political subversion, espionage, etc. As it grew, many sub-branches were formed, the most notorious of which was Department b4. Amt IVb4 of the RSHA, headed by Adolf Eichmann and devoted to the 'final solution' of the Jewish 'problem'. Gestapo agents operated throughout the occupied territories and co-operated fully in the round-up of civilians for despatch to the Konzentrationslager (concentration camps, also known as KZ), and the capture of those who escaped or avoided the round-ups. Gestapo agents were also located at most if not all KZs.

The Gestapo was commanded by Heinrich Müller, nicknamed 'Gestapo Müller', and was itself sub-divided into several sections dealing with aspects such as enemies of the state, religious sects, counter-intelligence, the occupied territories and even frontier policing. Gestapo personnel, like the Kripo, carried a warrant disc. In their case, it was in nickel rather than bronze, and the inscription over the bearer's number was 'Geheime Staats Polizei'.

AUXILIARY POLICE

The sheer scale of police and security operations on the Eastern Front meant that the combined resources of the military, the police and the SS

Theodor Eicke, the infamous commander of the *Totenkopf* Division. Eicke personally participated in the killing of Ernst Röhm on the night of 2 July 1934.

were inadequate for the task, and as early as the winter of 1941, suitable members of the local citizenry were accepted into an auxiliary police formation which became known as the Schutzmannschaft. These units came under the control of the Höhere SS- und Polizeiführer in the area in which they were recruited.

Theoretically, recruitment was on a voluntary basis for a period of six months, though it does seem that few who joined were ever given the option of leaving, or indeed any option at all about their service. It would seem that most recruits joined for purely opportunistic reasons. By volunteering to serve the Germans, these men avoided becoming victims themselves. It also ensured that they were at least paid and well fed compared with their countrymen, and put them in a position where they could perhaps protect their families and friends, and also, of course, settle a few old scores with any enemies.

Schutzmannschaften were organized into battalions of three, later four, companies of around 120 men, plus headquarters elements, three rifle platoons and a machine-gun platoon. This gave the Schutzmannschaft battalion a strength of between 500 and 700 men. Each company had a command cadre of German officers and senior NCOs who appear to have been drawn primarily from the Polizei, Sicherheitspolizei and SS. It is estimated that within a year of the formation of the Schutzmannschaft, there were over 50,000 former Soviet citizens serving the German state as auxiliary policemen.

As auxiliaries in the control of the Sicherheitspolizei, men from the Schutzmannschaft accompanied German troops in considerable numbers of punitive actions against the civil population, the suppression of the Warsaw Uprising being a prime example. Indeed, it seems that the Schutzmannschaft were often left to do the 'dirty' work that some Germans had no stomach for. Many of the auxiliaries had no compunction against carrying out the foulest of deeds against their countrymen, especially the Jews.

SS SECURITY UNITS

The task of policing Germany's conquered territories dramatically expanded the need for security units. A number of troops from the notorious SS-Totenkopfverbände (Death's Head Units) – those responsible for running the concentration camp system – operated behind the German lines in Poland and Russia. On the outbreak of war, SS-Totenkopfstandarten *Oberbayern*, *Brandenburg* and *Thüringen* moved into Poland. The first two operated behind the 10. Armee in Upper Silesia, and Thüringen followed behind the 8. Armee further south.

These units were tasked with 'cleansing and security' operations, but were little more than death squads tasked with hunting down Poles who had been added to Himmler's death lists: communists, intellectuals and Jews. The fact that they were never really intended for genuine security duties is reflected in the fact that when the army command in their area ordered them to take part in actual anti-partisan actions, they refused. A considerable number of complaints were made by army units that became aware of the behaviour of these troops. Furious protests were lodged by Generaloberst Blaskowitz, commander of 8. Armee, but the weak-willed commander-in-chief of the army, Generaloberst Brauchitsch, was too afraid to press the complaints with Hitler. Nothing was done to curb the excesses of these units until they were eventually recalled at the end of the year for absorption into the newly formed SS-*Totenkopf* Division.

This division was commanded by SS-Gruppenführer Theodor Eicke, whose *Totenkopf* units had been formed to provide guards for the concentration camps. The division itself, although displaying considerable bravery in action, was subsequently to be dogged by allegations of atrocities committed by its troops. Two *Totenkopf* Standarten (the 8th and 10th) were subsequently grouped together to form SS-Infanterie Brigade (mot) 1. This unit was active in the central sector of the Eastern Front behind Heeresgruppe Mitte (Army Group Centre) and is mentioned in several 'post-action' reports as giving assistance in 'security' sweeps by the Einsatzgruppen against 'partisans'.

A Soviet soldier identifies his brother as one amongst 200 Russians shot dead by the SS at Wülfel on 8 April 1945, killed on a death march from the Liebenau labour camp, near Hanover.

Polish civilians are led away by SS troops during the Warsaw uprising, spring 1943. The uprising was put down by a mixture of Waffen-SS Panzergrenadiers plus Ordnungspolizei regiments and SD and Gestapo officers, as well as regular Wehrmacht troops.

As we have seen, the police and security services, under the umbrella control of the SS, were a dark heart of the Nazi regime. They ranged from the local policeman overseeing civil order in a rural German village, through to fully militarized units combating partisans in the forests of Russia. With Himmler in overall control of the police, however, the Nazi ideology was able to permeate down through all strata of police service; those personnel who were not, at least publicly, in sympathy with the Nazi regime were unlikely to last long in their jobs.

SS SYMBOLISM

One reason for the notoriety of the SS has to be the unsettling nature of its imagery. Although the claim that the SS was an occult organization is taking things too far, it is certainly the case that Himmler and many of his subordinates saw the SS as something akin to a military religious brotherhood, along the lines of the Teutonic Knights of old. For this reason, the Allgemeine-SS in particular developed a forbidding visual presence that has few equals throughout history.

THE DEATH'S HEAD

Of all SS uniform trappings and accoutrements, the one emblem which endured throughout the history of the organization and became firmly associated with it was the death's head or *Totenkopf*. It has often been assumed that the death's head was adopted simply to strike terror into the hearts of those who saw it. In fact, it was chosen as a direct and emotional link with the past, and in particular with the elite military units of the Imperial Reich. Medieval German literature and romantic poems were filled with references to dark forces and the symbols of death and destruction, a typical example being the following short excerpt from an epic work by the 15th-century writer Garnier von Susteren:

Behold the knight
In solemn black manner,
With a skull on his crest
And blood on his banner...

In 1740, a jawless death's head with the bones lying behind the skull, embroidered in silver bullion, adorned the black funeral trappings of the Prussian king, Frederick Wilhelm I. In his memory the Leib-Husaren Regiments 1 and 2, elite Prussian Royal Bodyguard units which were formed the following year, took black as the colour of

Civilian captives are led off on their journey to Auschwitz. The police NCO on the right wears the pre-war tunic with open collar, quite different to the military-style tunic with high fastening collar worn by the NCO standing in the doorway in the background.

US soldiers inspect a bull whip used by a concentration camp guard. The revelations as concentration and extermination camps were liberated by the Allies increased the likelihood of SS soldiers being hunted to destruction, rather than allowed to surrender.

their uniforms and wore a massive *Totenkopf* of similar design on their *Pelzmützen* or busbies. The State of Brunswick followed suit in 1809, when the death's head was adopted by its Hussar Regiment 17 and the third battalion of Infantry Regiment 92. The Brunswick *Totenkopf* differed slightly in design from the Prussian one, with the skull facing forward and situated directly above the crossed bones.

During World War I the death's head was chosen as a formation symbol by a number of crack German army units, particularly the stormtroopers, flamethrower detachments and tank battalions. Several pilots, including the air ace Leutnant Georg von Hantelmann, also used variants of it as personal emblems. Almost immediately after the end of hostilities in 1918 the death's head appeared again, this time painted on the helmets and vehicles of some of the most famous Freikorps. Because of its association with these formations, it became symbolic not only of wartime daring and self-sacrifice but also of post-war traditionalism, anti-liberalism and anti-Bolshevism. Nationalist ex-servicemen even had death's head rings, cuff links, tie pins and other adornments privately made for wear with their civilian clothes.

It is not surprising, therefore, that members of the Stosstrupp *Adolf Hitler* eagerly took the *Totenkopf* as their distinctive emblem in 1923, initially acquiring a small stock of appropriate army surplus cap badges. Their successors in the SS thereafter contracted the firm of Deschler in Munich to restrike large quantities of the Prussian-style jawless death's head, which they used on their headgear for the next 11 years. As Hitler's personal guards they liked to model themselves on the Imperial Bodyguard Hussars, who had become known as the 'Schwarze Totenkopfhusaren' or 'Black Death's Head Hussars', and were fond of singing their old regimental song with its emotive verse:

In black we are dressed,
In blood we are drenched,
Death's head on our helmets.
Hurrah! Hurrah!
We stand unshaken!

When, in 1934, the Prussian-style *Totenkopf* began to be used as an elite badge by the new army Panzer units (which were, after all, the natural successors to the Imperial

15 April 1945; the commandant of Altendorn slave labour camp is led away by his US captors. All told, the Allgemeine-SS presided over nearly 15 million slave labourers during World War II, giving them huge resources of free manpower, almost all cruelly treated.

cavalry regiments), the SS devised its own unique pattern of grinning death's head, with lower jaw, which it wore thereafter. The 1934-pattern SS-*Totenkopf* ultimately took various forms – right-facing, left-facing and front facing – and appeared on the cloth headgear of all SS members and on the tunics and vehicles of the SS-Totenkopfverbände and SS-*Totenkopf* Division.

It was the centrepiece of the SS death's head ring, and could be seen on dagger and gorget chains, mess jackets, flags, standards, drum covers, trumpet banners and the SS and Police Guerrilla Warfare Badge. Moreover, because of its direct associations with Danzig, where the Prussian Leib-Husaren Regiments had been garrisoned until 1918, it was selected as the special formation badge of the SS-Heimwehr Danzig and the Danzig Police and Fire Service. Himmler wanted his men to be proud of their heritage, and there is no doubt that the honourable military associations of the German Death's Head were well used to that end. It became an instant status symbol in the Third Reich, and an inspiration to those who were granted the privilege of wearing it.

It is worth mentioning that the *Totenkopf* was also borne by several Wehrmacht elements such as the Kavallerie Regiment 5, the Infanterie Regiment 17, the naval Küstenschutz Danzig, and the Luftwaffe's Schleppgruppe 4 and Kampfgruppe 54 during World War II. (Moreover, many elite units of other nations have likewise used the death's head emblem at various times. These include the British Royal Navy submarine service and 17th Lancers, Mussolini's bodyguard, certain US special forces, Imperial Russian cossacks, Polish tank crews, Finnish cavalry and the French security police, to name but a few. Bulgaria even had a Military Order for Bravery in World War I which was graded 'With Skulls'.)

THE RUNES

Alongside the *Totenkopf*, the *SS-Runen* or SS runes represented the elitism and brotherly comradeship of the organisation, and were consciously elevated to an almost holy status. Indeed, as SS men marched off to war in 1939 they sang their battle-hymn *SS Wir Alle* ('We Are All SS'), which included the line 'Wir alle stehen zum Kampf bereit, wenn Runen und Totenkopf führen' ('We all stand ready for battle, inspired by runes and death's head').

The word 'rune' derives from the Old Norse 'run', meaning 'secret script'. Runes were characters that formed the alphabets used by the Germanic tribes of pre-Christian Europe for both magical and ordinary writing. There were three major branches of the runic alphabet and a number of minor variants, and some runes doubled as symbols representative of human traits or ideals, much as the Romans used oak and laurel leaves to denote strength and victory. In AD 98, in his work *Germania*,

Himmler inspects the inmates of a concentration camp. Himmler actually witnessed some mass executions, but was nauseated and had to leave the acts of murder to countless others.

the historian Tacitus described in detail how the Germans engaged in divination by runes. In the 19th and early 20th centuries, runes began to be re-examined by the fashionable '*Völkisch*' or 'folk' movements of northern Europe, which promoted interest in traditional myths, beliefs and festivals. Among these groups was the Thule Society; and through his association with its activities during 1919–20 Heinrich Himmler began to look back to the mystical Dark Ages for much of his inspiration. He had always had a fascination for cryptic codes and hidden messages, so it was doubly appropriate that he should tap many of the ideas in pagan symbolism and adopt, or adapt, certain runes for use by his SS.

All pre-1939 Allgemeine-SS recruits were instructed in runic symbolism as part of their probationary training. By 1945, 14 main varieties of rune were in use by the SS, and these are described from A to N below and shown in the accompanying illustrations.

UNIFORMS AND INSIGNIA

The earliest Nazis wore normal civilian clothing and were distinguished only by their crudely hand-made *Kampfbinde,* or swastika armbands, worn on the left upper arm. With the advent of the paramilitary SA in 1921, however, it became necessary to evolve

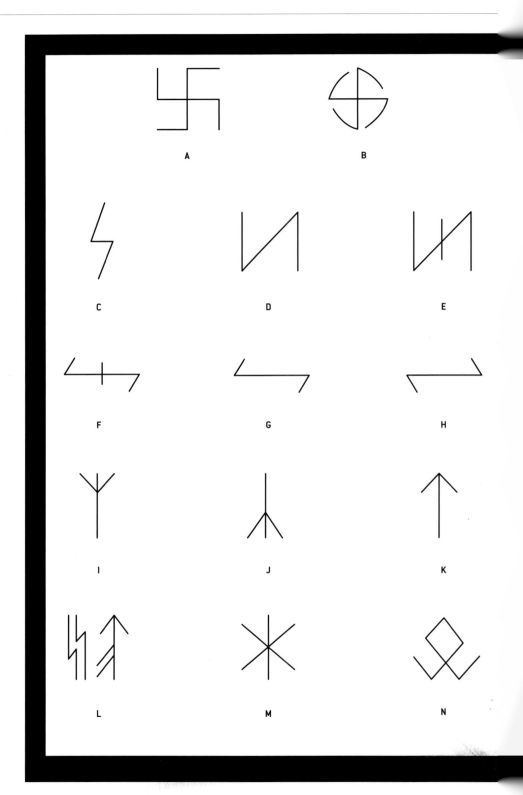

(A) The Hakenkreuz

The *Hakenkreuz* or swastika was the pagan Germanic sign of the thundergod Donner or Thor. During the 19th century it came to be regarded as symbolic of nationalism and the racial struggle, and in the post-1918 period was adopted by several Freikorps units, primarily the Ehrhardt Brigade. As the senior badge of the Nazi Party and state, it inevitably featured on many SS accoutrements, either static (i.e. standing flat) or mobile (i.e. standing on one point to give the appearance of an advancing movement). An elongated version of the mobile swastika was used by the Germanic-SS in Flanders.

(B) The Sonnenrad

The *Sonnenrad* or 'sunwheel' swastika was the Old Norse representation of the sun, and was taken up as an emblem by the Thule Society. It was later used as a sign by the Waffen-SS divisions *Wiking* and *Nordland*, many of whose members were Scandinavian nationals, and also by the Schalburg Corps, which was in effect the Danish branch of the Allgemeine-SS.

(C) The Sig-Rune

The *Sig-Rune*, also known as the *Siegrune*, was symbolic of victory. In 1933 SS-Sturmhauptführer Walter Heck, a graphic designer employed by the badge manufacturing firm of Ferdinand Hoffstütter in Bonn, drew two *Sig-Runes* side by side and thus created the ubiquitous 'SS-Runes' insignia used thereafter by all branches of the organization. (The SS paid him 2.50 Reichsmarks for the rights to his design!) Heck was likewise responsible for the 'SA-Runes' badge, which combined a runic 'S' with a Gothic 'A'.

(D) The Ger-Rune

The *Ger-Rune* was symbolic of communal spirit, and featured as a variant divisional sign of the Waffen-SS division *Nordland*.

(E) The Wolfsangel

The *Wolfsangel* or 'wolf hook' was originally a pagan device that supposedly possessed the magical power to ward off werewolves. It then became a heraldic symbol representing a wolf trap, and as such appeared, and still features, on the coat-of-arms of the city of Wolfstein. During the 15th century it was adopted as an emblem by peasants in their revolt against the mercenaries of the German princes. It was thereafter regarded as being symbolic of liberty and independence, although it was also known as the 'Zeichen der Willkür' or 'badge of wanton tyranny' during the Thirty Years' War. The *Wolfsangel* was an early emblem of the NSDAP, and was later used as a sign by the Waffen-SS division *Das Reich*.

(F) The Wolfsangel (variant)

A squat version of the *Wolfsangel* was the badge of the Weer Afdeelingen (WA), the Dutch Nazi Party's equivalent of the German SA, and was also used by the Germanic-SS in the Netherlands. It was later adopted by the Waffen-SS division *Landstorm Nederland*, which comprised Dutch volunteers.

(G) The Opfer-Rune

The *Opfer-Rune* symbolized self-sacrifice. It was used after 1918 by the Stahlhelm war veterans' association and was later the badge which commemorated the Nazi martyrs of the 1923 Munich Putsch. It also formed part of the design of the SA Sports Badge for War Wounded, which could be won by disabled SS ex-servicemen.

(H) The Eif-Rune

The *Eif-Rune* represented zeal and enthusiasm. It was the early insignia of specially selected SS adjutants assigned personally to Hitler and, as such, was worn by Rudolf Hess in 1929.

(I) The Leben-Rune

The *Leben-Rune* or 'life' rune symbolized life and was adopted by the SS Lebensborn Society and Ahnenerbe. It likewise featured on SS documents and grave markers to show date of birth.

(J) The Toten-Rune

The *Toten-Rune* or 'death' rune represented death, and was used on documents and grave markers to show date of death.

(K) The Tyr-Rune

The *Tyr-Rune*, also known as the *Kampf-Rune* or 'battle' rune, was the pagan Germanic sign of Tyr, the god of war, and was symbolic of leadership in battle. It was commonly used by the SS as a grave marker, replacing the Christian cross. A *Tyr-Rune* worn on the upper left arm indicated graduation from the SA-Reichsführerschule, which trained SS officers until 1934. It was later the specialist badge of the SS Recruiting & Training Department, and an emblem of the Waffen-SS division *30 Januar*, which comprised staff and pupils from various SS training schools.

(L) The Heilszeichen

The *Heilszeichen* or 'prosperity' symbols represented success and good fortune, and appeared on the SS death's head ring.

(M) The Hagall-Rune

The *Hagall-Rune* stood for unshakable faith (in Nazi philosophy), as expected of all SS members. It featured on the SS death's head ring as well as on ceremonial accoutrements used at SS weddings.

(N) The Odal-Rune

The *Odal-Rune* symbolized kinship and family and the bringing together of people of similar blood. It was the badge of the SS Rasse- und Siedlungshauptamt, and emblem of the Waffen-SS division *Prinz Eugen*, the first SS unit recruited from the *Volksdeutsche* community. The finer symbolic points of these runes were never generally appreciated by the majority of men who wore them, as instruction in their meaning ceased around 1940.

Hitler drives amidst rejoicing *Leibstandarte* soldiers after the victory in Poland in 1939. The *Leibstandarte* remained one of Hitler's elite divisions throughout the war, but showed a ready attitude to torching villages during the Polish campaign.

a uniform specifically for its members. At first their dress lacked any consistency and was characteristically Freikorps in style, generally taking the form of field-grey army surplus or windcheater jackets, waist belts with cross-straps, grey trousers, trench boots, steel helmets and mountain caps. Many SA men simply retained the uniforms they had worn during the 1914–18 war, stripped of badges. The swastika armband was the only constant feature, sometimes bearing a metal numeral or emblem to indicate unit identity, and a metal 'pip' or cloth stripes to denote rank. In 1923 members of the Stabswache and Stosstrupp *Adolf Hitler* wore similar garb with the addition of a Prussian-style death's head on the cap, usually surmounted by the *Reichskokarde*, a circular metal cockade in the imperial colours of black, white and red. After the failure of the Munich Putsch and the banning of the SA and the Stosstrupp, the men continued to wear their old uniforms as members of the clandestine Frontbanne, adding a steel helmet badge to the centre of the swastika armband.

At the end of 1924, Leutnant Gerhard Rossbach, formerly one of the most famous of the Freikorps and SA leaders, acquired a bargain lot of surplus German army tropical brown shirts in Austria. When the NSDAP was reconstituted and the SA reactivated in February 1925, Hitler kitted his men out with these readily available shirts and had ties, breeches and képis made to match. Thus, by chance circumstances rather than design, brown became the adopted colour of the SA and the Nazi Party in general. When the Stosstrupp was re-formed in April of the same year, under the auspices of the SA, its members too were issued with brown shirts. To distinguish them from the SA proper, however, they retained their death's heads and wore black képis, black ties, black breeches and black borders to the swastika armband.

By 9 November 1925, when the term Schutzstaffel was adopted, the brown shirt with black accoutrements was firmly established as the 'traditional uniform' of the SS. The vast majority of SS men, who were also members of the NSDAP, wore the Nazi Party badge on their ties.

On 9 November 1926, the rapidly expanding SA introduced collar patches or *Kragenspiegel* to indicate unit and rank, replacing the badges and stripes formerly worn on the armband. The right patch bore unit numerals and the left patch a Stahlhelm-style system of rank pips, bars and oakleaves. By contrasting the colour of the patch with that of the numerals, an attempt was made to reflect the state colours of the district in which the unit concerned was located, e.g. Berlin SA men wore black and white patches, Hamburg SA men red and white, Munich men blue and white, and so on. This arrangement proved difficult to sustain and the colour combinations ultimately underwent a number of changes. SA unit patches were particularly complex, accommodating not only Standarte, specialist and staff appointments, but also Sturmbann and Sturm designations.

In August 1929, the SS likewise introduced collar patches to denote rank and unit. As with the SA, rank was shown on the left patch, or both patches for Standartenführer and above, with unit markings on the right patch. However, the SS system was much simpler than that of the SA. All SS collar patches were black in colour with white, silver or grey numerals, pips, bars and oakleaves. Moreover, the unit collar patches were restricted to indicating Standarte, specialist or staff appointment. To show Sturmbann and Sturm membership the SS devised their own complicated system of 'cuff titles', narrow black bands worn on the lower left sleeve. Within every Fuss-Standarte, each Sturmbann was assigned a colour which bordered the upper and lower edges of the cuff title. The prescribed Sturmbann colours were: Sturmbann I – green; II – dark blue; III – red; IV (Reserve) – light blue. The number and, if appropriate, honour name of the wearer's Sturm appeared embroidered in grey or silver thread on the title. Thus a member of the 2nd Sturm, 1st Sturmbann, 41st SS-Fuss-Standarte would wear a green-bordered cuff title bearing the numeral '2', in conjunction with the number '41' on his right collar patch. A man in the 11th Sturm 'Adolf Höh', 3rd Sturmbann, 30th SS-Fuss-Standarte would sport a red-edged cuff title with the legend '11 Adolf Höh', and regimental numeral '30' on the right collar patch.

All members of Allgemeine-SS cavalry units had yellow-edged cuff titles, while those of signals and pioneer formations had their titles bordered in brown and black, respectively. A relatively small number of cuff titles bore Roman numerals or designations relating to staff or specialist appointments. During the autumn of 1929, at the same time as the new SS collar patches and cuff titles were being manufactured and distributed, a small sharp-winged eagle and swastika badge, or *Hoheitsabzeichen,* was introduced for wear on the SA and SS képi in place of the *Reichskokarde.* SS bandsmen's uniforms were further modified by the addition of black and white military-style 'swallows' nests' worn at the shoulder.

At the end of 1931 the SS adopted the motto 'Meine Ehre heisst Treue' ('My Honour is Loyalty') following upon a well-publicized open letter which Hitler had sent to Kurt Daluege, commander of the Berlin SS, after the Stennes Revolt, declaring in his praise: 'SS Mann, deine Ehre heisst Treue'. Almost immediately, a belt buckle incorporating the motto into its design was commissioned and produced by the Overhoff firm of Lüdenscheid to replace the SA buckle hitherto worn by all members of the SS. The new buckle was circular in form for officers and rectangular for lower ranks, and continued in wear unchanged until 1945.

In May 1933 shoulder straps or *Achselstücke* were devised for wear on the right shoulder only. These straps were adornments to be used in conjunction with the collar insignia already in existence and indicated rank level (i.e. enlisted man or NCO/junior officer/intermediate officer/senior officer) rather than actual rank.

In February 1934 a silver *Ehrenwinkel für Alte Kämpfer* (Chevron for the Old Guard) was authorized for wear on the upper right arm by all members of the SS who had joined the SS, NSDAP or any of the other Party-affiliated organizations prior to 30 January 1933. Qualification was later extended to include former members of the police, armed forces or Stahlhelm who fulfilled certain conditions and transferred into the SS. The traditional brownshirt uniform of the SS therefore developed almost continually over 11 years and incorporated many additions or alterations at specific times. These can be of great assistance in dating period photographs. With the advent of the black uniform the traditional uniform was gradually phased out, and it was not generally worn after 1934, except on special ceremonial occasions by members of the SS Old Guard.

RIGHT: Here we see Reichsführer-SS Heinrich Himmler in 1937. SS officers had the option of purchasing leather overcoats for winter wear. Himmler very much favoured them, and could often be seen in one, sporting the distinctive collar patches of his rank and the silver-grey lapels worn by Oberführer and above. To his right is an SS-Unterscharführer in walking-out dress, c. 1938. Members of the Stammabteilungen, or Supplementary Reserve Detachments, wore SS uniform with distinctive silver-grey collar patches and cuff titles. On the left is an SS-Rottenführer, SS-Reiterstandarte 6, summer 1939. He wears the white linen summer uniform newly authorized for wear between 1 April and 30 September each year. Crossed lances feature on both the unit collar patch and the specialist sleeve diamond, while the cuff title is edged in distinctive cavalry yellow. (Osprey Publishing © Paul Hannon)

THE BLACK UNIFORM

A major change to SS uniform was made in 1932, in response to a government demand that the SA and SS should adopt a more 'respectable' outfit as a condition of the lifting of a ban on political uniforms. On 7 July that year a black tunic and peaked cap, harking back to the garb of the imperial Leib-Husaren, were introduced for the SS to replace the brown shirt and képi. These items were made available first to officers, then to lower ranks, and were worn side-by-side with the traditional uniform during 1933 while all members were being kitted out. By mid-1934 sufficient quantities of the black uniform had been manufactured for it to be in general use. The new SS uniform was designed by SS-Oberführer Professor Karl Diebitsch, in conjunction with Walter Heck, who devised the SS-Runes emblem. The tunic comprised a standard four-pocket military-style jacket, the lower two pockets being of the slanted 'slash' type, with a four-button front. There were two belt hooks at the sides and two false buttons at the rear to support the leather waist belt. Insignia were the same as those created for the traditional uniform, and the tunic was worn over a plain brown shirt. The new SS peaked caps were again military in appearance, silver-piped for generals and white-piped for others, with velvet bands and silver cap cords for officers and cloth bands and leather chin straps for lower ranks. As with the képi, a 1929-pattern eagle was worn above a Prussian-style death's head on the cap. Several minor variants of the black uniform were produced in 1933, including types with three buttons down the front and box-pleated pockets in the tunic 'skirt'; but the whole outfit was formalized and standardized by mid-1934, when the new SS-style *Totenkopf* with lower jaw was introduced.

During the remainder of the 1930s, the black service uniform was developed as the SS organization expanded. Items of clothing began to bear the inspection and production stamps of the SS clothing works and RZM makers, examples being 'VA' (the SS-Verwaltungsamt or Administrative HQ), 'Beste Massarbeit' (best quality mass production), 'Vom Reichsführer-SS befohlene Ausführung' (made in accordance with the instructions of the Reichsführer-SS) and 'RZM M1/52' (the code used by the firm of Deschler on their SS cap badges). Greatcoats were produced; and a series of specialist arm diamonds or *Armelrauten* devised for wear on the lower left sleeve. Imperial-style 'pork-pie' field caps (known as *'Krätzchen'* or 'scratchers' because of their rough texture), forage caps and steel helmets began to be worn from 1934 on military manoeuvres, at drill training and during guard duty.

On 21 June 1936, a new and larger SS cap eagle replaced the old 1929 pattern, at the same time as the introduction of a series of SS swords and the SS chained dagger. Also around that period, white shirts were authorized for wear under the black tunic on ceremonial occasions. For evening functions such as parties, dances and so on, there were black mess jackets for officers and white 'monkey suits' for waiters, all sporting full SS insignia. Finally, as from 27 June 1939, officers were provided with an all-white version of the service uniform for walking-out during the summer period, officially defined as running from 1 April to 30 September each year. The white uniform was also extended to other ranks, but, with the exception of cavalry troopers, was seldom worn.

Full-time SS men were regularly issued with items of uniform and equipment. So far as part-timers were concerned, however, all uniform articles had to be purchased by the SS members themselves at their own expense. The only exceptions were free replacements for items lost or damaged during the course of duty. If an SS man wished to acquire a new tunic, for example, he could either buy it direct from a tailoring shop that was an approved sales outlet of the RZM, i.e. an authorized dealer in Nazi Party uniforms and equipment, or else place a pre-paid order with his local Trupp or Sturm which would, in turn, arrange to requisition a tunic on his behalf from one of the clothing stores run by the SS administrative authorities. The latter regularly produced price lists which were circulated to all SS formations for the attention of would-be buyers.

Gauleiter Arthur Greiser was the governor of the Nazi-occupied territory of Wartheland. Also an SS-Obergruppenführer, he exemplified how the Allgemeine-SS was able to dominate important political offices in occupied lands.

The gradual introduction of the grey service uniform, combined with the sudden reduction in the number of active part-time Allgemeine-SS men because of enhanced conscription at the outbreak of war, led to a surplus of black uniforms building up in SS stores after 1939. In 1942 the police collected most of the unwanted black Allgemeine-SS uniforms in Germany and sent them east to the Baltic States, Poland and the Ukraine for distribution to the native auxiliary police units being raised there. All SS insignia were removed, green facings added, and new badges stitched in place. The remainder of the surplus black uniforms in Germany were shipped west and issued to the Germanic-SS in Flanders, Holland, Norway and Denmark, who again attached their own insignia. Consequently, very few black Allgemeine-SS tunics survived the war with their original German badges intact.

THE GREY UNIFORM

From 1935, field-grey uniforms in the same style as the black service uniform were issued to members of the *Leibstandarte Adolf Hitler* and SS-VT for wear during their everyday duties. Simultaneously, an earth-brown uniform of identical cut was authorized for SS-Totenkopfverbände men serving in concentration camps. The new uniforms immediately proved to be eminently suited to the nature of the tasks performed by these full-time militarized units. Thereafter, members of the *Leibstandarte*, SS-VT and SS-Totenkopfverbände donned the black uniform only on ceremonial occasions and for walking-out.

In 1938 the Allgemeine-SS followed suit by introducing a very elegant pale grey uniform for its full-time staff, thus bringing the whole SS organization into line with the general war footing of the other uniformed services. The new outfit was identical in style to the black uniform, but bore an SS-pattern shoulder strap on the left shoulder as well as one on the right, and replaced the swastika armband with a cloth version of the 1936-pattern SS eagle. They were never issued with grey outfits and so continued to proudly wear the black uniform whilst on duty in Germany. By 1944, however, that most impressive of all uniforms, which had been such a status symbol in the pre-war days, had become an object of derision since its wearers were increasingly thought of as shirking military service. The German civil population revered the Waffen-SS, whom they affectionately dubbed the 'White SS', because of their frontline sacrifices, and despised the part-timers, the so-called 'Black SS'. The grey uniform fulfilled its function by providing the full-time and senior Allgemeine-SS membership with a shield, albeit a psychological one, against such criticism: in the eyes of the public, they were 'White SS'.

DAGGERS AND SWORDS

The SS service dagger, or *Dienstdolch,* was introduced along with its SA counterpart by the interim Chief of Staff of the SA and Himmler's then superior, Obergruppenführer von Krausser, under SA Order No. 1734/33 of 15 December 1933. Black and silver in colour, it bore the SS motto on the blade and runes and eagle on the grip, and its general design was based on that of a style of 15th–17th century Swiss and German sidearms, usually referred to today as the 'Holbein' style. Worn by all ranks of the Allgemeine-SS with service and walking-out dress, the SS dagger was presented to its owner at the special ceremony held when he graduated from SS-Anwärter to SS-Mann. It was not issued at any other time, or en masse like the daggers of the SA. Each SS-Anwärter paid the full cost of his dagger, usually in small instalments, prior to its presentation. On 17 February 1934, SS-Gruppenführer Kurt Wittje, Chief of the SS-

Amt, forerunner of the SS–Hauptamt, forbade the private purchase or 'trading-in' of SS daggers on the open market. Henceforth, daggers could only be ordered from manufacturers through the SS–Amt, for issue via the three main SS uniform distribution centres at Munich, Dresden and Berlin, which regularly processed requisitions received from the various Oberabschnitte Headquarters. Moreover, it was made a disciplinary offence for an SS man to dispose of or lose his dagger, on the grounds that it was a symbol of his office. In that way it was assured that no unauthorized person could buy or otherwise acquire an SS dagger.

As of 25 January 1935, members dismissed from the SS had to surrender their daggers, even though they were personal property paid for by their own means. In cases of voluntary resignation or normal retirement, however, daggers could be retained and the person in question was given a certificate stating that he was entitled to possess the dagger.

Jürgen Stroop (centre, in field cap) was the SS commander of forces involved in the liquidation of the Warsaw ghetto in 1943. He gave a full account of the destruction in a book chillingly titled *Es gibt keinen jüdischen Wohnbezirk in Warschau mehr!* (The Warsaw Ghetto is No More!).

SS soldiers form up on parade in 1935. By this point in history, SS membership numbered well over 200,000 people.

Only the finest makers of edged weapons were contracted to produce the 1933-pattern SS dagger. These included Böker & Co., Carl Eickhorn, Gottlieb Hammesfahr, Richard Herder, Jacobs & Co., Robert Klaas, Ernst Pack & Söhne, and C. Bertram Reinhardt. The earliest pieces from the 1933–35 period featured the maker's trademark on the blade, a dark blue-black anodized steel scabbard, and nickel-silver fittings, with the crossguard reverse stamped 'I', 'II', or 'III' to denote that the dagger had passed inspection at the main SS uniform distribution centre responsible for issuing it, viz. Munich, Dresden or Berlin respectively. During 1936–37 makers' marks were replaced by RZM code numbers, scabbards began to be finished with black paint, and the stamped inspection numerals were discontinued as the RZM had by then taken over entirely the regulation of quality control. Finally, from 1938, nickel-silver gave way to cheaper plated steel for the mounts and aluminium for the grip eagle. Despite the declining standard of materials used, a high-quality appearance was maintained and the daggers were consistent in their fine finish.

The SS dagger was suspended at an angle from a single leather strap until November 1934, when Himmler introduced a vertical hanger for wear with service dress during crowd control. However, the vertical hanger, while more stable, was too reminiscent of the humble bayonet frog, and in 1936 the single strap was reintroduced for both walking out and service uniforms; thereafter the vertical hanger was restricted to use on route marches and military exercises.

In September 1940, due to national economies, the 1933-pattern dagger was withdrawn from production for the duration of the war. A more ornate SS dagger, to be worn only by officers and those Old Guard COs and other ranks who had joined the organization prior to 30 January 1933, was introduced by Himmler on 21 June 1936. Generally known as the 'chained dagger', it was very similar to the 1933 pattern but was suspended by means of linked octagonal plates, ornately embossed with death's heads and SS runes, and featured a central scabbard mount decorated with swastikas. During the 1936–37 period, these chains and fittings, which were designed by Karl Diebitsch, were made from nickel-silver. Later examples were in nickel-plated steel, with slightly smaller, less oval-shaped skulls. Chained daggers bore no makers' marks and it is likely that only one firm, probably Carl Eickhorn, was contracted to produce them.

Each chained dagger had to be privately purchased from the SS administrative authorities in Berlin via the various Oberabschnitte headquarters, requisition forms being submitted regularly at the start of every month. Direct orders from individual officers were not entertained. In 1943, members of the security police and the SD were permitted to wear a knot with the chained dagger when it was being worn with field-grey uniform, and thus the SD became the only branch of the Allgemeine-SS to sport dagger knots. Production of the chained dagger was discontinued at the end of 1943 because of material shortages, and its wear was subsequently forbidden for the duration of the war. In addition to the standard 1933-pattern and 1936-pattern SS daggers, several special presentation variants were also produced. The first of these was the so-called Röhm SS Honour Dagger, 9,900 of which were distributed in February 1934 by SA Stabschef Ernst Röhm to members of the SS Old Guard. It took the form of a basic 1933-pattern dagger with the addition of the dedication 'In herzlicher Kameradschaft, Ernst Röhm' ('In heartfelt comradeship, Ernst Röhm') etched on the reverse side of the blade. Following the Night of the Long Knives, 200 similar daggers, etched 'In herzlicher Kameradschaft, H. Himmler', were presented by the Reichsführer to SS personnel who had participated in the bloody purge of the SA.

A very ornate and expensive SS honour dagger, with oakleaf-decorated crossguards, leather-covered scabbard and Damascus steel blade, was instituted by Himmler in 1936 for award to high-ranking officers in recognition of special achievement. When one was presented to the SDAP Treasurer, SS-Oberst-Gruppenführer Franz Xaver Schwarz, he responded by secretly commissioning the Eickhorn firm to produce an even more elaborate example, with fittings and chain hanger in solid silver, which he then gave to Himmler as a birthday present.

During the 1933–36 era, SS officers and NCOs engaged in ceremonial duties were permitted to wear a variety of privately purchased army-pattern sabres, often with silver rather than regulation gilt fittings. In 1936, however, at the same time as the introduction of the chained dagger, a series of standardized swords in the classic straight-bladed 'Degen' style was created specifically for members of the SS and Police, emphasizing the close relationship between the two organizations. There were minor differences between swords for officers and those for COs, while SS swords featured runes in their design and police examples the police eagle on the grip. Personnel attached to SS-Reiterstandarten retained the traditional curved sabre for use on

Displayed on the front cover of *Signal* magazine, Léon Degrelle was a new breed of Waffen-SS commander. A Walloon Belgian politician, he served in the German Army from 1941 and the Waffen-SS from 1943, receiving the Knight's Cross for his service.

horseback. SS NCOs could readily purchase their swords, via local units, from the SS administrative authorities. The officer's sword, on the other hand, which was referred to as the Ehrendegen des Reichsführers-SS or Reichsführer's Sword of Honour, was given an elevated status. It was bestowed by Himmler only upon selected Allgemeine-SS commanders and the graduates of the Waffen-SS Junkerschulen at Bad Tolz and Braunschweig. Manufacture of the Ehrendegen ceased in January 1941 for the duration of the war, and SS officers commissioned after that date frequently reverted to the old practice of carrying army sabres.

Still more exclusive were the so-called Geburtstagsdegen or 'birthday swords', given by Himmler to SS generals and other leading Nazi personalities as birthday presents. They were made to order by Germany's master swordsmith, Paul Müller, who was Director of the SS Damascus Blade School at Dachau, and featured hallmarked silver fittings and blades of the finest Damascus steel with exquisitely raised and gilded dedications from Himmler. Recipients included the German Foreign Minister, SS-Obergruppenführer Joachim von Ribbentrop, and the Führer of Oberabschnitt Nord, Wilhelm Rediess. It was even written into Müller's contract of employment that he could be recalled from leave should Himmler require a birthday sword made at short notice! Their production ceased at the end of 1944.

DECORATIONS

SS men were eligible for the whole range of orders, medals and awards created by the Nazi regime, which recognized both military and civil achievement as well as meritorious service to the NSDAP. Indeed, all SS candidates were expected to win the SA Military Sports Badge and the German National Sports Badge during their probationary training. In addition to these national honours, a small number of decorations were created specifically for the SS. Foremost among these were the SS Dienstauszeichnungen or long-service awards, instituted on 30 January 1938. The series comprised medals for four and eight years' service, and large swastika-shaped 'crosses' for 12 and 25 years. The Dienstauszeichnungen were intended primarily for members of the militarized SS formations, although full-time officials of the Allgemeine-SS were also eligible. Part-time members of the Allgemeine-SS, no matter how long their period of service, fell outside the award criteria and had to settle for one of the succession of NSDAP service decorations. Photographic evidence indicates that the SS Dienstauszeichnungen were not widely distributed and, in fact, it is likely that presentations ceased around 1941, for the duration of the war. Himmler appears to have been virtually the only senior SS leader to wear his decoration consistently.

THIS IS THE SITE OF
THE INFAMOUS BELSEN CONCENTRATION CAMP
Liberated by the British on 15 april 1945.

10,000 UNBURIED DEAD WERE FOUND HERE.
ANOTHER 13,000 HAVE SINCE DIED.
ALL OF THEM VICTIMS OF THE
GERMAN NEW ORDER IN EUROPE.
AND AN EXAMPLE OF NAZI KULTUR.

Belsen, 1945. Allied correspondents take down notes of what happened at the concentration camp. By this time, ex-SS servicemen were hunted figures.

An SS Marksmanship Badge was created prior to the outbreak of the war, for proficiency in rifle and machine-gun shooting; however, there is no evidence that the badge was put into production. Examples that exist in private collections, bearing the marks of the Gahr firm, are thought to be fakes. A Silver Clasp for female SS auxiliaries was instituted in July 1943 but, again, was never manufactured during the war.

THE DEATH'S HEAD RING

One of the most obscure yet potent of all SS uniform accoutrements was the Totenkopfring der SS, or SS death's head ring, instituted by Himmler on 10 April 1934. The Totenkopfring was not classed as a national decoration as it was in the gift of the Reichsführer. However, it ranked as a senior award within the SS brotherhood, recognizing the wearer's personal achievement, devotion to duty, and loyalty to Hitler and his ideals. The story of the death's head ring gives an interesting insight into the general workings and philosophy of Himmler and the SS.

The concept and runic form of the ring was undoubtedly adopted by Himmler from Pagan Germanic mythology, which related how the great god Thor possessed a pure silver ring on which people could take oaths (much as Christians swear on the Bible), and how binding treaties were carved in runes on Wotan's spear. The death's head ring comprised a massive band of oakleaves deeply embossed with a Totenkopf and a number of symbolic runes. Each piece was cast, then exquisitely hand-finished by specially commissioned jewellers working for the firm of Otto Gahr in Munich (which also made the 'Deutschland Erwache' standard tops for the NSDAP). The ring started off as a strip of silver which was bent circular to the required finger size and then joined at the front. The death's head was formed from a separate piece of silver and was soldered to the front to cover the join. The larger the ring, the larger the space between the death's head and the two adjacent Sig-Runes. Each completed ring was finely engraved inside the band with the letters 'S.lb.' (the abbreviation of 'Seinem lieben' or, roughly, 'To dear ...') followed by the recipient's surname, the date of presentation and a facsimile of Himmler's signature.

Initially, the weighty silver ring was reserved primarily for those Old Guard veterans with SS membership numbers below 5,000, but qualifications for award were gradually extended until, by 1939, virtually all officers with over three years' service were eligible. Award of the ring could be postponed if the prospective holder had been punished for contravention of the SS Penal and Disciplinary Code. Certified lists of nominees for the ring, together with their finger sizes, were regularly submitted by the SS Abschnitte headquarters to the SS Personalhauptamt in Berlin, which processed the applications and duly awarded rings and accompanying citations on behalf of the Reichsführer-SS. Each citation read as follows:

I award you the SS Death's Head Ring.

The ring symbolizes our loyalty to the Führer, our steadfast obedience and our brotherhood and comradeship.

The Death's Head reminds us that we should be ready at any time to lay down our lives for the good of the Germanic people.

The runes diametrically opposite the Death's Head are symbols from our past of the prosperity which we will restore through National Socialism. The two Sig-Runes stand for the name of our SS. The swastika and the Hagall-Rune represent our unshakable faith in the ultimate victory of our philosophy.

The ring is wreathed in oak, the traditional German leaf.

The Death's Head Ring cannot be bought or sold and must never fall into the hands of those not entitled to wear it.

When you leave the SS, or when you die, the ring must be returned to the Reichsführer-SS. The unauthorized acquisition of duplicates of the ring is forbidden and punishable by Law. Wear the ring with honour!

H. HIMMLER

The ring, which was to be worn only on the ring finger of the left hand, was bestowed on set SS promotion dates. All awards were recorded in the Dienstaltersliste, or Officers' Seniority List, and the personnel files of the holders. All ring holders who were demoted, suspended or dismissed from the SS, or who resigned or retired, had to return their rings and citations to the SS Personalhauptamt. Those later accepted back into the organization would again qualify for the ring. When a serving ring holder died, his relatives could retain his citation as a keepsake, but had to return his ring to the SS Personalhauptamt which arranged for its preservation in Himmler's castle at Wewelsburg in permanent commemoration of the holder. Similarly, if a ring holder fighting with the Wehrmacht or Waffen-SS was killed in action, his ring had to be retrieved from the body by members of his unit and returned by the unit commander to the SS Personalhauptamt for preservation. In effect, the returned rings of dead SS men constituted military memorials and were cared for as such at Wewelsburg's ever-growing 'Schrein des Inhabers des Totenkopfringes' or 'Shrine to Holders of the Death's Head Ring'.

The death's head ring became so sought-after an honour that many SS and police men not entitled to wear it had a variety of unofficial 'skull rings' produced in gold and silver by local jewellers and even concentration camp inmates. Others wore their old death's head jewellery which had been popular in the Freikorps days. However, these lacked any runic symbolism and were rather vulgar representations of the real thing.

On 17 October 1944, the Reichsführer-SS cancelled further manufacture and presentation of the Totenkopf ring for the duration of the war. In the spring of 1945, on Himmler's orders, all the rings which had been kept in the shrine were blast-sealed into a mountainside near Wewelsburg, to prevent their capture by the Allies. To this day, they have never been found.

Between 1934 and 1944 around 14,500 rings were awarded. As at 1 January 1945, according to information compiled by the SD, 64 per cent of these had been returned to the SS on the deaths of their holders (i.e. those now buried at Wewelsburg), 10 per cent had been lost on the battlefield, and 26 per cent were either still in the possession of ring holders or otherwise unaccounted for.

FLAGS AND BANNERS

From 4 July 1926, the SS had the distinction of keeping the most revered flag in the Third Reich, the Blutfahne or 'Blood Banner', which had been carried at the head of the Nazi Old Guard during the Munich Putsch when they were fired upon by the police. It was spattered with the gore of those shot during the encounter, and was thereafter considered to be something of a 'holy relic'. SS-Truppführer Jakob Grimminger from the Munich SS detachment, a veteran of the World War I Gallipoli campaign and participant in the 1922 'Battle of Coburg', was accorded the honour of being the first official bearer of the Blood Banner, and retained that position throughout his career. The last public appearance of the Blutfahne was at the funeral of Adolf Wagner, Gauleiter of Munich-Upper Bavaria, in April 1944. By that time Grimminger had attained the rank of SS-Standartenführer, his association with the mystical flag having assured him a steady succession of promotions.

German police and local auxiliaries herd Jewish people in the Lodz ghetto. An unpalatable fact of SS and police power is that it was often supported by the efforts of local citizens, through either compulsion or enthusiastic volunteering.

Every Allgemeine-SS Standarte was represented by a banner or Feldzeichen, which was itself known as the regimental 'Standarte'. Somewhat reminiscent of the ancient Roman vexillum banner, it took the form of a wooden pole surmounted by a metal eagle and wreathed swastika, below which was a black and silver boxed nameplate bearing the title of the SS Standarte on the front and the initials 'NSDAP' on the back. From the box was suspended a red silk flag with a black static swastika on a white circle. The motto 'Deutschland Erwache' ('Germany Awake') was embroidered in bullion on the obverse, with 'Nat. Soz. Deutsche Arbeiterpartei – Sturmabteilung' on the reverse. The flag was finished off with a black/white/red fringe and tassels. Apart from the black name box, the SS Feldzeichen was identical to that of the SA.

When an SS unit achieved roughly regimental proportions it was awarded a Feldzeichen, in a mass pseudo-religious ceremony that took place each September as part of the annual SDAP celebrations. During the proceedings Hitler would present many new standards to regimental commanders and touch them with the Blutfahne that Grimminger was carrying alongside, so linking in spirit the most recent SS members with the martyrs of the Munich Putsch.

SS-Reiterstandarten carried similar but distinctive Feldzeichen which had the 'Deutschland Erwache' flag hanging from a wooden bar fixed at right angles to the standard pole. In place of the name box these cavalry standards featured a black patch, or Fahnenspiegel, on the flag cloth, bearing crossed lances and the unit designation in silver. Each SS Sturmbann was represented by a Sturmbannfahne or battalion flag, which took the form of a brilliant red ground with a large black mobile swastika on a white circular field, with black and silver twisted cord edging. In the upper left corner, or canton, a black Fahnenspiegel was embroidered in silver thread with the Sturmbann and Standarte numbers in Roman and Arabic numerals respectively. The majority of these SS flags were made by the firm of Fahnen-Hoffmann, Berlin. SS standard-bearers initially wore a 'heartshaped' SA-style metal gorget or Kornet, dating from 1929, upon which was affixed a gilded eight-pointed sunburst surmounted by a facsimile of the centrepiece of the SA belt buckle. In 1938 a new and unique SS-pattern standard-bearer's gorget appeared, crescent-shaped and featuring a large eagle and swastika and a suspension chain decorated with runes and death's heads. SS flag-bearers also wore a massive bandolier in black, with silver brocade edging.

Command flags, or Kommandoflaggen, in the shape of rigid pennants on flag poles, were carried as unit markers at large parades or, in smaller versions, were flown from the mudguards of staff cars and other vehicles. They were square, rectangular or triangular in form depending upon designation, and were made of black and white waterproof

cloth with rustproof silver thread. Command flags were usually covered in a transparent celluloid casing during bad weather. Each SS Oberabschnitt was required to keep on hand one official vehicle flag and one command pennant for the Reichsführer-SS, for use in the event of a 'flying visit' by Himmler. Other Kommandoflaggen included those for the Heads of SS Hauptämter, SS Oberabschnitte and Abschnitte commanders, the leaders of Standarten, Reiterstandarten, Sturmbanne, SS stores and Inspectorates, and senior Sponsoring Members.

Heinrich Himmler appoints Jonas Lie as head of the Germanic SS in Norway, May 1941. He also acted as the collaborationist Minister of Police between 1941 and 1945.

ABOVE: 1: Schalburgmand, Schalburg Corps, Denmark, 1944. The Schalburg Corps was, in all but name, the Germanic-SS in Denmark, and the uniform worn by its members reflected that fact. 2: SS-Obergruppenführer Hanke; Breslau, April 1945. On 28 April 1945, Himmler was expelled from the Nazi Party and all his government offices for attempting to negotiate an armistice with the Western Allies. Hitler subsequently appointed Karl Hanke, an Allgemeine-SS Obergruppenführer and Gauleiter of Lower Silesia, as the new Reichsführer-SS, although Hanke had by that time abandoned his post in the besieged city of Breslau and never received word of his promotion. 3: A Volkssturm NCO, clutching his *Panzerfaust* and ready to die for the cause in spring 1945. The *Panzerfaust* was a short-range weapon, but was capable of destroying most Allied tanks. (Osprey Publishing © Paul Hannon)

THE GERMANIC-SS

Himmler saw the cornerstone of the Greater German Reich as being an SS organization with native branches in each of the Western occupied territories. He envisaged the ultimate creation of a new western Germanic state to be called Burgundia, grouping the Netherlands, Belgium and north-east France, which would be policed and governed solely by the SS according to the SS code and would act as a buffer to protect Germany proper from invasion. The general aim was to attract all the Nordic blood of Europe into the SS, so that never again would the Germanic peoples come into mutual conflict.

To that end, Himmler established a replica of the German Allgemeine-SS in Flanders in September 1940. This Allgemeene-SS Vlaanderen was joined two months later by the Dutch Nederlandsche-SS and in May 1941 the Norges-SS was formed in Norway. Members of these organizations retained their own languages and customs, and came under the jurisdiction of their own national pro-German political leaders. In the autumn of 1942, however, these formations were amalgamated to become branches of a new all-embracing Germanic-SS under Himmler's direct orders. They were retitled Germaansche-SS in Vlaanderen, Germaansche-SS en Nederland and Germanske-SS Norge. After the raising in April 1943 of the Danish Germansk Korpset, later called the Schalburg Corps, the Germanic-SS was complete, with a total active membership of almost 9,000 men. Their primary wartime task was to support the local police by rooting out partisans, subversives and other anti-Nazi elements.

The black uniform of the Germanic-SS in Flanders was virtually identical to that of the Allgemeine-SS. The only points of difference were that the peaked cap featured a large elongated swastika instead of the SS eagle, and a black diamond bearing the SS runes was worn on the left upper arm instead of the swastika armband. Rank insignia were worn on the left collar patch like that of the Allgemeine-SS, while the right collar patch was blank. On the lower left sleeve a black and silver cuff title bore the legend 'SS-Vlaanderen', and the belt buckle featured SS runes in a circle of oakleaves. In civilian clothes, members of the Germanic-SS in Flanders could wear a circular lapel badge with a white swastika on a black background, while Patron Members had their own diamond-shaped badge bearing the SS runes and the letters 'B.L.'. Members of the Vlaanderen-Korps, the reserve branch of the Flemish SS, wore a similar uniform, but were not entitled to sport the peaked cap or arm diamond; they had forage caps with a silver swastika on the left side, and their cuff titles read 'Vlaanderen-Korps'.

Moreover, their belt buckles had only a semi-circle of oakleaves around the runes. Members of the Germanic-SS in the Netherlands were similarly attired. A regimental number appeared on the right collar patch, with SS runes on the right upper arm. A triangle bearing a silver Wolfsangel on a red and black background was worn on the left sleeve, and a silver Wolfsangel also appeared on the peaked cap instead of the SS eagle All ranks wore a blank cuff title on the lower left sleeve.

The uniform of the Germanic-SS in Norway represented a departure from the norm for the Allgemeine-SS. It consisted of a ski cap, tunic, ski trousers or breeches, and mountain boots. Peaked caps were never worn by the Norwegian SS, and jackboots were seldom seen either. On the left upper arm was worn the so-called 'sun eagle' of Vidkun Quisling's Norwegian Nazis, in silver and black, above a cuff title bearing the legend 'Germanske-SS Norge'. A silver sunwheel swastika appeared on the right collar patch, with SS runes on the right upper arm. The Schalburg Corps in Denmark adopted a black uniform conforming with that of the Allgemeine-SS, and rank insignia were again the same although the nomenclature used was that of the Danish police. The main points of difference were that the SS cap eagle was replaced by a winged sunwheel swastika, and a sunwheel swastika also featured on the right collar patch and on the belt buckle. A Danish heraldic shield, comprising three blue lions on a yellow field with red hearts, was worn on the upper left arm above a cuff title bearing the word 'Schalburg'. On ceremonial guard duty, a highly polished black German steel helmet was worn with a large white sunwheel swastika on the right-hand side. For more active purposes, the corps was armed with light infantry weapons and supplied with a more practical khaki field uniform. A so-called Schalburg Cross bearing the corps motto 'Troskab vor Aere' ('Our Honour is Loyalty') was instituted late in the war, and at least one posthumous award is recorded. (It is reported that boxes of these crosses were strewn across the street outside the Schalburg Corps HQ at the Freemasons' Lodge in Copenhagen at the end of the war, and were eagerly picked up by passers-by.)

In addition to the regular Germanic-SS formations, the Allgemeine-SS established its own Germanische Sturmbanne or Germanic Battalions in the areas of the Reich where there were large concentrations of workers imported from the Nordic countries. These foreigners in Germany numbered several hundred thousand by the end of 1942, and posed a major problem for German internal security. To assist in their control, Flemish and Dutch SS officers and men, most of them fresh from frontline service in Russia, were employed by German firms to engage upon a propaganda campaign in the factories. They succeeded in persuading such a large number of their compatriots to join the local Allgemeine-SS that seven Germanic Battalions were set up in the major industrial areas of Berlin, Brunswick, Dresden, Düsseldorf, Hamburg, Nuremberg and Stuttgart. Service in the Germanische Sturmbanne was voluntary and unpaid, and was performed either after work hours or at weekends. Uniforms were supplied by the Allgemeine-SS, and comprised the standard outfit minus the tunic; insignia were worn on the shirt, in the manner of the old SS traditional uniform. It is not known if members were permitted to wear any special badges indicative of their national origin, but it would appear doubtful.

The Allgemeine-SS was in many ways the engine that drove National Socialism once Hitler was firmly established in power from 1933. If we include its authority over the police, its vast industrial power and its pernicious racial doctrines, its influence was felt in many areas of civilian life, both within Germany and within the occupied territories. Yet the Allgemeine-SS would come to be regarded with some distaste as the war went on, not least because many of its personnel hid safely behind a desk, while the Waffen-SS bled out on the frontlines.

THE WAFFEN-SS SOLDIER

The Allgemeine-SS, for all its immense power, has generally been overshadowed in historical focus by its combat counterpart, the Waffen-SS. The Waffen-SS, as we shall see, is an organization of contradictions. On the one hand, for example, it fielded some of the finest combat divisions in the German military system, sent to bolster the toughest sectors of the frontline and known for their fanatical spirit of resistance. Conversely, some of the late-war Waffen-SS formations were little more than cannon-fodder, brutally handled by vengeful Soviet forces surging into the Third Reich from the east. Another example, which shall form a large part of the discussion in remaining chapters, is that the Waffen-SS was part of an organization that prided itself on racial 'purity', yet came to be manned to a large degree by foreigners from the conquered territories.

In the remaining chapters of this book, we will chart the rise and fall of the Waffen-SS, from the victors of 1941 to the hunted of 1945. Before moving through that history, however, in this chapter we will take a more general look at the Waffen-SS soldier, his uniform, equipment, motivations, background, beliefs, tactics, leaders and other issues. As we shall see, the Waffen-SS soldier was born from a unique fusion of ideology and militarism, a combination of factors that could make him one of the most formidable of battlefield warriors.

APPEARANCE

In general terms, and certainly during the early part of the war, the Waffen-SS grenadier wore much the same clothing and carried the same personal equipment as his counterpart in the army. There were minor variations, for example in the exact cut and styling of tunics, sidecaps and field caps; rank insignia were totally different because the Waffen-SS used essentially the same rank structure as the old SA stormtroopers. The national eagle was worn on the left arm instead of on the chest and because almost all of the Waffen-SS divisions were named as well as numbered, black cuff titles were worn on the lower left sleeve.

The most distinctive item of German combat dress, worn by all ranks, was the *Stahlhelm* (steel helmet). Although its shape gave it the nickname 'coalscuttle', it was actually a very practical item, offering protection to the ears and the neck as well as the skull. A tribute to the soundness of its design is that the modern American combat helmet is virtually identical in shape. The standard M35 helmet was made of steel and weighed around a kilogram depending on size. The suspension consisted of an aluminium band covered in leather; this was adjustable to give a comfortable fit as were the black leather chinstraps. A variety of camouflaged helmet covers were also issued, but we shall return to the subject of camouflage later.

Young members of the *Totenkopf*, seen in Berlin in December 1939. The *Totenkopf* Division had been formed only three months previously.

Comfortable clothing is very important if a combat soldier is to operate at maximum efficiency, and the Waffen-SS introduced several ideas to enhance that efficiency. These ideas have subsequently been imitated by the armed forces of many other nations. Over his cotton, aertex or woollen underclothing, the Waffen-SS grenadier wore a grey woollen shirt designed for warmth and ease of movement. Unfortunately, the material had a high wood fibre content, making it scratchy to wear; it also wore out quickly with repeated washing, so later cotton shirts were introduced which were much more practical and popular.

Trousers and tunics were also designed with practicality as well as smartness in mind. Both were made of a wool/rayon mixture, which was extremely hard wearing. The trousers were straight-legged and high-waisted, being supported by braces rather than a belt, although this changed later in the war. The single-breasted tunic, belted at the waist, had four large pockets for carrying personal effects or extra rounds of ammunition.

A variety of field service caps were produced, the most common until 1943 being the sidecap or *Feldmütze,* which was similar in style to those worn by the soldiers of

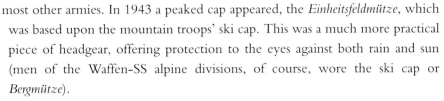

most other armies. In 1943 a peaked cap appeared, the *Einheitsfeldmütze*, which was based upon the mountain troops' ski cap. This was a much more practical piece of headgear, offering protection to the eyes against both rain and sun (men of the Waffen-SS alpine divisions, of course, wore the ski cap or *Bergmütze*).

For cold-weather conditions, the men were issued with a thick woollen calf-length greatcoat, double-breasted for extra protection against the wind. An even thicker version was available for sentries, who needed the extra protection if they were to stay alert. Even these proved inadequate in the arctic conditions of the Russian winter, so by the autumn of 1942 thick, warmly-lined parkas with hoods were being issued. These had drawstrings around the front of the hood and at the waist to help keep the wind out. A sheepskin cap with ear flaps was also introduced. For footwear, the Waffen-SS started the war wearing the standard German calf-length black leather marching boot (*Marschstiefel*), while officers were entitled to taller riding boots (*Reitstiefel*). Experience with frostbite in Russia led to the introduction of a felt overboot, as well as thick mittens in place of the standard woollen gloves, which were hopelessly inadequate. As the war progressed a more practical lace-up ankle boot (*Schnürschuh*) was introduced, based on the mountain troops' climbing boots; these were normally worn with canvas gaiters. They gave greater support to the ankle, enhancing the men's mobility.

CAMOUFLAGE CLOTHING

Production of all uniform items for the Waffen-SS was carried out at concentration camps, particularly Dachau and Buchenwald. This included the camouflage clothing pioneered by the Waffen-SS and which was their most distinctive trademark. Several examples are shown in the accompanying illustrations, but

LEFT: An SS-Unterscharführer of the SS-VT Standarte 1 *Deutschland*, France, June 1940. Holding his early-pattern sidecap with triangular embroidered SS eagle on its left side while he wipes sweat from his face, this CO is dressed in the standard field-grey tunic and trousers which became regulation wear for the Waffen-SS after 1937. He wears standard thigh-length iron-nailed leather marching boots and carries a 7.92mm Kar 98k rifle, while on the front of his belt is the wooden holster-stock for a 9mm C 96 Mauser automatic pistol. (Osprey Publishing © Jeffrey Burn)

because this style of clothing was so important, it is worth looking at more closely.

The Waffen-SS were among the first German units to use what has become known as 'disruptive pattern' clothing, designed to help the men blend in with their background surroundings and make them less visible to their enemies. The idea of camouflage itself is, of course, hardly new, but in the modern sense only dates from the turn of the century when the British Army belatedly decided that red tunics made the men marvellous targets and adopted khaki, a practice which, with variations in shade, was rapidly copied by most other armies. Khaki, or the German field grey-green equivalent, are practical, neutral shades, but the Waffen-SS decided this was not going far enough. What was needed was a form of garment to allow the men to blend in not just with different types of countryside, but with seasonal changes in the coloration of grass and foliage.

From the very outbreak of war in September 1939, most Waffen-SS combat troops wore a loose, thigh-length pullover smock over their

A Waffen-SS sniper prepares to take a shot. The standard weapon of most Waffen-SS soldiers was the Kar 98k rifle, a basic but rugged and accurate 7.92mm bolt-action weapon.

service tunic. Made of a rayon/cotton mixture, it was generously cut for ease of movement, and could be pulled tight at the waist with a drawstring, offering a degree of extra protection against the wind. The collarless head opening also had a drawstring, as did the cuffs, emphasizing the baggy appearance which was quite deliberate and a further form of camouflage in itself. Early pattern smocks had two chest vents to allow the wearer to reach the pockets in his tunic underneath, but it was soon found that this was impossible when webbing was worn, as it had to be, over the smock, so they were discontinued. Loops were also frequently sewn to the shoulders, upper arms and helmet cover to allow foliage to be attached as extra camouflage.

The smocks were reversible, and printed in a variety of patterns to match the changing seasons: light and dark green for spring, two shades of green and a purplish brown for summer, and three shades of russet and brown for autumn. Quantity fabric printing of such complexity had never been tried before, and special dyes and techniques had to be invented. Early smocks were screen printed, but because this took time, especially since the smocks also had to be waterproofed, later versions were machine

Various patterns of Waffen-SS camouflage. 1: Early-pattern camouflage smock. 2: Late-pattern camouflage smock. 3: *Zeltbahn* – this triangular piece of kit was extremely useful, being small and light enough to be carried as part of the assault equipment and serving as a poncho, windbreak or part of a tent. 4: army-pattern reversible winter tunic. 5: Waffen-SS-pattern reversible winter tunic. (Osprey Publishing © Jeffrey Burn)

printed. The patterns were carefully designed to break up the wearer's outline, with small hard-edged splodges of colour outlined in contrasting colours, so that a man standing still in a wood or hedgerow became virtually invisible. There were four basic patterns used as the war progressed, which for convenience are generally referred to as 'plane tree', 'palm tree', 'oakleaf' and 'pea', although none gave significantly greater camouflage protection than the others, so the reasons for the changes seem to have been merely experimental.

In 1942 work began in designing a new uniform for the Waffen-SS grenadier. The result was the M43 drill camouflage uniform. This consisted of a single-breasted jacket and trousers in a rayon mixture, camouflage printed on one side only, the coloration being predominantly dull yellow with green and brown splodges. The M44 suit which followed the M43 was made of coarse herringbone twill which was not as warm. The waterproof qualities of the M44 were also inferior to the M43. The introduction of the M44 field uniform marked the final stage in the simplification and deterioration of the dress of Germany's armed forces.

By 1944, shortages of materials and the need to make economies forced the army and the Waffen-SS to adopt a different type of tunic and trousers. The M44 field blouse (*Feldbluse*) was shortwaisted, closely resembling the British Army's battledress blouse. It was made from *Zeltbahn* material for cheapness, and was distinctly shoddy in appearance and less warm than earlier tunics. The accompanying trousers were also waist length and tighter fitting, being held up with a belt instead of braces.

The *Zeltbahn* itself had been developed by the army, but was adopted by the Waffen-SS. It was a simple triangle of material printed in camouflage colours which could be worn as a poncho in wet weather. The edges had holes for drawstrings, and three or more *Zeltbahnen* could be tied together to form a pup tent. When not in use, it was carried rolled on the back along with the soldier's other personal equipment.

EQUIPMENT

The basis for all field equipment was a set of adjustable black leather 'Y' straps which passed from the front of the waistbelt either side of the chest and over the shoulders, converging on a steel ring between the shoulder blades. From this ring a single strap joined to the belt at the centre of the back. The waistbelt itself carried three leather

This SS soldier in Normandy is armed with a *Panzerfaust* anti-tank weapon. The shaped-charge warhead was capable of defeating 200mm of armour.

ammunition pouches for the Kar 98 rifle either side of the buckle. The pouches themselves were made as units of three, and clipped to the 'D' rings which fixed the 'Y' harness to the belt.

Full infantry kit, the M39 pack, was rarely worn in combat by Waffen-SS grenadiers as they were principally shock troops, lightly equipped for mobility and going into action carrying a minimal amount of equipment. When worn – as on the march prior to an engagement – the pack harness was also attached directly to the 'D' rings and to the top of the frontal straps at roughly collarbone level by means of press studs, passing round the waist and under the armpits. To this network was first fixed a canvas backpack, approximately square in shape, which contained the man's washing kit, toothbrush, rifle-cleaning gear, field rations, tent pegs, a length of rope and spare clothing. His mess tin kit was strapped to the back of the pack and his *Zeltbahn* or greatcoat wrapped around its top and sides in a neat but heavy roll. The weight of full kit made it impractical for it to be carried in combat.

Entrenching tools and bayonets were another matter, and formed part of the assault kit. The entrenching tool was a simple wooden-handled spade carried in a leather case on the left hip, suspended from the waistbelt. Early versions were square-bladed and did not have a folding handle, while later versions had a triangular point which made a useful improvised weapon, as well as a hinged stock. The harness for both types involved a folding leather three-sided sheath for the blade, the first pattern being secured by a looped leather strap around the top of the handle, the latter by both horizontal and vertical buckled straps.

The bayonet and scabbard were usually strapped to the back of the first pattern entrenching tool; they could, of course, be worn attached simply to the waistbelt, in between the ammunition pouches and the entrenching tool for quick and easy access. This was necessary with the second pattern spade arrangement because it was awkward to get at the spade without first removing the bayonet.

To counterbalance this array, the grenadier carried a canvas bread bag slung from his waistbelt on his right hip. This carried provisions, his field cap when bareheaded or wearing his helmet, and any other oddments which would not fit in elsewhere. The

RIGHT: 1: M35/40 helmet and camouflage cover. The standard field-grey steel helmet with crimped edge, being worn with a summer-pattern camouflage cover. 2: *Schiffchen* field cap. Replacing the earlier-pattern side cap, this had a scalloped brim and national eagle sewn at the front above the *Totenkopf* device. 3: M43 *Einheitsfeldmütze*. Largely replacing the earlier side cap, certainly from 1943 onwards, this more practical form of headgear was based on the mountain trooper's cap (*Bergmütze*) which had a shorter visor. 4: Camouflaged field cap. This was a lightweight version of the *Einheitsfeldmütze* in camouflage material and usually lacking both buttons and insignia. 5: Fur cap. Produced to help counter the bitter cold of the Russian winters, this was a fur-lined felt cap with deep ear flaps and a chin string which could be used to tie the flaps at the crown when the weather was warmer. It was not issued with any insignia although men often sewed their own on. (Osprey Publishing © Jeffrey Burn)

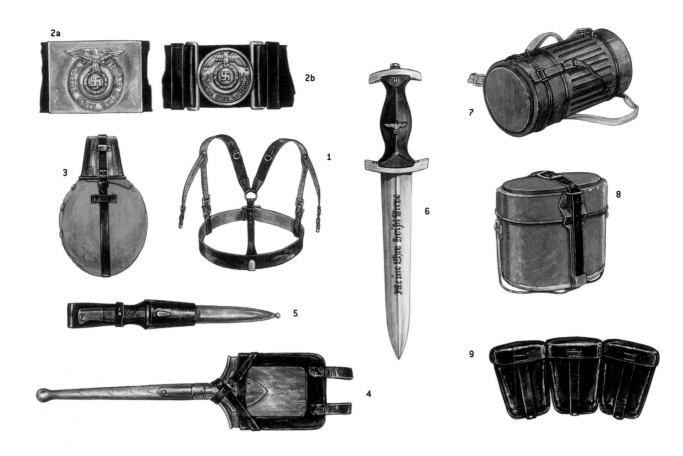

Waffen-SS infantry equipment. 1: Riflemen's 'Y' straps with 'D' rings and belt. 2a: NCO and other ranks' belt buckle. 2b: Officer's belt buckle. 3: M1931 field flask and drinking cup; 4: Small entrenching tool with 'closed-back' carrier. 5: S84/98 bayonet and dismounted sidearm carrier. 6: 1936-pattern SS dagger. 7: M1938 gasmask case. 8: M1931 cook pot. 9: M1911 cartridge pouches. (Osprey Publishing © Jeffrey Burn)

bag itself had two metal rings on its outer straps, one of which was used to attach the kidney-shaped water canteen. The grey-painted fluted metal gasmask container was not attached to the webbing, but slung around the neck on a canvas strap. It could be in a canvas sack with or without a gas cape. The widespread use of gas was never a serious threat and the gasmask case rapidly became a convenient container for a variety of personal items, particularly those which needed to be kept dry, such as tobacco. When going into combat, the grenadier would abandon much of the above kit and substitute a canvas 'A' frame, leaving his pack and greatcoat in a truck or dugout and retaining just his mess kit, water bottle, *Zeltbahn* (optional, depending on the weather), bread bag (probably stuffed with grenades instead of rations), entrenching tool and bayonet. The Waffen-SS were flexible in deciding what should be carried into action, but regulations stipulated that the gasmask container was not optional.

WEAPONS

Grenadiers equipped with submachine guns or, later, assault rifles, did not wear the Kar 98 ammunition pouches on the front of their waistbelts. Instead, they wore two sets of elongated triple pouches in leather or canvas for their weapon's magazines. These were slanted sideways because of their length, clearing the top of the thighs so as not to get in the way when a man was running. Members of machine-gun crews carried no ammunition pouches, but were instead equipped with holstered automatic pistols for self-defence. In fact, within the Waffen-SS as a whole, the carrying of a personal weapon such as a pistol or a submachine-gun (SMG) in addition to or instead of the issue rifle became something of a cachet.

A pistol is really of little value in a combat situation, having limited range and accuracy, but being small can be carried conveniently by personnel in armoured fighting vehicles, as can SMGs, whereas a rifle would be too unwieldy. However, a pistol is a great morale-booster and a single man so armed can often force the surrender of several opponents if they are shocked and demoralized, as happened quite often in France and during the early period of the advance into Russia. A pistol is also a last defence against capture, and soldiers of the Waffen-SS in Russia became well aware that a bullet was generally preferable to the latter fate. Pistols and submachine guns are also useful in close-quarter fighting, as when clearing a building, in dense woods where it is difficult to use a longer-barrelled weapon, or in trench fighting. (In fact, Hugo Schmeisser designed the world's first true submachine gun, the MP 18, specifically for trench warfare.) Finally, pistols are also symbols of authority and hence would normally be worn by officers and military policemen as a standard part of their uniform.

The most common pistols in service in 1939–40 were the famous 9mm P 08 Luger and the more modern P 38 Walther, which was put into production in 1938 to replace the former weapon, being cheaper to manufacture. It was also a more practical design, with a lock to prevent accidental firing even with the safety switch 'off'. This was

Waffen-SS troops in Poland man a 5cm leichter Granatwerfer 36 mortar. This weapon was complicated to use and had an ineffectual maximum range of just over 500m.

Troops of SS-TV *Ostmark*, seen here in April 1939. *Ostmark* was originally formed in September 1938 as a guard force for the concentration camp at Linz.

much appreciated by the troops, because there had been several accidents with the Luger when it was field-stripped with a round accidentally left in the chamber. The Walther, on the other hand, even had a pin indicator that could be felt in total darkness and which showed if there was a round in the chamber. In fact, the Walther P 38 was such a good weapon that Oberführer Heinrich Gartner, head of the Waffen-SS Procurement Office, tried unsuccessfully to divert all production to the Waffen-SS.

Waffen-SS officers were frequently seen equipped with the smaller Walther PP or PPK. Being designed for police use, they were easily concealed, for example at the small of the back, and could be missed in anything other than a thorough body search. The same could not be said for one of the Waffen-SS grenadier's other most popular weapons, the 9mm C 96 Mauser. Popularly known as the 'broomhandle' Mauser because of the shape of its grip, this ingenious handgun remains one of the finest combat handguns ever made and has become a valued collector's item.

While the Luger and Walther P 38, each with eight-round box magazines, could only be fired single-shot and had an effective combat range of little more than 25m, the Mauser could take a 20-round magazine and could be fired fully automatic like a submachine gun (or, in German parlance, machine pistol) with a range of several hundred metres. To enable it to be fired at this range, it had an ingenious hollow

RIGHT: As the Waffen-SS progressed through the war, they received much-improved items of uniform, kit and weaponry. Of particular note here is the kneeling infantryman's StG 44 automatic rifle, designed specifically for delivering effective fire over practical combat ranges of up to 400m. (Osprey Publishing © Jeffrey Burn)

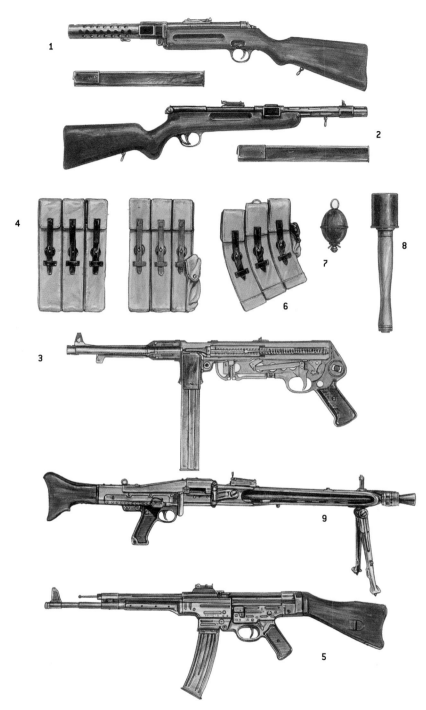

ABOVE: Weapons of the Waffen-SS. 1: 9mm Schmeisser (Haenel) MP 28 submachine gun. 2: 9mm Bergmann MP34/35 submachine gun. 3: 9mm MP 38 and 40 submachine gun. 4: Leather and canvas MP 38/MP 40 magazine packs. 5: 7.92mm MP 43 assault rifle. 6: Leather and canvas MP 43 magazine pouches. 7: M1939 Eiergranate. 8: M1924 Stielhandgranate. 9: 7.92mm MG 42 machine gun. (Osprey Publishing © Jeffrey Burn)

wooden stock which doubled as its holster and could also accommodate cleaning tools. Unfortunately, when fired in the fully automatic mode, the Mauser was impossible to aim accurately because of the sharp barrel rise, but the hail of lead it spouted was guaranteed to send opponents diving for cover.

The latter is one of the chief attributes of all submachine guns. The Waffen-SS used several types of these, but had a definite preference for some over others. In 1940 there were four basic types, the 9mm MPE, MP 28, MP 34/35 and MP 38, with the MP 40 just coming into service. All were short-barrelled, with 20- or 32-round box magazines, a high rate of fire and an effective combat range of around 150m. However, the Waffen-SS preferred the old MP 28 to the more modern designs because of its superior manufacturing quality and because its magazine slotted into the side of the receiver instead of underneath it. This meant it could be fired from the prone position much more easily.

The same was true of the MP 34 and MP 35 produced by the Danish Bergmann company, which had been taken over following the occupation of Denmark in April 1940 (a campaign in which the Waffen-SS did not take part). The Waffen-SS, short of weapons at the time because of restrictions imposed by the army (see below), were delighted to be allowed to take over the entire production of the Bergmann SMGs, making this weapon uniquely their own.

Other extremely popular non-German weapons used by the Waffen-SS included the 9mm Browning Hi-Power automatic pistol manufactured by Fabrique Nationale in Belgium. This had a 13-round magazine, making it a much more effective combat weapon than a Luger or Walther, as well as having a more comfortable grip. After the invasion of the Soviet Union in June 1941, captured Russian PPD and PPSh-41 submachine guns were also pressed into service in large numbers. Home-grown submachine guns were generally reserved for junior officers and NCOs rather than the rank and file.

While submachine guns were popular with the Waffen-SS, the principal weapon used by them up to 1943–44 was the German Army's standard 7.92mm Kar 98 rifle, a traditional breech-loader with a five-round magazine sharing almost identical characteristics with the British Lee-Enfield and the American Springfield. Later, the grenadiers eagerly seized the new MP 43/StG 44 assault rifle. The world's first true assault rifle, combining the traditional rifle's virtue of range and accuracy with a submachine gun's high rate of fire, this had been introduced after combat experience had shown that most firefights took place at under 400m.

The Waffen-SS placed great emphasis on laying down saturation firepower, so tried wherever possible to have a greater concentration of heavy support weapons – machine guns and mortars – than was army practice. German industry provided two particularly

Flemish Waffen-SS troops load an MG 34 machine gun: the gunner has just opened the top cover, and his assistant is inserting a belt of 7.92mm rounds.

fine weapons for this purpose, the 7.92mm MG 34 and MG 42. Rightly regarded as the best machine guns ever made, these had a phenomenal rate of fire and the further advantage of being able to use 75-round saddle drum magazines in place of conventional belts.

Other weapons available to the grenadiers included 'egg' and 'stick' hand grenades; anti-personnel and anti-armour mines and rifle grenades; 5cm and 8cm mortars; and flamethrowers. The 5 and 8cm mortars were later supplemented by 12cm mortars after experience in Russia had shown the need for a weapon capable of throwing a heavier round to greater range.

At the beginning of the war the infantry had no effective weapons against enemy tanks. In the 1939–40 campaigns this did not matter too much, because French and British tanks were poorly deployed and rarely a threat. In Russia things were totally different, and in response to demand from the frontline troops Dr Heinrich Langweiler devised a very simple but extremely effective weapon capable of stopping any tank then in existence. The *Panzerfaust* ('armour fist') was a single shot weapon comprising a

RIGHT: In the summer of 1941, a Waffen-SS soldier hands out bread to his unit. The man on the right is a section leader, indicated by his MP 40 submachine gun and his binoculars. (Osprey Publishing © Jeffrey Burn)

MANUFACTURE AND MAINTENANCE

As already noted, all Waffen-SS uniforms (other than those tailored privately) were produced in the concentration camps. The German Jewish community included a large number of skilled tailors and seamstresses, and although they were denied all civil rights, it was not the SS Economic Administration Department's policy to let their talents go to waste. (Printing of the actual camouflage material was carried out by specialist private contractors, however.) In the field, each Waffen-SS soldier was issued with needle and thread to effect running repairs, while men who had been cobblers in civilian life found their own talents in demand from their comrades-in-arms who needed their boots re-soled. Weapons, of course, were manufactured in factories and there is little point in describing the details of these processes. In the field, each man had hand tools (screwdriver, spanner, etc) and cleaning materials for his personal weapons, while more drastic repairs were carried out in mobile field workshops following closely behind the front line.

hollow charge warhead expelled from a simple metal tube. The fin-stabilized grenade had a range of only 30m, requiring nerves of steel to use, but could penetrate 140mm of armour plate. Subsequently, both range and armour penetration were improved and the *Panzerfaust* was so successful that production peaked at 200,000 units a month. The second infantry anti-tank weapon, introduced during 1943, was the *Panzerschreck* ('armour battleaxe'). Essentially a copy of American bazookas captured in Tunisia, it was a hollow tube firing a solid fuel rocket with an 88mm hollow-charge warhead. Because the diameter of a hollow charge warhead is the critical factor in determining armour penetration, it was a far more effective weapon than the 60mm bazooka, and could penetrate 100mm of armour plate. At 120m its range was better than that of the *Panzerfaust*. The weapon's only drawbacks were that the flare of the rocket launch gave the operator's position away to the enemy, so he had to be prepared to roll away rapidly to avoid retribution. In addition the operator had to wear a gasmask to protect his face from the backblast. Subsequently, a small shield incorporating a sight was added. In action, the *Panzerschreck* was crewed by two men, operator and loader, who both normally carried three of the fin-stabilized rockets on their 'A' frame harness.

PSYCHOLOGY AND TRAINING

Before looking at the training which all Waffen-SS infantrymen had to go through, it is important to look at the reasons men enlisted in the Waffen-SS in the first place, rather than the army; and at the factors that made them such tough and often fanatical fighters, earning themselves that description, 'soldiers of destruction'.

ABOVE: Training, 1934–37. 1: SS-Schütze, 1934. His headgear is the Imperial-style field cap known as the *Krätschen*.
2: SS-Oberscharführer, SS-Standarte *Germania*, 1936. The instructing NCO wears the SS-VT's new 'earth-grey' (*erdgrau*)
service uniform, officially introduced from November 1935. 3: SS-Untersturmführer, *Leibstandarte SS Adolf Hitler*, 1937.
This second lieutenant wears the earliest style of field-grey (*feldgrau*) uniform, introduced in that year. (Osprey
Publishing © Stephen Andrew)

The SS leadership understood the propaganda value of the Waffen-SS, and combat cameramen selectively recorded the action. Here we see one such man, on operations with the *Leibstandarte* Regiment in Russia, 1941.

The men who volunteered for the Waffen-SS swore a distinctive oath, affirming total loyalty to the person of Adolf Hitler rather than to the state. It went as follows and is a key factor in understanding the psychology of the Waffen-SS soldier:

'I swear to thee Adolf Hitler

As Führer and Chancellor of the German Reich

Loyalty and bravery.

I vow to thee and to the superiors whom thou shalt appoint

Obedience unto death

So help me God.'

What, then, did motivate a man to join the Waffen-SS and swear such an oath, rather than going into the regular army? There are many individual answers. For example, the later Kommando leader Otto Skorzeny (see Chapter 4) originally wanted to join the Luftwaffe, but opted for the Waffen-SS instead when he found out that his height would preclude him from serving as aircrew. But more often the answer was simple ambition and the desire to belong to an elite. After the reintroduction of conscription in 1935, the army's standards were obviously lowered. (Prior to this, the Reichswehr had been restricted to a mere 100,000 men, which meant that recruiting officers could pick and choose.) An ambitious man who realized his own limitations would, quite naturally, prefer to be a big fish in a small pond rather than a small fish in a large one.

Army leaders also realized this, and exercised tight controls over the number of men eligible for national service whom they would permit to join the SS. Seeing what was happening, as noted in the previous chapter, Hitler put the entire SS on to the police rather than the army budget. This gave the army more money to play with and helped reduce their animosity towards the growth of the SS, an animosity based on the fact that the army was traditionally the sole arms bearer for the state and undiminished by the fact that the pre-war Waffen-SS was a relatively tiny organization.

There were two other significant differences between volunteers for the Waffen-SS and for the army. Although the SS physical requirements were higher (see below), their educational ones were lower. Nearly half of all Waffen-SS recruits had received only minimal schooling, and officer candidates especially were accepted with far lower academic qualifications than their counterparts in the army. This, of course, made them more amenable both to the tight discipline and to ideological indoctrination. (It should be noted that these remarks apply only to the Waffen-SS and not to, for example, the SD, which attracted a high proportion of young lawyers and administrators with university degrees.)

The other difference is that the majority of volunteers for the Waffen-SS came from rural areas, whereas the bulk of the army's ranks were composed of city dwellers. This process of natural selection vindicated itself later in a way which seems rather surprising, until you remember that fifty-odd years ago rural living conditions were far more primitive and, literally, closer to the earth than they are today. Thus it soon became apparent, particularly in Russia, that the majority of men in the Waffen-SS divisions were more comfortable living in the field, and more adept at field- and woodcraft, than their urban comrades-in-arms. Since one of the basic requirements of a soldier is to survive in order to be able to fight, this was a not insignificant asset.

Recruits for the Waffen-SS – at least in the early days, before wartime demands forced a relaxation of standards – had to satisfy stringent physical and moral conditions. 'Sepp' Dietrich, the commander of the LSSAH, wanted mature men rather than pimply teenagers, so only recruited from those aged between 23 and 35, at least 1.8m tall, and in peak physical condition. No man was accepted if he had a criminal record, and he had to be able to prove pure 'Aryan' ancestry with no 'taint' of Jewish blood. Until the need to replace casualties forced him to relax his own standards, Dietrich would not even accept a man into the *Leibstandarte* if he had a single tooth filled. He was determined that the regiment would be the toughest, fittest and most highly disciplined unit in the Führer's service, and right to the very end it attracted the cream of volunteers for the Waffen-SS.

When Hitler assumed power in 1933, a rush of waverers – the 'March Violets', who had previously sat on the political fence – practically fell over each other in their

A recruit to the Hitlerjugend signs a statement affirming his Aryan ancestry. Both the army and the Waffen-SS competed to pull in the best recruits from the HJ.

enthusiasm to join the NSDAP, the SA and the SS. Following the emasculation of the SA in 1934, the SA would never again pose a threat. But Himmler had a problem within the SS itself, because the rush of newcomers to their ranks were not of the old calibre. So, over the next few months he initiated a ruthless house cleaning process, expelling from the SS large numbers of 'Johnny-come-latelies' on grounds of alcoholism, criminal records, homosexuality or the inability to prove pure 'Aryan' ancestry, thus restoring to the survivors the status of an elite.

Initial enlistment was 25 years for officers, 12 for NCOs and four for other ranks, and candidates were only permitted to apply for officer training after serving at least two years in the ranks, unless they had previous equivalent service in the army. Despite these lengthy periods, and despite the tough physical, racial and moral entry requirements, there was no shortage of volunteers. Unfortunately, in the early days, what the Waffen-SS badly lacked was experienced officers, and this was to be a contributory factor in their high casualty rate during the 1940 campaign.

Initial training was carried out in depots outside each regiment's home town; for example, the *Totenkopf* Division was based at Dachau, Standarte *Deutschland* was at Munich, while *Germania* was at Hamburg. But to begin with there was no consistency, so in 1936 Himmler created a Waffen-SS Inspectorate headed by a highly experienced former army officer, Paul Hausser. Brand new officer training schools were built at Bad

Tolz and Braunschweig with light and airy barracks and classrooms. Hausser was helped in initiating the training programme by two men in particular: Felix Steiner and Cassius Freiherr von Montigny.

Steiner had been a member of a Stosstruppe, or assault troop, during World War I. These assault troops had consisted of small bodies of volunteers armed to the teeth not only with the first submachine guns but also with improvised weapons such as clusters of grenades wrapped around a single stick, shields like a medieval knight, and entrenching tools with their edges sharpened like razors. They were true light infantry, just as the Waffen-SS grenadiers were to become, going into action in daring trench raids unencumbered by the usual weight of kit, just carrying weapons, ammunition and water bottles. This, Steiner decided, would be the style of the SS; let the army provide the cannon fodder ...

Montigny, a World War I U-boat skipper, had similarly strong ideas on discipline. Between them, he and Steiner were determined to create a force of men who would

The NS-Ordensburg Vogelsang (Vogelsang National Socialist Castle) was a training ground for SS personnel in the 1930s – their education would be both military and political.

be tough, ruthless and self-disciplined, and to a large degree they succeeded. What they also created was a force of men who were almost recklessly brave and totally callous where human life was concerned, factors which were to have repercussions on the battlefield in the form of a number of appalling atrocities.

The training programme evolved for the *Deutschland* and *Germania* Standarten was broadly followed by the *Leibstandarte*, although, because of their ceremonial duties, the men in the latter regiment had to endure a great deal more 'spit and polish'. Similarly, the same programme was followed in only slightly modified form when Theodore Eicke began the transformation of part of the SS-Totenkopfverbände into the *Totenkopf* Division.

The normal day's routine began at 0600hrs with the recruits dressed in PE kit being put through an hour's callisthenics before breakfast, which usually consisted of porridge and mineral water. (This was partly due to Himmler's own dietary fanaticism and partly to the fact that the SS Economic Department had the monopoly on both these products.) After breakfast, the men changed into fatigues or service dress, depending on the day's programme. Of all the aspects of military training, weapons training received the greatest emphasis. First the men had to learn how to strip, clean and reassemble their rifles. This took place in the classroom, the instructor using a large wall chart showing the weapon in exploded view to explain the function of each part. Then the men had to practise on their own rifles, repeating the process endlessly, day after day, until they could do it blindfolded. They were shown how to clear blockages and effect simple field repairs. Then it was out on to the firing butts for target practice at steadily increasing ranges. Those who proved 'gun shy' or who simply had no aptitude despite patient encouragement were eased out into administrative or other tasks, because the SS obviously needed signallers, clerks, cooks and so on as much as any other army does.

Once the men were familiar with their weapons, they would begin learning infantry assault techniques, charging at sandbags with fixed bayonets. The instructors put great emphasis on aggression, constantly stressing fierceness in the attack both as a means of winning battles quickly and of minimizing casualties. To this end the men were taught the techniques of unarmed combat by qualified martial arts instructors and, later, when they

RIGHT: Figures from the Waffen-SS training schools, 1941–42. 1: SS-Oberscharführer instructor, SS-Junkerschule Tölz, c. 1941. This NCO instructor's shoulder straps, piped in infantry white, bear the white metal letters 'JS' over 'T' – the initials of the academy at Bad Tölz; and his cuffband displays its name in Gothic script, 'SS-Schule Tölz'. 2: SS-Standartenoberjunker, SS-Junkerschule Tölz, c. 1942. Although his appearance is more impressive than that of the instructor, this veteran senior NCO is in fact an officer candidate undergoing instruction. His uniform and insignia show a mixture of officer and NCO features. 3: SS-Unterscharführer instructor, SS-Unterführerschule Radolfzell, c. 1942. The uniform of this sergeant on the staff of one of the NCO training schools is distinguishable from (1) by the shoulder strap letters 'US' over 'R', and the cuffband with the Gothic script title 'SS-Unterführerschule'. 4: SS-Musiker, SS-Musikschule Braunschweig, c. 1941. Still wearing his Hitlerjugend brassard – a practice confirmed by photographs – this young bandsman undergoing training at the Brunswick music school wears an enlisted quality M1936 field blouse and M1940 field cap. (Osprey Publishing © Stephen Andrew)

were sufficiently skilled to be able to practise against each other without causing injury, they would fight mock battles using rifle and bayonet, or just the bayonet on its own.

To further encourage aggression, boxing featured as a major part of the curriculum, helping the men to get over the instinctive fear of being hurt and teaching them that getting your own blow in first is the best way of avoiding just that. In fact, sport played a major part in the Waffen-SS training programme, much more so than in the army. All forms of field and track sports were encouraged, not just for relaxation as in the army, but as part of the training itself, as a means of enhancing physical fitness and reflexes. And, of course, there were endless route marches and cross-country runs, both with and without full kit, to develop stamina and endurance.

Before getting out into the air again the men would have a hearty midday meal, followed by a 'make and mend' session during which barracks were scoured, boots cleaned, uniforms pressed and repaired and any other chores attended to. In the evening, the recruits could read, write letters, play cards or chess – the latter game being particularly encouraged because of the way it helps develop both logical thinking and mental flexibility. Those recruits lucky enough to have secured a pass could go into town so long as they first passed a rigorous examination by the duty officer of the guard.

So far, apart from those already noted, there was little difference between the training of a Waffen-SS soldier and his army counterpart. What they had to endure additionally was formal lectures at least three times a week covering the policies of the NSDAP and intense indoctrination in SS philosophy, particularly the theories of racial superiority which destined them to rule over the *Untermensch* – the so-called 'sub-human' Jews, gypsies, Freemasons and communists. Slavs were rapidly added to the list once the invasion of the Soviet Union became a reality, but shortly afterwards the SS hierarchy began changing its mind. Latvians, Lithuanians and Estonians, it was decided, were not 'Slav' but essentially 'Germanic'. So, it turned out, were Ukrainians, Azerbaijanis and anyone else who hated Moscow, almost regardless of their origins, because casualties created such a huge manpower demand.

Into this melting pot would also flow Indians and Palestinians, as well as men from every European country (Britain not excepted although in tiny numbers), who all swore variants of the basic Waffen-SS oath and adherence to its motto, 'Meine Ehre heist Treue', which can be translated either way as 'my loyalty is my honour', or 'honour is my loyalty'. Thus, its initial idealism diffused, the Waffen-SS actually became a polyglot organization whose members fell far short of the standards demanded by Hausser, Dietrich, Steiner and the remainder of the 'old guard'. While those original standards were high, they did not go far enough as far as Himmler was concerned. He was virulently anti-Church (Theodore Eicke was even more so), even though he adopted many practical Jesuit principles in the organization and creed of the SS, to such an

Waffen-SS troops receive mail from home. During Operation *Barbarossa*, letters and photos sent home by Waffen-SS personnel would provide incriminating later testimony of atrocities on the Eastern Front.

extent that Hitler called him 'my Ignatius Loyola' after the founder of the Society of Jesus. This anti-Christian campaign was never wholly successful and almost half the men in the original Waffen-SS regiments remained churchgoers despite peer criticism and insult (the figure was only 31 per cent in the Totenkopfverbände).

What the ideological lectures aimed at producing were men who firmly believed in their own destiny as missionaries of the new 'Aryan' order that would rule the world. They were thoroughly indoctrinated in Nazi philosophy, so that they would know what they were fighting for. While many believed in this, others were more cynical and believed purely that they were fighting to make their country strong again, as well as forming part of an elite. This, coupled to their allegiance to the Führer, goes most of the way towards accounting for the almost suicidal courage and determination of the Waffen-SS soldier on the battlefield. Certainly, few were taken in by Himmler's SS mythology, based on his readings of early German history reinforced by a mystical belief in reincarnation, in the old pagan Nordic gods and in runic symbolism. Yet, having said that, the award of the SS-*Totenkopfring* was one of the most coveted of all awards.

Once the Waffen-SS recruit had survived this basic training and ideological and 'spiritual' indoctrination, he could – like a trainee soldier anywhere – get down to learning more complex tasks. In particular, and more so than in any contemporary armed force before the emergence of the British Commandos and the American Rangers, for example, Steiner and his team of instructors intended that the SS grenadier would be able to handle himself and his weapons competently under any conceivable battlefield situation, by day or night, regardless of terrain or weather. Individual training still continued, but increasingly gave way to unit training, first at the squad level of eight men and gradually broadening out into exercises at company, battalion and regimental level. Finally, full-scale exercises would be held involving the whole of a division.

The only way in which this training differed from the army's was, as we have seen, in the emphasis on aggression and overwhelming firepower. The Waffen-SS had plenty of the former but, as we shall see later, initially at least were hampered in acquiring the latter. They were in a situation rather like the army's *Panzerwaffe* – knowing what they wanted, but unable to get enough in sufficient time. This situation changed as the war progressed and Hitler came to place increasing reliance on his Waffen-SS divisions to 'get the job done', giving them priority in the issue of new equipment; but to begin with it was far from true.

At the first two levels, the training programme taught the integration of squad and company support weapons – the machine guns, mortars, flamethrowers and, later,

The Waffen-SS caught the imagination of the German public; they seemed to represent the heroic face of National Socialism. Here we see a set of stamps, depicting a Waffen-SS mortar team in action.

ABOVE: *Panzerfaust* training. A young 17-year-old grenadier from the 12. SS-Panzer Division *Hitlerjugend* is being shown how to use the *Panzerfaust* by a grizzled Unterscharführer. Most of the *Hitlerjugend* officers were drawn from the *Leibstandarte*, and this sergeant proudly retains the cuff title of his parent formation. (Osprey Publishing © Jeffrey Burn)

Panzerfäuste and *Panzerschrecke*. This involved learning games theory, although it was not described as such at the time. What games theory tells you, for example, is that a bolt-action rifle fired at a 1m-square target at a range of 200m has a seven out of ten probability of hitting, assuming average marksmanship. The same theory tells us that a submachine gun or assault rifle fired on automatic has only a two in ten probability, and a machine gun on a bipod mount three in ten. What this does *not* mean is that a machine gun is less effective than a bolt-action rifle, because the equation does not take into account that a machine gun can be pouring 500-plus rounds into the same target area in the time it would take to aim about 15 rifle shots. Viewed like this, the machine gun will get 150 hits on the target, the rifle only ten or so. Increasing the distance beyond 200m (assuming the weapon is capable of doing this) affects its basic accuracy by $A = a (200/D)$, when 'A' is the new base accuracy of the weapon at the increased range, 'a' is the original accuracy figure (e.g., seven out of ten) and 'D' is the new distance to the target.

Games theory coupled to empirical research gives many such equations and the Waffen-SS grenadier was hardly expected to learn them, merely how to put them into practice to give the best results depending upon the tactical circumstances. Thus, sometimes a single-shot rifle is the best weapon, sometimes a submachine gun and sometimes a machine gun.

Small-unit tactical training therefore encourages the individual soldier to experiment with different combinations to gain the best results based on his judgement of terrain, weather, visibility, his own men's abilities and the capability and weapons effectiveness of the enemy. Some factors are obvious – that increasing range diminishes accuracy, for example, or that laying down saturation fire will keep your enemy's head down while allowing you to get on with the approach to the objective. Understanding such basics is fairly simple, putting them into practice effectively a matter of experience, and to give their men that experience Hausser, Steiner and their staffs made great use of live ammunition in exercises, a technique which at the time attracted strong criticism from the army hierarchy because of the inevitable accidental casualties it caused. In the long run, however, such exercises certainly *saved* lives, because once they went to war the men of the Waffen-SS were not unnerved by the simple fact of being under return fire. The efficacy of live-firing exercises is proven by their almost universal adoption elsewhere after the Waffen-SS pioneered the way; but at the same time it must be admitted that such training can produce over-confidence, and this could account (along with the inexperienced leadership already noted) for some of the Waffen-SS's heavy casualties during their early campaigns.

Apart from the matter of live firing, Waffen-SS training differed from that of the army in two other important ways. In the first place, although total discipline was demanded and ruthlessly enforced, training was designed to produce inner discipline and self-reliance. Only a soldier who knows that his comrades have been through the same treadmill will trust them, and vice versa. And in the second place, Steiner in particular strove to break down the traditional Prussian barriers between officers and men, encouraging them to talk and exchange ideas as equals when off duty and to address each other as *Kamerad* rather than by rank. This was no easy process, because class distinctions had far from disappeared from the Germany of the 1930s, but the process was helped by the fact that the NSDAP had created a new class of people who were appointed on merit rather than through an accident of birth. This meant that a man like 'Sepp' Dietrich, for example, and others like him who could barely have expected to rise to senior NCO rank in the army, could become colonels and generals within the Waffen-SS. It was a reversion to Napoleon's old principle of 'a marshal's baton in every private's knapsack' (on top of which, Hitler fully recognized the truth of one of Napoleon's other adages – 'give me enough medals to hand out and I'll win you any battle', and by introducing such awards as the Knights Cross of the Iron Cross had

Troops of the *Leibstandarte Adolf Hitler* sit atop an armoured vehicle, next to a pintle-mounted MG 34 machine gun.

gone a long way towards creating an army which could only be defeated by 'bigger battalions', not by skill).

There was more to the success of the Waffen-SS than this, however. In a very real sense, the men had an esprit de corps more comparable to that of regular British Army regiments than most German Army ones. Because they were formed as a deliberate elite, and recruited and trained as such, and awarded regimental cuff titles, they had a far stronger bond with their parent regiment than an army conscript did with his. They were also volunteers, emphasizing – as in the British Army – their professionalism in their own minds. And they shared the same love of sports, which might seem a minor point, but perhaps is not.

One way in which they definitely differed from the British (or German) Army of the time was in the relationship between officers and enlisted men, not least because every Waffen-SS officer had had to have served at least two years in the ranks or completed equivalent service elsewhere. Officers themselves were positively encouraged to discuss their decisions and orders (after the event, of course, not at the time; no effective military machine can be operated as a democracy). This was designed to enable their men to understand why they were asked to do things in a certain way, and help build confidence in the officers to whom they had sworn 'obedience unto death'.

At least 15 Panthers would be left in La Gleize and Stoumont after the withdrawal of Kampfgruppe *Peiper* in the Ardennes. This Panther Ausf. G belonged to SS Panzer-Regiment 1; it was a Panzerbefehlswagen, a command tank, equipped with an extra radio set (either the FuG 7 or the FuG 8) in addition to the usual FuG 5. (Osprey Publishing © D. Parker/ R. Volstad)

Theodore Eicke, when he began training up the *Totenkopf* Division at Dachau, went still further, instructing junior officers that they were to take some of their meals in the other ranks' and COs' messes, and even introducing suggestion boxes through which his men could leave ideas or air complaints anonymously.

Himmler wanted the Waffen-SS to be a brotherhood, an extended family, and this resulted in the men learning to trust their officers as well as each other, with little of the 'them and us' attitude prevalent in most other armies at the time. Regrettably, these ideals began to break down later, when the Waffen-SS began accepting volunteers from the occupied countries.

TACTICS

The basis of German military philosophy at the beginning of the war and through to 1942 remained that of what we now call *Blitzkrieg* ('lightning war'), and was repeated on both the grand and the small scale: particularly, it must be noted, within the Waffen-SS, with their emphasis on aggression and speed.

Like all successful concepts, that of *Blitzkrieg* was simplicity itself although it is still often misunderstood, even today. The idea was to mass sufficient force against one sector of the enemy line in order to achieve superiority, break through and *keep moving* as rapidly as possible to keep the enemy off balance while secondary attacks either side

WAFFEN-SS PANZER DIVISION

Of all Hitler's armoured forces, it was probably the elite divisions of the Waffen-SS that gained the greatest fame, or notoriety, as Panzer divisions. A total of seven Waffen-SS divisions were either established as, or converted to, Panzer division status. It has often been suggested that Waffen-SS divisions were given unfair priority in re-equipping with the latest, improved versions of various armoured vehicles. There is, however, little evidence to support this theory, as elite army units such as *Grossdeutschland* were also equipped with the best tanks available. It is more likely that the best equipment available was given first to those units that would make best use of it, i.e. those that were the most aggressive and daring in the attack and most tenacious in defence, and the Waffen-SS Panzer divisions certainly qualified on both counts.

Many of the Panzer units of the army adopted special unofficial unit insignia, which was worn on the side of the headgear in the same manner as the 'tradition' badges worn by U-boat crews. Probably the best known of these is the running greyhound of the 116 *Windhund* Panzer Division, but there were many others. Some units also produced their own newspapers or periodicals to foster a sense of common identity and build morale.

Soldiers of the SS *Germania* regiment take a breather from operations in France in 1940. They are wearing the screen-printed early-pattern camouflage smock issued to the Waffen-SS.

of the breakthrough point prevented him from transferring reinforcements. It was this idea of continuous movement with an almost total disregard for flanks which made the *Blitzkrieg* concept work so well in those early years, since the Germans' opponents were unable to respond quickly enough – despite having an overall superiority in manpower, guns and tanks – to check the tidal wave of men and machines. The 1940 campaign in France and the Low Countries is perhaps the best example of these failings.

Blitzkrieg relied upon the *integrated* use of all weapons systems, and was greatly assisted by the fact that German military organization was built on the modular system, with plug-in replacements. The Waffen-SS used the same principle with élan, but one significant difference did emerge between themselves and the army. This lay in their loyalty to their parent regiment. An army soldier, unless he was himself a member of an elite formation such as the *Grossdeutschland* Division, did not particularly care which unit he fought within. There was no fierce loyalty, by and large, such as existed within the Waffen-SS for their 'own' unit. This made interchange of personnel more difficult, because a man would be reluctant to move to a different regiment (except by the prospect of promotion); so the formation of *ad hoc* Kampfgruppen (battlegroups) was much more rare within the Waffen-SS than within the army. Men preferred to stay with their own unit even if it had been decimated.

It was inevitable that this feeling should extend down to company and squad level, men who had trained together and learned to trust each other trying to stick together because they knew how their comrades thought and acted, what their strong and weak points were. This, again, is true in most armies, but was particularly so in the Waffen-SS and some of the elite formations of other nations. And what it all boils down to tactically is that the men of the Waffen-SS – at whichever structural level you care to pick – acted as a team. The machine gunners and mortar crews would lay down as high a concentration of firepower as possible, enabling the rest of their section to crawl, or dash where there was cover, towards the objective. Then the grenades would be hurled, the building or trench saturated with gunfire, and the squad would move on, trusting to their companions in flanking units to watch their backs if their own progress had been slower. In this way, small Waffen-SS units often outstripped the main advance of their parent unit by miles, sacrificing security for the speed and surprise of sustained momentum.

A classic example of this is Fritz Klingenberg's almost single-handed capture of the Yugoslav capital of Belgrade during Operation *Strafe* (Punishment) in 1941. Hauptsturmführer Klingenberg, a graduate from Bad Tolz, was commanding the second company of the *Reich* Division's motorcycle reconnaissance battalion at the time, and was keenly aware that his unit was flanked by the army's crack *Grossdeutschland* Regiment. The result was a race to see who was best, the army or the Waffen-SS, with Belgrade the winner's prize. As it turned out, it was rather a race in slow motion, because the spring rains had turned Yugoslavia's largely unpaved roads into a quagmire of glutinous mud in which the motorcycles bogged down all too frequently. Nevertheless, thanks to finding a bridge which had not been demolished over the Vlasecki Canal, Klingenberg and his men managed to reach the pivotal town of Alibuna in front of their rivals during the evening of 11 April. Despite the late hour, they were ordered to push on another 20km to Pancevo, arriving at midnight. The following day, despite their exhaustion, Klingenberg forced his men on, but they were hampered by the lack of bridges over the River Tamis, which allowed leading elements of the *Grossdeutschland* Regiment to catch up with them. Klingenberg's goal on the far side of the swollen rivers Tamis and Danube was tantalizingly in sight, but seemed unreachable until pioneers arrived with rubber assault boats. Klingenberg went out on a personal recce in search of an alternative, and to his delight found an abandoned motor boat. It was in a very dilapidated condition and crossing the rivers in such a craft was fraught with peril, so Klingenberg called for volunteers to accompany him. Almost every man in his company raised their hands, but the boat would only carry a few, and in the end he selected ten of his best.

Crossing the Danube with this tiny task force, Klingenberg marched into Belgrade itself. Astonishingly, there was no resistance, although when Klingenberg reached the German Mission in the city centre he found it besieged by an angry crowd. Klingenberg set up his two machine guns and the crowd hurriedly dispersed. Inside

ABOVE: Putting training into practice, Ardennes 1944. Muffled in reversible white winter parka and overtrousers with no insignia, a Hitlerjugend soldier is equipped with a second-pattern *Panzerschreck* with shield (the shield prevented the soldier receiving facial burns from rocket ignition). His loader, slapping his shoulder to indicate the weapon is loaded, has a pair of anti-tank Tellermines. (Osprey Publishing © Jeffrey Burn)

the mission, Klingenberg summoned the city's mayor by telephone and demanded his surrender, threatening to call up an air strike if he did not receive immediate obedience. This was pure bluff, because he did not have a radio, but the mayor was not to know this and hastily signed a surrender document. Shortly afterwards, leading elements of the 11. Panzer Division arrived in the city, believing themselves first. Their chagrin, and the celebrations in *Reich* Division's headquarters when the news was confirmed, can be well imagined. Klingenberg himself was awarded the Knight's Cross for his achievement.

This story is illuminating in several respects. It demonstrates the determination of the Waffen-SS to show that they were better than the army. It shows their will, aggression and audacity. And it is a small-scale example of *Blitzkrieg* tactics in operation.

DEFENSIVE TACTICS

As the war progressed, such tactics became increasingly impossible. When Russian resistance stiffened and then turned to the offensive, the Waffen-SS had to acquire new skills. Aggression alone was no longer enough, the lightning strikes and rapid advances no longer feasible. Now the Waffen-SS grenadiers had to learn to endure in the face of an implacable and numerically superior foe whose equipment was in some respects also becoming superior. It was impossible in Russia, given the vast distances involved, to hold a continuous frontline from the Baltic to the Black Sea, so what were known as 'hedgehog' tactics evolved. A division would occupy a cluster of villages, each held in company or battalion strength. In a sense it was like the old infantry 'square' of Napoleonic times designed to repel cavalry. The Russian attacks swirled round the 'hedgehogs' and were fired into from the flanks and rear until they were exhausted. Mere companies of Waffen-SS men held out against attacks by whole divisions. They were not always successful, of course, and there are many instances reminiscent of the French Foreign Legion's stand at Camerone, when, finally out of ammunition, the surviving grenadiers would charge their opponents with fixed bayonets and die to a man. They had, after all, vowed 'obedience unto death'.

During the long retreat from the summer of 1943 – by which time the cream of the SS grenadiers, mounted in armoured half-tracks instead of tanks, had been renamed Panzergrenadiers – the Waffen-SS proved itself as skilful in defence as in the attack. Rushed from one trouble spot to another like a mobile fire brigade, they succeeded time and again in stemming the Russian tide and inflicting enormous casualties. But they suffered in turn, and the new cadres of young replacements – the original age limits having been abandoned – were totally unprepared for conditions on the Eastern Front.

Crew members of the *Hohenstaufen* Division take a break on their PzKpfw IV tank. The Waffen-SS Panzer divisions were known for their innovative and flexible tactics, and their rapid creation of improvised battlegroups, which often had two Panzer battalions as their core.

LOGISTICS

A peculiarity of the Waffen-SS is the struggle they had to acquire modern arms in the early days because the army insisted they needed everything industry could produce for themselves. As we have seen, this actually worked to their advantage in some respects, such as their acquisition of Bergmann submachine guns. The *Leibstandarte*, Hitler's bodyguard, had no problems in obtaining whatever they wanted, simply because Der Führer insisted on it. The SS-VT (which later provided the nucleus for the *Das Reich* and *Wiking* Divisions) also managed to get most of what they needed, although there was a shortage of artillery to begin with. But the army was opposed to helping Eicke in any way, and only grudgingly, under pressure from Hitler, agreed to accept a few of his men for specialist training, at the signals school in Halle, for example. But for weapons and equipment Eicke had to scour his own concentration camp stores and other SS depots, even resorting to 'borrowing' a couple of old howitzers used for training purposes at Bad Tolz.

As 1939 drew to a close, thanks to Himmler's constant entreaties to Hitler, Eicke's *Totenkopf* Division gradually began to come together. Much of his equipment was Czech, but there was nothing wrong in this because the Czech arms industry was one of the finest in the world; in fact, during the 1940 campaign, roughly a quarter of the army's tanks were also Czech. What annoyed Eicke was the fact that when Himmler managed to acquire a dozen Skoda 15cm artillery pieces, they went to the SS-VT instead of the *Totenkopf*. Nevertheless, the eminent American historian George H. Stein makes the following interesting comment. On 4 April 1940 the commander of the 2. Armee, General Freiherr Maximilian von Weichs, paid his first visit to the new formation which had been placed under his command:

> In their opening conversation with Eicke, Weichs and his staff revealed their ignorance ... They were under the impression that the 'Totenkopf' Division was organized and equipped like a Czech foot division, and were very much surprised to discover it was really a modern, motorized infantry division. At a time when only seven of the Army's 139 infantry divisions were motorized, this was indeed a command to be proud of. Weichs' inspection of the troops left him visibly impressed, and he completed his visit in a frame of mind far different from that in which he had arrived.

Weichs was not the only high-ranking army officer to be impressed by the *Totenkopf*. Later in the war, Germany's greatest general, Generalfeldmarschall Erich von Manstein, came to consider it the finest unit under his command. After the Waffen-SS had proved itself in the 1940 campaign and Hitler authorized further expansion, army reluctance to help gradually receded. Then, as Hitler came to place increasing reliance on the fighting ability and loyalty of his Waffen-SS formations, they actually began to receive priority in the allocation of new equipment. This led to the popular but totally untrue myth that the reason for the Waffen-SS's success was because it was better equipped than the army. It was not, although it did de-centralize its weapons allocation, which could have fostered that impression, because each squad of eight men had at least one machine gun, so a platoon of three squads had a minimum of three plus at least one mortar. Similarly, of the three or four platoons in a company, one would be a support platoon equipped entirely with machine guns and mortars, in line with the Waffen-SS's emphasis on maximum firepower to achieve results. In the army, although the basic organization was the same, machine guns were only allocated at platoon rather than squad level. The Waffen-SS could never acquire enough automatic weapons from

The Waffen-SS armoured forces were rightly feared by Allied troops for a combination of tactical excellence and advanced tank technology. Here we see the *Hitlerjugend* Division in Normandy, 1944, manning PzKpfw V Ausf G Panthers.

Waffen-SS troops manhandle an Opel Blitz truck along a muddy road in Poland, 1939. As with the German Army, the Waffen-SS experienced crucial logistics problems as the war went on, particularly on the Eastern Front.

official sources for its satisfaction, so the bounty of captured weapons following the mass encirclement battles during the initial phases of the Russian campaign was welcomed with open arms. Kar 98s were thrown away in favour of Tokarev self-loading rifles, PPD and PPSh-41 submachine guns and Degtyarev light machine guns, all adding to the Waffen-SS's already formidable firepower. These weapons proved their value in particular during the vicious street fighting which characterized such a large part of the Russian campaign.

The German manufacturing and supply organization was, by and large, remarkably efficient, but it became strained beyond its limits in Russia. During the first winter of 1941–42, for example, there was never enough warm clothing because the high command had incorrectly predicted the campaign would be over in six weeks. As a result, the men had to acquire whatever they could, the result being that virtually all pretence at uniform disappeared as they wrapped themselves in 'commandeered' fur and sheepskin coats and hats.

The basis of the German supply organization was the railway system, although petrol was brought forward in convoys of tanker trucks. Everything else – food, ammunition, medical supplies, etc – was transported to railheads and thence to depots from which individual battalions and companies collected their requirements in their own trucks. Unfortunately, this system frequently broke down, either because of the weather or because of partisan attacks on the railway lines and convoy routes. The Luftwaffe helped as much as possible, but lacked enough aircraft with sufficient payload to be of more than marginal help, especially since the weather all too often prevented flying at all. This meant that the supply administrators had to put the emphasis on ammunition, with everything else given second priority, so for food the men all too frequently had to forage for themselves as so many armies have had to do throughout history.

FAMOUS COMMANDERS

Although extremely unpopular except with his own troops, Theodor Eicke epitomized several characteristics of the Waffen-SS, particularly brutality. Many other men were of totally different character and showed other characteristics; during the battle for Arnhem in September 1944, for example, the commander of II SS-Panzer Korps, Wilhelm Bittrich, ordered his men to give captured British paratroopers not only medical attention, but chocolate and brandy as well. (The ironic fact that these came from captured British supply containers does not detract from the generosity of the deed.)

Broadly speaking, taking their leadership as examples, one can group the men of the Waffen-SS in four categories. Among the 'butchers', alongside Eicke, one could place Friedrich Kruger, last commander of 6. SS-Gebirgs-Division *Nord*, who had earlier terrorized the population of Cracow while commandant there from 1939 to 1944; or Heydrich's former deputy Bruno Streckenbach, who commanded the Latvian 19. Waffen Grenadier Division der SS with particular brutality. Kurt 'Panzer' Meyer, the miner's son, falls into this category too, and

RIGHT: An Obersturmführer of the *Totenkopf* Division, Russia, summer 1944. Illustrated during the long 'advance to the rear' in which the Waffen-SS divisions acted as a mobile fire brigade to stem the Soviet advance, this war-weary officer wears the 'old style' officer's cap without stiffening, the 1943-pattern tailored camouflage jacket and 1944-pattern trousers, a typical field combination given the usual supply vagaries. For weaponry, he carries a 9mm Erma MPE submachine gun and has a holstered Walther P 38 on his belt. (Osprey Publishing © Jeffrey Burn)

Waffen-SS troops man a 3.7cm
Flak gun. Such weapons could
provide either anti-air cover or,
when the barrel was levelled,
devastating fire against ground
targets.

Waffen-SS troops man a 3.7cm Flak gun. Such weapons could provide either anti-air cover or, when the barrel was levelled, devastating fire against ground targets.

was responsible for a massacre of Canadian prisoners while commanding 12. SS-Panzer Division *Hitlerjugend* in 1944.

The second category includes professional officers of the old school, such as Paul Hausser, Felix Steiner, Herbert Gille, Wilhelm Bittrich and Georg Keppler. Bittrich, mentioned above, was formerly in the Luftwaffe, but transferred to the Waffen-SS because it offered the prospect of more rapid promotion. Before assuming command of II SS-Panzer Korps in 1944 he had earlier led 8. SS-Kavallerie and 9. SS-Panzer Divisions. He survived the war with the rank of full general. Herbert Gille similarly ended the war with the rank of general, having commanded 5. SS-Panzer Division *Wiking* during the furious fighting on the Russian Front during 1943–44, and later IV SS-Panzer Korps. Felix Steiner, who, as we have seen, fought as an infantryman during World War I, was director of education at the War Office before transferring to the Waffen-SS in 1935. During the course of the war he actually commanded army formations on two occasions, III Panzer Korps in 1942 and 11. Armee during the siege of Berlin in 1945.

Josef 'Sepp' Dietrich really falls into no category. Uneducated and bluntly outspoken, he had really very little idea of military command and owed his success to his early support of Hitler and the part he played in the Röhm Purge in 1934. After commanding the *Leibstandarte* since its formation, he became commander of I SS-Panzer Korps (succeeding Hausser) from 1943 to 1944, and 6. SS-Panzer Armee during the Battle of the Bulge and the last-ditch offensive in Hungary in 1945. Sentenced to 25 years' imprisonment for complicity in war crimes, he was actually released in 1955, still an unrepentant Nazi.

The third class are the foreign volunteers, such as the Romanian Artur Phleps; Woldemaras Veiss, former prime minister of Latvia; and best-known of all, Leon

Degrelle, the Belgian fascist leader who commanded the *Wallonien* Brigade (later Division) throughout the war, particularly distinguishing himself in the rearguard fighting during the breakout from the Cherkassy Pocket.

Finally there are the younger men who, if there is ever glamour in war, gave the Waffen-SS its glamour. These include Theodor Wisch, who assumed command of the *Leibstandarte* when Dietrich was given I SS-Panzer Korps; he was only 37 at the time. Badly wounded, he saw no further action after Normandy. Otto Kumm is another. Only 36 at the end of the war, he commanded the *Prinz Eugen* Division. Fritz Witt, who was killed by naval gunfire while commanding *Hitlerjugend*, had previously commanded a *Leibstandarte* battlegroup in Russia. And finally of course there is the hero of Belgrade, Fritz Klingenberg. After the invasion of Russia, he was appointed commander of the officer training school at Bad Tolz, where he himself had learned his trade. In 1945 he was given command of 17. SS-Panzergrenadier Division *Götz von Berlichingen* and was killed in action only days before the end of the war.

Having now painted a broad picture of the Waffen-SS soldier, we will move forward by looking at the specific campaigns in which they fought and bled. Like the rest of the German armed forces, the Waffen-SS experienced the swing from victors to vanquished, with the added ignominy that came from belonging to one of the most-hated organizations in the post-war world.

Josef 'Sepp' Dietrich congratulates men from the *Leibstandarte Adolf Hitler* following the campaign in France, 1940.

DAYS OF VICTORY

LEFT: Troops of the SS-Heimwehr Danzig — founded in the free city of Danzig in 1939 — take cover behind an Austrian armoured car during an assault on the Polish post office.

The Waffen-SS was, in some senses, a late-comer to the war. Although it did serve in the campaigns in Poland, the West and the Balkans in 1939–40, its contribution to those campaigns was physically tiny when compared to that of the broader Wehrmacht. Indeed, the German Army in particular always dwarfed the Waffen-SS in terms of scale. Yet from 1941, and the opening of Germany's campaign against the Soviet Union, the contribution of the Waffen-SS would grow exponentially, and it came to be regarded as the cutting edge of many of the Germany's offensives and defensive battles.

In the remaining chapters of this book, we will chart the rise and fall of the individual divisions of the Waffen-SS, from great formations such as the *Totenkopf* and *Das Reich*, through to some of the little-known later divisions that were obliterated within months of their formation. In this chapter, we look at the years 1939–42, in which the greatest of the Waffen-SS divisions were formed or were blooded in action. Note – the names

Another image of the SS-Heimwehr *Danzig* during their assault on the Polish post office in Danzig, September 1939. The unit is advancing under fire, sheltered by the ADGZ armoured car.

SS-TV non-commissioned officers pose for the camera c. 1938. The SS-TV personnel went on to a multitude of different roles, from concentration camp administrators to frontline combat personnel.

of the formations described below frequently changed during their evolution. Describing all these changes would be deadening, so here the honour title is often used as shorthand for the formation in various stages of evolution.

1. SS-PANZER DIVISION *LEIBSTANDARTE ADOLF HITLER*

The *Leibstandarte* was the original Waffen-SS formation. It traced its origins to the bodyguard known as the SS-Stabswache Berlin, formed in March 1933 to protect Hitler. Its official designation was changed several times before, in November 1933, becoming the *Leibstandarte Adolf Hitler* (LSSAH), essentially translated as 'Adolf Hitler Lifeguard Regiment'. Unlike most other units, which recruited in a specific home region, the regiment took its personnel from throughout Germany; only the best physical candidates were accepted for this high-profile unit. Special insignia – the SS runes collar patch rather than the unit number worn by Allgemeine-SS units, the distinctive cuffband bearing Hitler's signature, and white leather dress belts and accoutrements worn on parade – set the *Leibstandarte* apart from all others. The unit was initially about ceremony as much as muscle. It provided honour guards on many state occasions, as well as providing sentries for Hitler's new Reichskanzlei (Reich

Leibstandarte troops during fighting at Sacharzow, Poland, in 1939. Although the Germans faced tough resistance from the Poles at times, the outcome of the invasion was never in doubt.

Chancellery) in Berlin. Its home was the former Imperial Prussian cadet barracks at Berlin-Lichterfelde. Its members' impeccable appearance and precision drill earned them the somewhat derogatory nickname of the 'Asphalt Soldiers' – good for parades, but unproven on the field of battle.

Reorganized into a motorized regiment in late 1934, the *Leibstandarte* took part in the re-occupation of the Rhineland, the *Anschluss* with Austria, and the occupation of the Sudetenland and Czechoslovakia. In September 1939, the *Leibstandarte* was put to the ultimate test when it went into battle for the first time during the invasion of Poland, for which it was attached to the army's Panzer Division *Kempf*. In action at Lodz, Warsaw and Modlin, the regiment fought well, but sustained more than 400 casualties fending off determined attacks by Polish cavalry and infantry, which sometimes came to hand-to-hand combat.

LEFT: Officers of the early Waffen-SS, 1939–40. 1: SS-Sturmbannführer, SS-VT, seen wearing service dress in 1939. 2: SS-Brigadeführer und Generalmajor der Waffen-SS, late 1940. 3: SS-Hauptsturmführer of artillery, SS-Verfügungs Division, summer 1940. (Osprey Publishing © Jeffrey Burn)

The battle for Poland cost the *Leibstandarte Adolf Hitler* more than 400 casualties, as the regiment faced tougher-than-expected resistance from Polish troops.

In March 1940 an artillery battalion was added in the first of many moves to increase the strength and military effectiveness of Hitler's own 'personal' regiment, a unit of which he was intensely proud. During the campaign in the West the *Leibstandarte* acquitted itself well. It crossed the Yssel river near Zutphen, covering over 75km in a single day, and performing with a level of enthusiasm for battle that was to become its trademark. The LSSAH took part in the encirclement and seizure of Amsterdam, the unit's satisfaction over this successful action being somewhat dampened when Luftwaffe General Kurt Student was shot and wounded by *Leibstandarte* soldiers who mistook him for one of the enemy. In recognition of its performance the LSSAH was given the honour of having the '*Führerstandarte*', Hitler's personal banner, as its regimental flag.

Yet the *Leibstandarte* also began to gather the reputation for brutality that would eventually come to define the SS in general. On 28 May 1940, the *Leibstandarte* was closing in on the British Expeditionary Force's perimeter around Dunkirk. Outside the village of Wormhoudt, the car in which 'Sepp' Dietrich was driving came under heavy fire and burst into flames. Dietrich flung himself into a culvert for shelter, rolling in the mud to protect himself from the heat, but it was to be five hours before his men eliminated the resistance and rescued him. Incensed at the thought that their bluff, coarse but beloved commander had been killed, the men of *Leibstandarte* threw themselves at the defenders of Wormhoudt, some 330 men of the 2nd Royal Warwickshire and Cheshire Regiments and the Royal Artillery. About 80 men were taken prisoner by Haupsturmführer Wilhelm Mohnke's company from the regiment's 2nd Battalion, whose own commander had been badly wounded. The men were herded into a barn, whereupon their guards began hurling hand grenades into their midst, shooting down those who tried to escape. Someone finally called a halt to the slaughter, but there were only 15 survivors. The culprit was not identified until 1988, by which time he was an elderly retired businessman.

In April 1941 the *Leibstandarte* excelled itself in the invasion of Greece. *Leibstandarte* took part while *Reich* was heading for Belgrade. The division's reconnaissance battalion was in its rightful place in the van of the attack. However, it encountered far stiffer opposition from the tough Greek and British Empire troops opposing it, and at one point the battalion, commanded by Kurt 'Panzer' Meyer, became pinned down by heavy and accurate machine-gun fire while trying to force a way through the Klissura Pass. Seeing his men's reluctance to move out of the shelter of the rocks behind which they were crouching, Meyer resorted to the desperate expedient of pulling a pin from a grenade and rolling it towards their feet. 'Never again,' he said later, 'did I witness such a concerted leap forward as at that moment.' The pass was captured and, like Klingenberg, Meyer was awarded the Knight's Cross.

It was, however, with the invasion of the Soviet Union in July 1941 that the *Leibstandarte* was to be put to its greatest test; now a brigade just under 11,000 strong, it formed part of Heeresgruppe Süd. After advancing through Cherson it captured Taganrog, and in November, Rostov, where it took more than 10,000 prisoners. Here, SS-Hauptsturmführer Heinrich Springer earned the Knight's Cross of the Iron Cross for his daring seizure of the vital bridge over the River Don. As the end of the year drew near, however, the impetus of the advance faltered and Soviet resistance grew. Counter-attacks put the *Leibstandarte* in danger, but Hitler refused to countenance a general withdrawal. Nevertheless, the SS was forced back out of Rostov, and into a number of grim winter defensive engagements in the area of the Donetz Basin as the Soviets counter-attacked in considerable strength.

Despite the failure of the German campaign, *Leibstandarte* had greatly enhanced its reputation as a first-class combat unit, drawing praise from army generals who had formerly regarded the Waffen-SS with some disdain. A good example of the formation's combat vigour can be seen in its final defence along the Don River at Rostov, on 25 November 1941.

From their headquarters more than 1,400km behind the front, Hitler, Fritz Halder (Chief of the Army General Staff) and most of the Reich's leadership believed 1. Panzer

ABOVE: Operations in France, 1940. The *Leibstandarte* soldier in the background wears the black uniform of the Panzer arm. The soldier to the left is a junior officer in the *Totenkopf* Division, while the other individual is an NCO from the SS-VT Standarte 2 Germania. (Osprey Publishing © Jeffrey Burn)

Armee should be able to push past Rostov and on to Stalingrad and the Caucasus before the weather forced a halt to *Barbarossa*. Never a strong German suit, Wehrmacht intelligence did not see how the Red Army could offer much of a challenge after battles like Kiev and the Sea of Azov. Somehow Heeresgruppe Süd scraped together enough fuel and ammunition during the first half of November to continue the advance past the Mius River. On 17 November, von Kleist's men moved out. On that same day, Marshal Timoshenko launched his own limited counter-attack. Neither Soviet resistance, poor logistics nor harsh weather could deny III Panzer Korps, however. They entered Rostov on 20 November and cleared the city of defenders two days later. General Paul von Kleist had no enthusiasm for staying in Rostov and presently requested permission to evacuate. At the end of an exposed salient, weakened from five months campaigning and with its logistics unimproved, his Panzer army was in no position to put up a serious fight. On the south edge of the city overlooking the Don River the 300 men of *Leibstandarte*'s motorized division's reconnaissance battalion under Sturmbannführer Kurt 'Panzer' Meyer held an 8km front. They had had only three days to improve their positions by digging into the rock hard earth and stacking blocks of ice in front of them.

Troops of the *Leibstandarte* are here seen manning a half-track mounted Flak 30 anti-aircraft gun, although the decimation of the Soviet Air Force during the early phases of *Barbarossa* meant they had few aerial targets.

Early on 25 November, Marshal Timoshenko loosed his Fifty-Sixth Army against III Panzer Korps' defences in and around Rostov. At 0520hrs on a dim and freezing morning, parts of three rifle and one cavalry division assaulted the German line. The mile-wide Don was frozen solid and supported all but the heaviest vehicles. T-34 tanks provided support fire from the far bank. Soviet riflemen of the 343rd Rifle Division attacked in battalion strength with bayonets fixed to their Moisin Model 1891 rifles standing straight up, screaming 'Urrah!' and often with their arms linked. The German troops' weaponry included the standard M1934 Karabiner 98k rifle and MG 34 light machine guns, with officers also carrying the Walther P 38 sidearm. These small arms were supported by a few Pak 38 50mm anti-tank guns. Some of the SS troops wore issued snow smocks, some improvised snow camouflage, while others had nothing but their standard wool uniforms. The Soviet infantry attacked in three waves. Successive lines stumbled over piles of dead from earlier attacks, each getting closer to the defenders on the bluff above the river who fought desperately to keep control of the Don River bridge. Finally the fourth wave broke through the 2nd and then 1st Companies of SS men. Assault guns with German infantry immediately counter-attacked. They captured 400, mostly wounded, while more than 300 Red Army soldiers lay dead on the battlefield. Total cost to the *Leibstandarte* Division was two dead and seven wounded.

The commander of III Panzer Korps is recorded as saying of the LSSAH, 'This truly is an elite unit.' This reputation was not achieved without cost, however: more than 5,200 of the brigade's soldiers had become casualties.

In June 1942 the *Leibstandarte* – much weakened after a year of brutal combat and a Russian winter – was pulled from its defensive positions along the Mius River and moved to France, where it was greatly reinforced and re-formed as a mechanized or Panzergrenadier division. The new division spent some months forming up and training before moving to occupation duties in the southern (Vichy) part of France – occupied by Germany in retaliation for the surrender of the French Army in North Africa to the Anglo–American landings in November. During this period the *Leibstandarte* was given

LEFT: The *Leibstandarte* at war, 1940–43. 1: SS-Schütze, 1940. This infantry enlisted man serving with the LSSAH in Holland and France wears for field service an old 1937 field-grey SS tunic with slanted skirt pockets, still displaying the collar cord. By this date most of these tunics had been modified with dark green collar facing, making them closer in appearance to the regulation army M1936 field blouse. 2: SS-Schütze, Panzerspähzug, 1940. This private of the regiment's armoured car reconnaissance troop wears an army issue black *Panzerbekleidung*, the special uniform for members of armoured vehicle crews. Headgear is the Panzerschutzmütze, a wool beret fitted over a padded crash-helmet; the embroidered insignia in white on black are of unique pattern. His jacket collar and shoulder straps are piped in the rose-pink branch colour of the Panzertruppe; the 'LAH' cyphers are machine-embroidered in silver-grey thread. Note that he still wears old-pattern collar patches edged with black and aluminium twist cord. 3: SS-Scharführer, SS-Sturmgeschütz Abteilung 1, 1943. This assault gun commander wears the field-grey version of the special uniform for crews of armoured vehicles, issued to armoured units other than tanks. (Inset) The 'LAH' shoulder strap cypher in bronzed metal. (Osprey Publishing © Stephen Andrew)

France, summer 1942. A Waffen-SS unit drives through a peaceful French village. Many Waffen-SS formations were sent to France from the Eastern Front for necessary periods of rest and refit.

its own detachment of the new PzKpfw VI Tiger heavy tanks, being a early recipient of this most powerful of World War II battle tanks.

2. SS-PANZER DIVISION *DAS REICH*

This division originated from the combining of the existing SS-VT Regiments *Deutschland*, *Germania* and *Der Führer* with the sappers and signallers of the SS-Pioniersturmbann and the SS-Nachrichtensturmbann. The SS-VT was created in March 1935 from previous units of SS-Politische Bereitschaften, and the first of the SS-VT regiments (designated Standarten at that time), *Deutschland*, was formed in Munich in September of that year. One year later a second regiment, *Germania*, was founded in Hamburg; and following the *Anschluss* with Austria a third, *Der Führer*, was created in Vienna.

The various SS-VT units, with the exception of *Der Führer*, which was still forming, served during the Polish campaign under army command. The *Deutschland* regiment was attached to the army's Panzer Division *Kempf*, part of Heeresgruppe A striking south into Poland from East Prussia, whilst *Germania* was allocated to Heeresgruppe B in the south. *Deutschland* acquitted itself well during attacks on the Polish defensive positions of the Mlava Line, in particular the seizure of Höhe 192, which required attacks up-hill against fiercely defended enemy positions. The regiment also took part in the defeat of the Polish fortresses on the Modlin Line, the soldiers of *Deutschland* receiving glowing praise from General Kempf for their performance in battle.

Unlike its sister regiment, *Germania* was not used as a cohesive unit, but split up and attached piecemeal as separate detachments to support various army units. The decision not to group the various SS units that took part in the Polish campaign into a single force was deliberate: Hitler wished to appease senior elements of the Wehrmacht who opposed any growth in the power and influence of the armed SS in parallel with the traditional armed services. However, given the performance of these units in the field, in October 1939 Hitler ordered the formation of the SS-Verfügungs Division under SS-Obergruppenführer Paul Hausser, a highly experienced former professional army officer. The new division would include, in addition to regiments *Deutschland*, *Germania* and *Der Führer*, the SS-Artillerie Regiment, SS-Pioniersturmbann, SS-Nachrichtensturmbann, reconnaissance and anti-tank detachments.

The new formation attacked through Holland in April 1940 to link up with paratroopers who had dropped at Rotterdam. Although the various SS-VT units had been formed into a division, during this initial stage of the Western campaign individual units were once again allocated to support various army units. It was the *Der Führer* Regiment that led the invasion force, storming across the River Yssel despite the Dutch having blown the bridge, establishing a bridgehead and capturing the town of Westervoort. The regiment advanced more than 100km in just one day. Other units faced much tougher resistance, but although suffering serious casualties they still succeeded in overcoming enemy fortifications protecting the Meuse–Waal Canal. *Der Führer* continued to impress with its first-class performance, passing Utrecht and storming on through Amsterdam to Zandvoort on the coast. Subsequently, the separated SS-VT units came together at Marienbourg, and the division struck westwards to eliminate Dutch forces holding out in Walcheren. The Dutch were in excellent defensive positions and supported by artillery and naval units off-shore. Leading the attack, the *Deutschland* Regiment took heavy casualties, which only ended with a Dutch withdrawal rather than a successful German assault.

On 22 May the division struck out towards Calais. While bivouacked for the night en route the SS troops were attacked by French units attempting to break out of the encirclement at Dunkirk. The French were held, though the fighting was extremely tough, and once they had regained the initiative the SS-VT succeeded in destroying numerous tanks and took several hundred prisoners. The division crossed the La Bassée Canal the following day and held the bridgehead they established against British counter-attacks. The advance continued with *Der Führer* and *Germania* striking through the Nieppe forest and pushing the British back. At this time *Deutschland* was forcing a crossing over the Lys Canal, and holding against powerful British armoured attacks; the day was saved by the timely arrival of the *Totenkopf* Division.

On 1 June, the division was pulled out of the line to regroup and prepare for the second stage of the assault on France that began four days later; the SS-VT struck southwards through Orleans and seized Angoulême. This second phase saw the division primarily engaged in mopping-up actions until the French capitulation on 25 June. It is estimated that SS troops took the surrender of over 30,000 prisoners during this period for the loss of less than 35 of their own men. Several members of the SS-Verfügungs Division were decorated with the Knight's Cross for their parts in this campaign.

In July 1940 the division moved to occupied Holland, where it spent several months before returning to France; it was originally earmarked to take part in the proposed invasion of Great Britain. During this period the division lost a number of its most experienced soldiers, transferred to provide a cadre for the new *Wiking* Division then being formed; in December 1940 the *Germania* Regiment was removed and replaced by SS-*Totenkopf* Infanterie Regiment 11. Later that month the division was officially renamed as SS-Division *Das Reich*.

The *Reich* Division remained in France until March 1941, when it was ordered to the Balkans. It would not be there for long, before it was assigned to a far larger operation. On 22 June 1941, the *Reich* Division formed part of Heeresgruppe Mitte, under Generalfeldmarschall von Bock, during the invasion of the Soviet Union. Not being in the first wave, when it finally moved it found the going slow on the heavily congested roads. The division saw its first action in Russia on 28 June when it ejected Soviet forces from the village of Starzyca, though only the timely arrival of reinforcements prevented the spearhead units being cut off during an enemy counter-attack. *Reich* advanced into the heart of central Russia, crossing the Beresina, skirting the notorious Pripet Marshes, to Mogilev and Smolensk, and captured and defended Yelnya against determined counter-attacks. On 8 August, the division was temporarily relieved for a period of rest and refitting near Smolensk.

By September, *Reich* was back in the forefront of the advance, taking Sosnitza and assisting in the capture of Kiev and over 665,000 Soviet prisoners. After another brief rest and the arrival of replacements for casualties, by 19 October the division was heavily involved in Operation *Taifun* (Typhoon), the advance on Moscow. After capturing Gshatsk and holding it against furious counter-attacks, *Reich* pushed on and took Mozhiask and Istra; by early December divisional elements had taken the Moscow

LEFT: SS-Verfügungs Division, 1940. 1: SS-Unterscharführer, SS-Standarte *Deutschland*. This seasoned NCO, as a squad leader, has added binoculars and a mapcase to his rifleman's equipment. 2: SS-Schütze, SS-Standarte *Germania*. This rifleman typifies the appearance of soldiers from this unit during the Westfeldzug. His helmet has been daubed with mud, a simple and effective alternative to the camouflaged cover. 3: SS Hauptstürmführer, SS-Pioniersturmbann. This engineer captain wears the typical M1936 field-grey, green-collared field blouse as used by his army counterparts. (Osprey Publishing © Stephen Andrew)

Reich Division motorcycle troops mark the way for following divisional units. The German advance into Russia in 1941 took *Reich* to the outer suburbs of Moscow itself.

suburb of Lenino and could actually see the domed roofs of the Kremlin. However, the onset of winter, heavy losses through combat attrition, and the fanatical defence of their capital by Soviet troops then drained the impetus out of the German advance. With Moscow tantalizingly just out of their grasp, the Germans were forced onto the defensive. *Reich* had ultimately reached a point just 16km from the centre of Moscow, but had suffered heavy casualties in the process: it is estimated that by this point only 40 per cent of its original personnel remained.

The weakened division then found itself battered by fierce Soviet attacks as the enemy began their winter counter-offensive. By January 1942, the *Der Führer* Regiment was down to a strength of fewer than 50 men as the exhausted formation clung on against Red Army pressure, and by the end of February the *Reich* Division was reclassified as a mere Kampfgruppe. It fought along the Volga river in March, holding until the enemy attacks finally began to ease. It was then allowed some much needed rest before, in June, being withdrawn from the front and returned to Germany for rebuilding as a Panzergrenadier division. From August 1942 until late January 1943 the division was posted to France on occupation duties, and took part in the occupation of Vichy France that winter.

3. SS-PANZER DIVISION *TOTENKOPF*

The *Totenkopf* Division, as noted in previous chapters, had its origins in the highly unsavoury units formed to guard the concentration camps, the SS-Totenkopfstandarten, after control of the camps passed from the SA to the SS in 1934. Head of the Concentration Camps Inspectorate was the equally unsavoury Theodor Eicke. Regiments were raised and located at several camps: Standarte I Oberbayern at Dachau, Standarte II Brandenburg at Oranienburg, Standarte III Thüringen at Buchenwald, and Standarte IV Ostmark at Mauthausen. The various SS-*Totenkopf* elements were collectively termed the SS-TV.

The SS-Totenkopfverbände were considered inferior to the SS-VT. Service in the latter counted towards an individual's liability for military service, whereas the former did not. Eicke had great ambitions for his *Totenkopf* troops, however; he gradually weeded out the poorest elements and improved their military capabilities, although their low priority as basically internal security personnel condemned them to second-rate equipment and obsolete or captured weapons.

On the outbreak of war Standarten *Oberbayern*, *Thüringen* and *Brandenburg* were sent into Poland to subjugate any resistance. This generally consisted of assisting the notorious SD Einsatzgruppen in rounding up Jews and other 'undesirables' behind the lines. In the area around Bydgoszcz, elements of *Brandenburg* alone executed 800 'suspect' Poles over just two days. The appalling behaviour of *Totenkopf* units in Poland

Following their victories in Poland, SS troops stand and observe the grave of Jozef Pilsudski, the former Polish prime minister and the General Inspector of the Armed Forces.

provoked vociferous complaints by the army, all of which were brushed aside. (The Einsatzgruppen operations are further discussed below.)

In November 1939 Hitler finally authorized combining the various *Totenkopf* regiments to form a third SS division. Problems with discipline were still rife, despite Eicke's brutal response to disobedience or insubordination. Training continued during the first months of 1940, although the new SS-*Totenkopf* Division was desperately short of vehicles and heavy equipment – so much so that Eicke had to beg, borrow and literally steal the necessary means to bring his units up to strength. The division was finally assigned to 2. Armee for the impending campaign in the West.

On the opening of the offensive on 10 May, to Eicke's disgust, *Totenkopf* was held in reserve, only being committed to action one week later. It advanced through southern Holland, Belgium and into France where, in action north-east of Cambrai, the division took more than 16,000 enemy prisoners. Its dubious reputation was worsened by the execution of captured French Moroccan troops, considered racially 'inferior'.

Subsequently *Totenkopf* was ordered to reinforce the German units that had punched through to the coast, cutting off the British Expeditionary Force (BEF) from the main body of the French Army to the south. In fact a major Anglo-French force, intent on breaking out of the encirclement, smashed right into the division. The light anti-tank weapons available to *Totenkopf* were no match for the Allied tanks, and the SS troops suffered significant casualties. Eicke's men had to resort to using heavy artillery pieces firing at the enemy tanks over open sights, and only the timely arrival of Stuka dive-bombers saved the day; the division had come perilously close to panic.

The *Totenkopf* was then tasked with advancing to the La Bassée Canal and seeking out a suitable crossing point for the main body of the German advance. Eicke ignored his orders and pushed on across the canal against stiff resistance. At this point Hitler's notorious 'halt order' was issued and Eicke was obliged to give up his hard-won bridgehead and withdraw his troops. His clear disobedience of specific orders resulted in a furious reprimand from General Hoepner, who accused him of being a 'butcher' who showed disregard for the lives of his men.

Just two days later the advance resumed, and Eicke had to recapture the area he had just relinquished, taking heavy casualties in doing so. His division faced further stiff

RIGHT: SS-*Totenkopf* Division, 1940–43. 1: SS-Oberscharführer, Feldgendarmerie, 1940. This senior NCO of military police wears an army issue M1936 field blouse with NCO's aluminium Tresse trim to the green-faced collar. 2: SS-Sturmbannführer of infantry, late 1941. 3: SS-Sturmmann of infantry, 1942. This soldier is the 'number one' of a machine-gun crew and carries the excellent MG 34, with the accompanying tool-box on his belt. 4: SS-Rottenführer, SS-Panzergrenadier Regiment 6, late 1943. This junior NCO displays the ribbons of the Iron Cross 2nd Class and the Winter 1941 East Front medal in his buttonhole, the Iron Cross 1st Class pinned to his left pocket above the Infantry Assault Badge, and on his upper left sleeve the shield awarded to those who took part in the battles of the Demjansk Pocket. (Osprey Publishing © Stephen Andrew)

An SS trooper plays to the camera on a farm in the Ukraine, 1942. This benign image conceals the sheer brutality with which the Waffen-SS often treated Ukrainian citizens.

resistance at Bethune and La Paradis, where the British defenders made the SS pay dearly for every yard of ground. The 4th Company of Standarte 2, commanded by Obersturmführer Fritz Knöchlein, was held up by a determined but isolated group of about 100 soldiers of the 2nd Royal Norfolk Regiment. Retreating through the little hamlet of Le Paradis, the Norfolks first tried to hold out in a farmhouse but were forced to evacuate it when Knöchlein's mortars set it alight. Realizing further resistance was futile, the men – who had attempted to find cover in a cowshed – raised a white flag. They were marched along a lane to a barn outside which two machine guns had been set up. Lined up in front of it, they were mercilessly gunned down. Despite SS troops going in with the bayonet to finish off any survivors, three escaped death and lived to see Knöchlein hanged for this atrocity in 1948. His excuse was that he could not spare men to guard prisoners if the momentum of the advance was to be sustained.

In the final days of the campaign, *Totenkopf* once again faced French forces that included Moroccan troops; significantly, here again the only surrenders that were accepted were from white French soldiers. Throughout the campaign in the West *Totenkopf* had suffered much higher casualties even than other SS units that were also gaining a reputation for reckless disregard for losses; Eicke's division lost more than 300 officers in just ten days' fighting. The human material – former political police thugs and Allgemeine-SS reservists, with inadequate military training – was one explanation for both the high casualties and the brutality towards prisoners; another was Eicke's ruthless ambition for his division.

After the conclusion of the campaign the division remained in France on occupation duties for almost a full year; it is reported that in comparison to its aggression in combat, it was involved in assisting local farmers to gather in their harvests. It was also formally declared part of the Waffen-SS proper, and received considerable reinforcements, including new recruits untarnished by service as concentration camp guards. Artillery, Flak and Ersatz (replacement) battalions were added.

For the invasion of the USSR in June 1941 the division was allocated to Heeresgruppe Nord (Army Group North), and attached to IV Panzergruppe. It advanced in the second wave through Lithuania and Latvia, mopping up resistance; and was involved in heavy combat against the defences of the Stalin Line, where Eicke was wounded when his field car went over a mine. *Totenkopf* met unexpectedly fierce resistance and suffered significant casualties. Despite this heavy fighting, however, the division's officer losses in over a month of fighting were 82, as opposed to 300 in just ten days in France. It had also taken a greater number of prisoners in this short period than it had in the whole of the *Westfeldzug*. Clearly *Totenkopf* had learned some lessons from its earlier mistakes. During August the division was involved in very heavy fighting on the approaches to Leningrad, and particularly along the Luga defence line. The Soviet Thirty-Fourth Army was annihilated, but *Totenkopf* suffered more than 4,000 casualties.

Waffen-SS troops advance through a shell-blasted and waterlogged landscape on the Eastern Front. Terrain and climate made the German operations in Russia and Ukraine logistically tortuous.

In late September 1941 the division bore the brunt of a massive Soviet counter-attack at Lushno, where its forces were thinly spread over a 24km front; the attacks were eventually repulsed, leaving *Totenkopf* battered but victorious. During these actions, SS-Sturmmann Fritz Christen earned himself one of the most richly deserved Knight's Crosses to be awarded to a soldier of the Waffen-SS. Christen's anti-tank unit was decimated by enemy attacks, and he manned his gun alone for three full days after the rest of his crew were killed. When relief troops arrived they found Christen alone, surrounded by about a hundred enemy corpses and 13 destroyed Soviet tanks. Christen received his award personally from Hitler, a rare honour for such a junior rank.

As the steam began to run out of the German advance the division, now severely weakened, was obliged to dig in and by the end of 1941 was fully on the defensive. During this period many of its troops were involved in anti-partisan operations during which no quarter was given or expected. Gradual combat attrition had now reduced *Totenkopf* to around 50 per cent strength.

In January 1942 *Totenkopf* came under attack when the Soviets launched a major counter-offensive that smashed its way through the army units on the division's flanks. There followed one of the great battles of the Eastern Front, with which the division would thereafter always be connected. *Totenkopf* became encircled with a number of army units around the town of Demjansk; greatly outnumbered, the German units held on tenaciously. The much-weakened *Totenkopf* was divided into two Kampfgruppen and, after Himmler's personal intervention, was reinforced by air with just 400 replacements; this assistance was as much for psychological as physical effect. By late March 1942 divisional casualties stood at just under 13,000, and 11 of its members had been awarded the Knight's Cross for gallantry.

In April 1942 a German attack forced a narrow relief corridor through to the besieged troops in the Demjansk Pocket. The normal establishment of a full strength infantry division was around 17,000 men; the total combined strength of the six divisions then at Demjansk, under overall command of SS-Obergruppenführer Eicke, stood at just 14,000. Although the encirclement had been broken, the ferocity of the fighting was unabated, and by August *Totenkopf's* divisional strength was down to just over 2,700 men. In November 1942 the division was withdrawn and transferred to France for rest and refitting. During this period it was upgraded to the status of a Panzergrenadier division.

RIGHT: Eastern Front, 1941–43. 1: SS-Unterscharführer despatch rider, 1941. 2: SS-Obersturmbannführer, winter surcoat, 1942–43. 3: SS-Hauptscharführer Kriegsberichter, c. 1944. It is thanks to the efforts of the prolific photographers of the SS war correspondents' branch that so many wartime photos of the Waffen-SS in action are available to us today. (Osprey Publishing © Stephen Andrew)

4. SS-*POLIZEI* PANZERGRENADIER DIVISION

The *Polizei* Division was formed in October 1939 by drafting approximately 15,000 members of the Ordnungspolizei and attaching army artillery and signals units. It underwent intensive training near the Black Forest until the spring of 1940, and during this period some elements of the division performed occupation duties in Poland. While all German police forces came under the authority of the SS, the formation was not considered to be on a par with true armed SS divisions, and this was reflected in the quality of equipment issued.

The division saw its first combat during the invasion of France and the Low Countries in 1940. It was initially held in reserve with Heeresgruppe C in the Rhineland, going into action on 9 June when it crossed the River Aisne. It fought around the Argonne Forest against French rearguard units, capturing the small town of Les Islettes. The campaign was brief, however, as the division was taken out of the line on 20 June. Soon afterwards the *Polizei* Division was transferred to East Prussia where it continued its training. In January 1941 control of the division passed from the police to the SS.

On 27 June 1941, the *Polizei* Division joined the German forces massing for the invasion of the Soviet Union, becoming part of the reserve of Heeresgruppe Nord. It went into action around Luga, losing over 2,000 dead and wounded in bloody fighting through difficult terrain of dense forests and mosquito-plagued swamps. By August the division, along with a number of army divisions, had finally managed to complete an encirclement of the Soviet forces at Luga; the town was captured at the cost of significant casualties, the divisional commander SS-Gruppenführer Arthur Mülverstedt being one of those killed in action.

In January 1942 the division was deployed along the Wolchow river, and the following month it was officially made part of the Waffen-SS, changing its Polizei insignia for regulation Waffen-SS insignia thereafter. Between January and March the SS-*Polizei* Division saw fierce fighting that resulted in the defeat of the Soviet Second Shock Army. The remainder of 1942 was spent on the Leningrad front. The division was beginning to gain a reputation for reliability, though it had by no means achieved elite status, but combat attrition saw the formation's strength steadily whittled down. In January 1943 the division came under Soviet attacks around the south of Lake Ladoga; the enemy eventually broke through the German defence lines in February, and forced the SS troops to retreat westwards to new defence positions at Kolpino. These were successfully held, but losses had been severe; at this point elements of the division were withdrawn to Silesia as the nucleus for a re-formed Panzergrenadier division, while the remainder were formed into a smaller Kampfgruppe. During the following month

ABOVE: *Polizei* Division, 1940–41. 1: SS-Oberschütze of artillery, 1940. Note that the use of the police helmet decal in place of the SS version was common during this period. 2: SS-Brigadeführer, 1942–44. 3: SS-Rottenführer, Greece, 1943. The *Polizei* Divison was issued with tan tropical uniforms during its spell of duty in the Balkans. (Osprey Publishing © Stephen Andrew)

the Dutch volunteers of the SS-Freiwilligen Legion *Niederlande* (SS-Volunteer Division *Netherlands*) were assigned to bolster its strength. This Kampfgruppe remained in constant action on the Eastern Front until May 1944, when it was finally disbanded.

5. SS-PANZER DIVISION *WIKING*

The *Wiking* Division is one of the earliest examples of Himmler's broadening of the ethnic diversity of the Waffen-SS. The division had its origins in an order issued by Himmler in September 1940 founding a division of 'Germanic' volunteers from the Netherlands, Denmark and Norway, and Belgian Walloons. In order to provide an experienced cadre for the new formation the *Germania* Regiment was transferred from the *Reich* Division, backed by Volunteer Regiments *Westland* and *Nordland*. It was initially named SS-Infanterie Division (mot.) *Germania*, but this instantly caused confusion with the regiment of the same name, and on 20 December the divisional title *Wiking* was formally bestowed.

Command of the new division was given to SS-Obergruppenführer Felix Steiner, a respected former army officer. In February 1941, the newly raised Finnish volunteer unit Finnisches Freiwilligen Bataillon der Waffen-SS was attached to *Wiking*; and several weeks of intensive training followed at Heuberg before, in April 1941, the formation was declared ready for combat deployment. In mid-May the new division moved into western Poland in preparation for its part in the attack on Soviet Russia, for which it was allocated to III Panzer Korps as part of Heeresgruppe Süd.

The *Wiking* Division saw its first combat around Tarnopol. By August 1941 it had reached Uman, where it participated in the massive encirclement that netted the Germans over 100,000 prisoners. Operating with the *Hermann Göring* Division, *Wiking* saw action at Korsun, and by 21 August was across the River Dnieper. Transferred to XIV Panzer Korps, *Wiking* advanced towards Oktjabrisk; but by the end of November it had been halted by an enemy counter-attack and forced onto the defensive on the Mius River as the onset of winter stalled the German advance.

In the New Year the division advanced from its positions along the Mius as the German offensive began afresh. That summer it took part in the deepest penetrations of the Russian campaign, the drive on Rostov on the River Don and the attempt to secure the Caucasus oilfields. By the end of 1942 and the onset of another winter *Wiking* had proven itself in combat well enough to warrant upgrading to the status of Panzergrenadier division. It took up positions along the Terek river, deep in the Caucasus. However, after the disaster at Stalingrad in January 1943 and the launch of the Soviet counter-offensive on the southern front *Wiking* was pushed back towards Manych, and was involved in heavy defensive actions around Izym.

6. SS-GEBIRGS-DIVISION *NORD*

This division had its origins in February 1941, when a number of SS-*Totenkopf* regiments were transferred to Norway for garrison duty. These were mostly Allgemeine-SS reservists of military service age. Subsequently, SS-Kampfgruppe *Nord* (mot.) was formed, from SS-Totenkopfstandarten (redesignated as SS-*Totenkopf* Infanterie Regimenter) 6 and 7 and a number of other units. This new battle group was attached to XXXVI Korps of Heeresgruppe Nord, to participate in Operation *Silberfuchs* (Silver Fox), intended to secure the liberation of Karelia – a region of Finland occupied by Soviet forces – and subsequently to take part in the invasion of the northern USSR. However, the 'battlegroup' had woefully inadequate training and preparation for combat, and would consequently suffer heavy casualties. Many of its gunners had had no opportunity to practise live firing; there had been no combined training of the infantry and artillery units; the strength and quality of the transport was low, and there were insufficient infantry support weapons. The brigade was not a cohesive force but rather a collection of disparate and inadequately equipped units, many of its officers and men hardly trained even in basic military skills.

On 6 June 1941 it was ordered to the Rovaniemi area of Finland. The Kampfgruppe had only recently concentrated near Kirkenes, and had to march the length of the Arctic Ocean Highway from Kirkenes on the Arctic Ocean to Rovaniemi not far from the Baltic coast. By 10 June its forward elements had reached their destination, but other units straggled in over a period of a week or so. Elements began moving towards the Soviet frontier near Salla on 17 June. On 24 June the order to advance finally arrived, the attack itself being further delayed until 1 July.

Nord was tasked with making a frontal attack on heavily defended enemy positions in front of Salla, as part of an attempt to cut a main railway line and isolate Soviet troops in the Kola Peninsula. The brigade would be supported by an assault by 169. Infanterie Division on the northern flank, while Finnish infantry drove deep behind enemy lines towards Allakurtti from Nord's southern flank. The SS troops were reinforced by the addition of the army tank battalion Panzer Abteilung 40, and both army artillery units and Stuka dive-bombers provided suppressive bombardment of Soviet positions prior to the assault. This softening-up barrage had only limited success; it did cause some damage to the enemy, but also started forest fires which severely hampered visibility and thus the subsequent artillery and air attacks. The advancing SS infantry were met by stubborn resistance and extremely heavy defensive fire; they were unable to advance far, and on 2 July the attack was called off. *Nord* had become badly scattered (although it should be mentioned that army units on their northern flank fared little better).

Nord spent the next two days regrouping in preparation for a resumption of the attack, but in the early hours of 4 July the Red Army launched a counter-attack with armoured support. Although this was eventually beaten off by the army and Finnish units on *Nord*'s flanks, reports that enemy tanks had broken through caused several companies of SS infantry to flee their positions. About a kilometre behind the line they met the Kradschutzen platoon on its way forward to check out the reports of enemy tanks. The motorcyclists were infected by the panic and, without checking further, reported that enemy armour had indeed broken through; as a result an entire regiment abandoned their positions, only being rallied when they reached the corps headquarters at Kelloselka.

It was intended to put the badly shaken troops into defensive positions while renewing the attack with other elements of both the SS-*Totenkopf* infantry regiments. Many of the latter simply got lost and failed to rendezvous; and the attack soon ran into heavy fire from enemy bunkers in the forest edge. The SS troops returned fire and eventually the enemy positions fell silent, but patrols sent out to confirm that they had been eliminated were unable to locate the concealed bunkers. Mistakenly assuming that they had been destroyed, the SS troops continued their advance, only to be brought under heavy fire while crossing open ground in front of the treeline. They were pinned down for several hours before being given authority to pull back. Over a period of nine days the battlegroup had lost 261 dead and 307 wounded (though they had taken over 250 enemy prisoners).

The lamentable performance of Kampfgruppe *Nord* was a direct result of their lack of training and inadequate leadership; the brigade had been thrown into battle to learn its craft the hard way, under fire, and against an extremely tough enemy. It was subsequently broken up into smaller sub-units which were subordinated to Finnish

SS security forces hang civilians on the Eastern Front. Permission to commit murder in Eastern Europe came from the very top. SS-Obergruppenführer Wilhelm Backe, the Reich Minister of Food, even designed a plan to strip food resources from the Soviet Union that would, according to his calculations, result in the starvation of 'tens of millions' of civilians.

forces attacking Soviet positions at Kestenga. The battle-hardened Finns were aware of *Nord*'s inexperience at all levels, and took direct control of the SS regiments. This was to be the first and only time that Waffen-SS troops were placed under command of an allied army. By 20 August the units of Kampfgruppe *Nord* had lost a total of 1,085 men to a combination of enemy action and dysentery.

After retraining under the tutelage of Finnish infantry, the brigade was rebuilt with younger, fitter soldiers from the Waffen-SS replacement system, and SS-*Totenkopf* Infanterie Regiment 9 was added. In September 1941 the Kampfgruppe was upgraded to divisional status, and all its fragmented sub-units were brought back under German command. While the original units remained in the line in Finland, January 1942 saw the formation of new elements at Wildflecken, which were trained as mountain infantry; they joined the former battlegroup – redesignated on 15 May as a mountain division – in Finland in August 1942.

RISING STARS

The first two years of World War II had been a time of severe learning for the Waffen-SS. It had experienced the harsh reality of combat in France and the Soviet Union, some of its units suffering near-catastrophic losses fighting against enemies classed as *Untermenschen* (subhuman) according to its twisted philosophy. Yet it had also proven that, when well led and properly equipped, it could fight and fight hard. The formation

Soldiers of the *Leibstandarte Adolf Hitler* open fire with a 2cm Flak 30 gun at ground targets during the Russian summer of 1941, as part of the operations of Heeresgruppe Süd.

was also producing a new generation of combat leaders, men who would take the reputation of the Waffen-SS to both highs and lows over the duration of its existence. Two such men are considered here.

SS-GRUPPENFÜHRER UND GENERALLEUTNANT DER WAFFEN-SS HERMANN FEGELEIN

Born in Bavaria on 30 October 1906, Fegelein was raised in Munich where his father, a retired officer, worked at a military riding school. After leaving university he fulfilled brief military service in 1925–26 with Reiter Regiment 17, then served in the police in 1927–29. He kept up a keen interest in equestrian sports, competing at international level. Thus when he joined the Allgemeine-SS in 1933 he was commissioned SS-Untersturmführer and assigned to the cavalry branch, and by July 1937, aged only 30, he was commander of the SS Main Riding School in the rank of SS-Standartenführer. A favourite of Himmler, he was allowed to retain this rank semi-officially when he joined the Waffen-SS in 1939 as commander of the new SS-*Totenkopf* Reiterstandarte 1. Deployed in Poland on security duties, the unit duly committed its first confirmed atrocities in October 1939.

This single regiment was gradually increased to brigade status, and served in the rear areas on the central sector of the Eastern Front from the early stages of Operation *Barbarossa*. During anti-partisan duties under Himmler's Kommandostab RfSS, Fegelein's SS-Kavallerie Brigade committed widespread war crimes in the region of the Pripet Marshes in summer 1941. Transferred to frontline duty, the brigade faced serious opposition in winter 1941/42, and fought well under 9. Armee command in desperate battles around Rzhev. Reduced to a 700-man battlegroup by March 1942, it was then progressively withdrawn to Poland by August that year, and SS-Standartenführer Fegelein was awarded the Knight's Cross on 2 March 1942. In May, Fegelein was given a staff posting as Inspector of SS cavalry, but returned to the front in December 1942 to lead a Kampfgruppe on the Don Front as part of Heeresgruppe B. On 20 December, Fegelein led an assault with two self-propelled guns on a Soviet corps HQ, capturing senior officers and important documents. Over the following two days Fegelein suffered two bullet wounds, and on 22 December he was awarded the Oakleaves.

Fegelein was promoted to SS-Brigadeführer und Generalmajor der Waffen-SS on 1 May 1942, and two weeks later took command of the SS-Kavallerie Division (later numbered 8., and titled *Florian Geyer*), which had been created by expanding his old brigade. Fegelein led the division with some success during 1943, on anti-partisan operations in central Russia and later in the frontline under Heeresgruppe Süd. He seems to have made up for his lack of staff training by relying upon competent and experienced subordinates, acknowledging his debt and assisting their careers. His personal bravery under fire seems to be well documented, and he qualified for the Close Combat Clasp in Silver. He was wounded again in September; and in January 1944, with the rank of SS-Gruppenführer, he joined the Führerhauptquartier (Fuhrer Headquarters) as Himmler's liaison officer with Hitler.

In June 1944 he married Gretl Braun, sister of Hitler's mistress Eva. He was wounded once again in the assassination attempt on Hitler on 20 July 1944, and on that very day was decorated by Hitler with the Swords in recognition of his command of the *Florian Geyer* Division. Despite his connections, however, Fegelein did not survive the paranoia that reigned in the Führerbunker in the closing days of the war, when Hitler was enraged to learn that Himmler – his 'loyal Heinrich' – had been exploring the possibility of secret negotiations with the Allies in the hope of saving his own neck. On 27 April 1945, Fegelein went missing from his post; he was apparently discovered with a mistress in a nearby apartment, drunk, in civilian clothes, and in possession of a substantial amount of money and false passports. He was dragged back to the Bunker and interrogated by the chief of the Gestapo, Heinrich Müller. Hitler ordered an immediate court-martial; and on 29 April, stripped of his insignia and decorations, Hermann Fegelein was shot by a firing squad of SS guards in the garden of the Foreign Office.

SS-OBERFÜHRER GEORG BOCHMANN

Georg Bochmann was born on 18 September 1913 in the Saxon town of Albenau. The son of a factory worker, he enlisted in the SS-Totenkopfverbände in April 1934. He was commissioned SS-Untersturmführer in 1936, and posted to SS-Totenkopfstandarte I *Oberbayern* based at Dachau. Eventually given command of 14. (Panzerjäger) Kompanie of the regiment within the new SS-*Totenkopf* Division, SS-Obersturmführer Bochmann served in the West in spring 1940. As noted, during this campaign the ill-trained and ill-equipped division suffered very heavy casualties, and some of its units earned a reputation for war crimes. With the upgrading and enlargement of *Totenkopf* a Panzerjäger Abteilung (anti-tank battalion) had been formed, and Bochmann, now an SS-Hauptsturmführer, commanded this unit in the invasion of the USSR in 1941, when it fought on the Leningrad front.

The battalion took severe casualties but performed much more efficiently than in 1940. Bochmann himself came to prominence during the encirclement of German forces, including the *Totenkopf*, in the Demjansk Pocket. In April 1942 Bochmann led his weary men in a successful break-out across the River Lovat and through enemy positions. They captured a number of Soviet artillery pieces in hand-to-hand fighting, during which Bochmann was seriously wounded, and reached German lines on 21 April. For this achievement Bochmann was decorated with the Knight's Cross on 3 May 1942.

When the *Totenkopf* Division, re-organized as 3. SS-Panzergrenadier Division, returned to Russia in February 1943, SS-Sturmbannführer Bochmann now commanded the mechanized infantry unit SS-Panzergrenadier Regiment 5 *Thule*, which saw heavy fighting under the new I SS-Panzer Korps. Bochmann was decorated with the Oakleaves on 17 May 1943, receiving the award personally from Hitler. He was subsequently given command of his division's SS-Panzer Regiment 3, and led the *Totenkopf* tank

PARTISAN INTERROGATION

The SS military police was a much smaller organization than that of the army and in general terms provided security at divisional level while in the field. Here we see the outcome of a search by Waffen-SS military police of a Russian farm. The wearing of the Anti-Partisan War Badge on the pocket shows that these men have been involved in several actions against partisan units. The two visible SMGs are the Erma-35 (left) and the MP28. (Osprey Publishing © Velimir Vuksic)

Waffen-SS men proudly display captured Red Army battle flags, while in the background sit hundreds of Russian prisoners; many of those prisoners would be worked to death in SS-run camps back in Germany and Poland.

regiment through the Kursk salient fighting of July, including the gigantic armoured clash at Prokhorovka. Much weakened, the division saw continual fierce combat against Soviet advances around Stalino, and then in the failed defence of Kharkov in August. Throughout the autumn of 1943 the division, now one of the most trusted in the order of battle, was used as a 'fire brigade', fighting successfully but at heavy cost to stem a number of Soviet thrusts. In November 1943 it was redesignated as 3. SS-Panzer Division, and Bochmann's regiment received an increased allocation of armour.

Brought back up to strength in June 1944 after operations in Romania, the *Totenkopf* was worn down again during desperate defensive fighting that summer in the face of the Soviet Operation *Bagration*, which forced Heeresgruppe Mitte back into Poland. In August 1944, Bochmann was temporarily posted to command SS-Panzer Regiment 9 in the new but elite 9. SS-Panzer Division *Hohenstaufen* fighting on the Western Front. He remained in this post until January 1945, when he took command of 18. SS-Freiwilligen Panzergrenadier Division *Horst Wessel*, with the rank of SS-Oberführer. This formation was markedly inferior to his previous commands, being raised largely from ethnic German conscripts from Hungary, though it was up to strength and relatively well equipped. Thrown into battle against the Soviet armies steamrolling through Silesia, *Horst Wessel* took a terrible mauling and was soon encircled by the Red Army near Oberglogau. As at Demjansk, Bochmann once again led a successful break-out, which saved a part of the division from certain annihilation. On 30 March 1945, Bochmann was summoned to the Führerhauptquartier and decorated with the Swords. He was then given command of 17. SS-Panzergrenadier Division *Götz von Berlichingen*,

Soldiers of the *Reich* Division (predecessor of the *Das Reich* Division) are seen in basic winter camouflage around Moscow in the winter of 1941/42. Only in the following winter would the German forces have adequate winter clothing.

a formation greatly weakened while fighting on the Western Front since June 1944. Bochmann led his new division in Bavaria and Austria for the remaining weeks of the war, only surrendering to US forces on 7 May 1945 when expressly ordered to do so by XIII Armee Korps.

Georg Bochmann died in retirement at the age of 60, and his funeral was attended by large numbers of his former soldiers.

THE EINSATZGRUPPEN

Although this book is not about the Holocaust per se, at this point in the narrative it is crucial to look at the early role of the SS in the implementation of Hitler's 'Final Solution'. The killings that took place in the Baltic States, Belorussia and the Ukraine in 1941 and 1942 are not laid squarely at the door of the Waffen-SS, but rather at the SD's specialist 'Einsatzgruppen'. Nevertheless, they can be seen as part of the totality of SS operations on the Eastern Front, a ghastly exercise in nothing more than militarized murder.

As early as September 1939, Reinhard Heydrich, in his capacity as Chief of the Security Police, had issued instructions for his Einsatzgruppen to take part in rounding up Jews from rural areas, to concentrate them in larger cities with good rail links to facilitate further 'measures'. No executions were mentioned at this point, and indeed the economic security of the occupied territories was to be fully considered, especially the needs of the army and businesses supplying the army; any Jews contributing to these concerns were to be 'emigrated' later. However, after the launch of Operation *Barbarossa* all pretence was set aside, and the Einsatzgruppen began their mass murders almost immediately.

Four Einsatzgruppen were formed to operate behind the frontlines, putting into effect the Nazi racial policies, rounding up partisans and generally disposing of those the Nazis considered 'undesirables'.

Einsatzgruppe A, commanded by SS–Brigadeführer Walter Stahlecker, operated in the northern sector of the Eastern Front. Its sub-units were Sonderkommando 1a, Sonderkommando 1b, Einsatzkommando 2 and Einsatzkommando 3.

Einsatzgruppe B, under the command of SS–Gruppenführer Artur Nebe, operated in the central sector and was divided into Sonderkommando 7a, Sonderkommando 7b, Sonderkommando 7c, Einsatzkommando 8, Einsatzkommando 9 and Vorkommando Moskau.

Einsatzgruppe C, commanded by SS–Brigadeführer Otto Rasch, operated around Kiev. Its sub-units were Einsatzkommando 4a, Einsatzkommando 4b, Einsatzkommando 5 and Einsatzkommando 6.

Einsatzgruppe D, commanded by Otto Ohlendorf, operated in the Ukraine and the sub-units were Einsatzkommando 10a, Einsatzkommando 10b, Einsatzkommando 11a, Einsatzkommando 11b and Einsatzkommando 12.

The Einsatzkommandos could then be further divided into individual squads or Teilkommandos.

The brutal face of the German occupation in Poland. Fifty-one Polish prisoners are executed by German troops in September 1939.

On the invasion of the Soviet Union, Einsatzgruppe A moved into Soviet-occupied territory from Gumbinnen in East Prussia, entering Lithuania two days later in the wake of the Wehrmacht's 18. Armee. The deportations and executions began almost immediately. By the start of July, the Einsatzkommandos had entered Riga. Having cut a swathe of terror and destruction through Latvia and Lithuania, the Einsatzgruppe entered the Soviet Union and was operational around Leningrad and Minsk, while maintaining bases in Latvia and Lithuania.

Einsatzgruppe B, following 9. Armee, operated in the Baltic states and in the Soviet Union around Minsk, where it was active around July and August 1941. Some of its Kommandos were responsible for mass executions in Byelorussia. Various elements were also stationed in Vitebsk, Mogilev and Smolensk. Einsatzgruppe C, meanwhile, moved into the eastern part of Galicia following the start of *Barbarossa*, and by early July had already organized an anti-Jewish pogrom in Lvov. Zlotchev and Tarnopol suffered a similar fate. By mid-July it was operating in the area around Kiev, where in September it organized the infamous slaughter of over 30,000 Jews at Babi-Yar. It carried out mass executions around Kharkov and Belgorod and was aiming to visit its attentions on Stalingrad but the defeat of 6. Armee here forced it on to the retreat. Einsatzgruppe D was attached to 11. Armee on the southern sector of the Eastern Front, advancing through Transylvania and eventually arriving at Simferopol in the Crimea. All along the western shores of the Black Sea, its personnel carried out mass executions, Sevastopol and Odessa being just two towns that suffered its attentions.

The Einsatzkommando personnel were made up from a mixture of SS, Gestapo, auxiliary police, Kripo and Orpo personnel, with a very small number of SD men. When members of the Sicherheitspolizei were selected for service with the Einsatzgruppen, it appears they were informed that their mission was to be one of putting down resistance and generally pacifying the areas to the rear of the advancing armies, a task which seemed perfectly logical and reasonable, so it is possible that some men may not have realized the types of actions that they were about to become

RIGHT: Eastern Security Auxiliaries. The central figure on this plate shows the typical appearance of a member of the Schutzmannschaft. Shown in the insets are: 1: Rank insignia worn by Schutzmannschaften on the field-grey uniform. 2: Sleeve chevrons worn on the black uniform. The ranks shown, from left to right, are, Unterkorporal, Vizekorporal, Korporal, Vize-Feldwebel and Kompanie-Feldwebel. 3: Cap insignia was an elongated diamond shaped swastika surrounded by laurel leaves. 4: The arm patch was similar to the cap insignia, but larger, and had the motto 'Treu, Tapfer, Gehorsam' ('faithful, brave, obedient') surrounding the swastika. 5: The Schutzmannschaft shoulder strap also featured the elongated diamond shaped swastika, with piping colours analogous to the colour of the woven sleeve emblem. 6: Schutzmannschaften operating in an administrative or non-combatant role wore uniforms devoid of any insignia, but were obliged, theoretically at least, to wear a special armband, with black text on green, indicating they were in the service of the security police. 7: Schutzmannschaften were ultimately issued with a full field-grey uniform with field cap. In this dress a full set of rank insignia was worn, in the positions shown. Note that no eagle with swastika national emblem was worn. (Osprey Publishing © Velimir Vuksic)

involved with. Clearly, however, from surviving testimony and documentary evidence, the officers leading the Einsatzgruppen, Einsatzkommandos and Teilkommandos were fully informed that their tasks would include rounding up and eliminating Jews and communists from the occupied areas.

It was policy to make 'every attempt to ensure' that what were described as 'reliable elements' of the local populace were encouraged to 'participate' in these actions. This gave the impression that the local indigenous population had taken matters into their own hands, with the Germans reluctant to interfere in 'internal' matters. The Einsatzgruppen therefore lost no time in identifying nationalists in the local community who were only too happy to be encouraged to begin a pogrom against the local Jews and settle scores with former communist functionaries and their sympathisers.

A report from Einsatzgruppe A in October 1941 contained the comment:

It was the task of the Sicherheitspolizei to set these 'self-cleansing' movements in motion and to direct them into the right channels in order to achieve the aim of this cleansing as rapidly as possible. It was no less important to establish as undeniable and proven fact for the future that it was the liberated populace itself which took the most

German security police, members of an Einsatzgruppe, herd Jewish civilians into a valley prior to their execution. The scene was photographed in Zdolbunow, Poland.

severe measures, on its own initiative, against the Jewish-Bolshevik enemy, without any instruction being evident.

Even at this early stage in the war, the Einsatzgruppen commanders were seeking 'scapegoats' upon whom the atrocities could be blamed.

Many such actions turned into gruesome 'carnivals' of death, with local inhabitants cheering and applauding the beating to death of their former neighbours, as the Einsatzgruppen looked on approvingly. It must also be said that members of Wehrmacht units in the locality also often came along to such events as spectators and occasionally took part in killings. In fact, an order was published by Generalfeldmarschall von Rundstedt forbidding this, and warning of severe punishments which would befall any army personnel who were discovered to have involved themselves. One set of promulgated orders included the strict instruction that 'Individual actions by members of the Wehrmacht or participation by members of the Wehrmacht in excesses by the Ukrainian population against the Jews is forbidden; they are also forbidden to watch or take photographs of measures taken by the Sonderkommandos.' The same orders specifically stated that any commander failing to ensure that his men followed these commands was failing in his duty of supervision and was 'to be severely punished'. Yet the fact remains that the pogrom on the Eastern Front could not have been implemented without the theatre support – sometimes active, sometimes tacit – of the Wehrmacht at various levels. Not all Wehrmacht commanders were as high-minded as von Rundstedt, and the sheer brutality of the war on the Eastern Front meant that German Army soldiers had plenty of opportunities to be as ruthless as their SS counterparts, whether executing Soviet 'partisans' out of hand in some isolated village or consigning hundreds of thousands of Soviet POWs to death by starvation and exposure. Few military formations came out 'clean' from the experience of the Eastern Front.

Of course, ultimately, the Einsatzgruppen themselves would become heavily involved in the killings alongside their locally recruited 'auxiliaries'. Clearly, many who had believed that they were to be used on genuine policing duties in support of the army found these tasks repugnant and some absolutely refused to take part. In fact, Himmler himself had foreseen such eventualities and had accepted that 'any man' who felt unable to endure the psychological stresses of such tasks would be returned home to Germany for other duties. As the German armies in Russia were forced onto the defensive and pushed back towards their own borders, special units were formed to try to erase any evidence of the activities of the Einsatzgruppen, including digging up the bodies of their victims and cremating them. Yet such was the scale of the crime, and such would be the magnitude of the eventual German defeat, that the SS was incapable of hiding all its secrets.

TURNING FORTUNES

LEFT: An SdKfz 222 of the 1. SS-Panzer Division *Leibstandarte* rumbles through the streets of Yugoslavia. Many SS units would be involved in vicious 'anti-partisan' action in Yugoslavia.

ESTABLISHED DIVISIONS

By the end of 1942, the Waffen-SS was becoming a truly veteran formation, its initial divisions having been bloodied both in the West and, more severely, in the East. The following accounts of the Waffen-SS' most distinguished divisions illustrate how Himmler's army was tested almost literally to destruction in 1943–44, a period in which the German armed forces faced not only the Soviet juggernaut, and continuing combat in Sicily and Italy, but from June 1944 Allied forces driving in from the West.

LEIBSTANDARTE

The war record of the *Leibstandarte* in 1943–44 perfectly illustrates the dire straits into which the Waffen-SS tumbled during the mid–late war years. In early 1943 the *Leibstandarte* was rushed back to the Eastern Front as Stalingrad fell and the whole military situation deteriorated. It formed part of I SS-Panzer Korps under Paul Hausser, tasked with preventing the city of Kharkov from falling to the Red Army. Outnumbered seven to one, Hausser refused to sacrifice his new corps just to satisfy another of Hitler's 'no-withdrawal' orders, and on 15 February the city was abandoned. The capture of Kharkov had left the enemy exhausted, however, while the Germans began to regroup. The German counter-attack was launched on 23 February, and after three weeks of bitter fighting the Soviets were once again thrown out of the city; more than 20,000

A Waffen-SS Tiger tank on the Kuban front, 1943. The Waffen-SS used the Tiger to considerable effect on both the Eastern and Western Fronts. SS tank commander Michael Wittman destroyed nearly 30 British armoured vehicles in a single Tiger during the battle of Villers-Bocage in June 1944

enemy troops were killed or wounded and over 600 Soviet tanks destroyed. The ferocity of the fighting had cost the LSSAH about 4,500 killed; the former Red Square in the centre of Kharkov was renamed 'Platz der Leibstandarte' in honour of the division.

Battlefield casualties had to be made up by a draft of former Luftwaffe soldiers, much to the irritation of the divisional commander, 'Sepp' Dietrich. Just as many of his best officers and NCOs were being transferred to form the cadre for the new 12. SS-Panzer Division *Hitlerjugend*, Dietrich was preparing to hand over command to Theodor 'Teddi' Wisch, as he himself took over from Hausser as corps commander.

Shortly thereafter the *Leibstandarte* took part in the summer offensive at Kursk, where it formed the spearpoint of 4. Panzer Armee. The division fielded 100 tanks, 12 of which were the impressive new Tigers. Launching its attack on 5 July, the *Leibstandarte* made good initial progress, reaching the second line of enemy defences by the early evening of the first day. The SS troops were involved in bitter hand-to-hand fighting as they cleared the enemy trenches. By 11 July the division had reached the River Psel, the last major obstacle before Kursk itself.

On the 12th the tanks of the SS formations clashed with Soviet armour in a major action near Prokhorovka. It was the first of several engagements around this little Russian town which built up over a number of days into the biggest armoured battle in history. Over 300 German and 400 Soviet tanks were destroyed without either side gaining any decisive advantage; the battle for the Kursk salient was still in the balance. However, news of the Allied landings in Sicily caused Hitler to cancel the offensive. The *Leibstandarte* was one of the units sent westwards to counter the Allied threat to Italy, handing over all its tanks to the remaining SS divisions before departing for warmer climes. It was a brief change of scene: following the overthrow of Mussolini and Italy's armistice with the Allies the *Leibstandarte* was involved in disarming Italian troops, but by October 1943 the division was heading east once again, by way of the Balkans.

In a further disorientating switch in theatre, by the end of the year the division was in fierce combat around Zhitomir; so furious was the defensive fighting that by the end of February the *Leibstandarte* had just three operational tanks remaining on strength. The LSSAH narrowly escaped annihilation after being surrounded in the Kamenets–Podolsk Pocket, but the remnants were rescued by the timely intervention of the 9. and 10. SS-Panzer Divisions, the *Hohenstaufen* and *Frundsberg*. The *Leibstandarte* was in a woeful condition, and in April 1944 was withdrawn to France for rest and refitting.

Thousands of new troops had refreshed the worn-out shell of this premier division by June 1944, and as the Allied invasion troops began landing in Normandy it was virtually at full strength once again. However, Hitler's insistence that the Normandy landings were only a feint resulted in the *Leibstandarte* being held in reserve for fully 23 days after D-Day, 6 June. Although some elements went into action earlier, the division

A Sturmgeschutz III Ausf G, of Panzerbrigade 150, Ardennes 1944. The five Sturmgeschütze III allotted to Panzerbrigade 150 on 24 November were engaged east of Malmédy with Kampfgruppe Y on 21 December: these StuG 40 Ausf.G were largely unmodified except for the addition of new side skirts, which did little to disguise them. They were painted in American olive drab and displayed white stars on the front glacis, on both sides of the body and on the side skirts. (Osprey Publishing © D. Parker/ R. Volstad)

A Panzerbrigade 150 SdKfz 250/5 given some basic markings modification for operations in the Ardennes, December 1944. (Osprey Publishing © D. Parker/ R. Volstad)

as a whole was not committed to battle until 6 July. Inserted into the frontlines around Caen, the LSSAH fought in many desperate defensive battles against overwhelming odds, in conditions of complete enemy dominance of the air, and often within reach of devastating Allied naval gunfire support. It took part in the attempted counter-offensive on Avranches, but was repulsed, losing large numbers of tanks to British Typhoon aircraft. By the end of August it had just managed to escape encirclement in the Falaise Pocket, but had lost all its tanks and artillery and suffered over 5,000 casualties. The division was then withdrawn to Germany for refitting; once again, the replacements received were no longer of the quality of the troops with which it began the war.

The following months were spent in a frenzy of activity. In December 1944 the division was separated into Kampfgruppen. Kampfgruppe Peiper had the heavy (King Tiger) tank battalion, a mixed battalion of PzKpfw IVs and PzKpfw V Panthers, with one battalion of Panzergrenadiers and artillery support; Kampfgruppe Sandig had the rest of SS-Panzergrenadier Regiment 2; Kampfgruppe Hansen consisted of SS-Panzergrenadier Regiment 1 plus anti-tank and artillery support; and Kampfgruppe Knittel had the reconnaissance battalion with artillery and pioneer support. Their

Ardennes, 1944. 'It's a long way to Tipperary, boys!', Peiper called out from his half-track to some American prisoners passing by between Stoumont and La Gleize (this actually happened at Baugnez). (Osprey Publishing © D. Parker/ R. Volstad)

Wearing thick winter coats, Waffen-SS troops man a trench on the Eastern Front in 1944. The soldier at the front is armed with an MP 40 submachine gun, a 9mm weapon feeding from a 32-round single-stack magazine.

mission was to play a leading part in the Ardennes counter-offensive.

Advancing on 16 December as the spearhead on the route designated 'Rollbahn D', SS-Standartenführer Joachim Peiper's command almost immediately ran into problems. The terrain through which they were travelling was totally unsuitable for the enormous King Tiger tanks; narrow, snow≠bound roads hampered progress, and Peiper's column found itself ensnarled in traffic jams. Severe fuel shortages were temporarily alleviated by the capture of the US fuel dump at Büllingen on 17 December, and Peiper's Kampfgruppe made real progress through Ligneuville and Stavelot; however, that afternoon troops assigned to guard duties shot 83 US prisoners at the Baugnez crossroads near Malmédy. The spearhead of the column ran into trouble again on 18 December when two of three bridges over the Amblève at Trois Ponts were blown just as the SS troops arrived. Peiper was forced to divert via La Gleize and used an intact bridge at Cheneux; but a clearing of the heavy cloud cover brought Allied air attacks.

Joined now by Kampfgruppe Knittel, Peiper's advance began to falter once more; each time a potential route was identified and the Germans raced for a bridge to take them out of the Amblève valley, US resistance would stiffen. On the 19th, Peiper captured Stoumont after bitter fighting, but attempts to push beyond the town were unsuccessful. Stavelot, in the German rear, was retaken by the Americans; now the Germans were forced to defend Stoumont and Cheneux against US counter-attacks, at heavy cost to both sides. By 24 December Peiper was almost out of fuel and ammunition; he had no hope of advancing and was in great danger of being cut off. Leaving a rearguard to hold off the enemy, he destroyed his heavy equipment and began to withdraw, reaching the Salm river and the main body of I SS-Panzer Korps the next day. On 29 December the various *Leibstandarte* Kampfgruppen were ordered to move from the northern flank of the Ardennes front to the southern. The fresh assault by the remains of LSSAH made little progress, however, and on 1 January 1945 the division was withdrawn to prepare for the next planned counter-offensive.

A well-known image of a Waffen-SS trooper manning an MG 42 machine gun. The MG 42 could fire at a rate of 1,200rpm, making it a devastating support weapon for infantry units.

DAS REICH

In January 1943, the newly retitled *Das Reich* Division returned to the Eastern Front, where it was thrown into heavy fighting in the defence of Kharkov. Hausser's withdrawal from the city (see above) enraged Hitler; but just one week later the SS divisions *Das Reich*, *Leibstandarte* and *Totenkopf* smashed their way back into Kharkov and routed the Soviets. It was a momentous victory for the Waffen-SS, made even more satisfying by the additional recapture of Belgorod.

No sooner were *Das Reich*'s troops rested after their great victory than they were thrown into battle again in the attack on the Kursk salient in July.

As part of II SS-Panzer Korps with General Hoth's 4. Panzer Armee, *Das Reich* struck into the southern part of the salient covering the right flank of the corps. Torrential rain had turned the roads into impassable quagmires so that the *Das Reich* infantry were forced to advance without essential armoured support, and were soon involved in fierce hand-to-hand combat. Air support from Stuka dive-bombers helped them seize their first objective, the village of Beresov and the heights overlooking it. Resistance soon stiffened, however, and the SS grenadiers came under punishing artillery fire and attacks from enemy aircraft. Despite fierce opposition, *Das Reich* made excellent progress until checked by a determined Soviet counter-attack at Prokhorovka on 8 July. *Das Reich* held the enemy at bay, supported by General von Richthofen's tank-busting Stukas, and along

A dead Waffen-SS trooper in Normandy, 1944. The tube around his neck contains a spare barrel for an MG 42 machine gun.

with the other Waffen-SS divisions of II SS-Panzer Korps they knocked out over 300 enemy armoured vehicles. Having contained this counter-attack *Das Reich* pushed forwards once again, and on 12 July became involved in the historic tank battle in the hills around Prokhorovka. Over the next few days the two opposing sides fought virtually to a standstill, with horrendous losses in both men and tanks on both sides. Although Soviet numerical losses were greater than German, they were in a position to make good these losses, a luxury the Waffen-SS units did not possess.

With the transfer of troops to the West to face the Allied invasion of Sicily, *Das Reich* went over to the defensive. In the second half of 1943 they fought many bitter battles along the River Mius, and defended once again the cities they had recently captured – Kiev, Zhitomir and Kharkov. Over the next five months the division was inexorably pushed back, losing control of Kiev in November. By the end of 1943 *Das Reich* had once more been reduced to Kampfgruppe status. Elements of the division were withdrawn to France for rest and refitting; and by late April 1944 the last units had arrived from the Eastern Front.

During this period the division's troops were sometimes used against French partisans. Brutalized by years of combat in the East, they were in no mood to take casualties from the maquisards, and reprisals for German deaths and the destruction of vehicles were often brutal. When the Allies landed in Normandy on 6 June 1944 the division was ordered to move to the frontline from its positions near Bordeaux. Along the way it was delayed by frequent acts of sabotage and subjected to harassing attacks, and responded furiously, executing 99 civilians in Tulle in retaliation for the deaths of some 40 German soldiers. The capture by the Resistance of SS-Sturmbannführer Helmuth Kampfe, CO of *Der Führer* Regiment's III Bataillon, was the ostensible excuse for the destruction on 10 June of the peaceful village of Oradour-sur-Glane near Limoges, and the murder of more than 640 civilian men, women and children, by 3rd Company of the regiment's 1st Battalion led by SS-Hauptsturmführer Kahn and the battalion commander, SS-Sturmbannführer Otto Dickmann.

On reaching the invasion front, *Das Reich*, still awaiting the arrival of some units in transit from the south, was split up and attached to army formations, seeing action predominantly against the British forces near Caen. It was in Normandy that one of the division's most famous soldiers scored a historic triumph. SS-Oberscharführer Ernst Barkmann, commander of a lone PzKpfw V Panther tank from SS-Panzer Regiment 2, was covering a crossroads near Le Lorey when a long column of at least 14 enemy tanks with supply trucks came into sight. In the action which ensued, despite the intervention of Allied fighter-bombers and his tank being damaged, Barkmann knocked out eight Sherman tanks and numerous trucks including fuel tankers, only withdrawing when his ammunition ran low.

The division suffered badly in the fighting against US forces around St Lô. In mid-August substantial numbers of German troops were caught in the Falaise Pocket, but *Das Reich* was one of the units that broke through the Canadian and Polish

A German armoured unit advances at Kursk in 1943. *Leibstandarte*, *Totenkopf* and *Das Reich* all suffered heavy losses in both men and armour during Hitler's failed Operation *Zitadelle*.

Scene of horror. The gutted church at Oradour-sur-Glane, France, where 247 women and 205 children died after the building was set alight by soldiers of the *Das Reich* Division on 10 June 1944.

encirclement to provide their trapped comrades with an escape route. *Das Reich* was subsequently withdrawn from the line for rebuilding, though many of the replacements were draftees from the Wehrmacht and a far cry from the quality of the division's original troops.

Das Reich was next committed, like *Leibstandarte*, to action during the ill-fated Ardennes offensive. Like other German units it suffered from lack of fuel and ammunition and the need to move heavy armour along totally unsuitable roads. The division captured key objectives at Manhay and Grandmesnil, but its success was short-lived and both towns were lost to American counter-attacks. The division's Panzer ace Ernst Barkmann raised his already impressive score, however, adding 15 more Shermans to his victory tally (though nine of these were simply abandoned by their crews at the approach of his lone Panther). In early January 1945 *Das Reich* was sent into reserve.

ORADOUR-SUR-GLANE

It was the death of the popular Sturmbannführer Helmuth Kampfe, CO of III Bataillon of the *Der Führer* Regiment – a predominantly Austrian unit – which provoked one of the worst of all the Waffen-SS massacres. During the evening of 9 June 1944, while *Das Reich* Division was en route to Normandy, Kampfe set out for his headquarters in his car. When he failed to arrive, men were sent out to look for him. His car was discovered abandoned, but of Kampfe there was no sign, nor was his body ever found. It can safely be assumed that he was ambushed by the *maquis* and killed. The following morning Kampfe's close friend Otto Dickmann, CO of I Bataillon, arrived at regimental headquarters in Limoges in a state of great excitement. Villagers in St Junien had told him that a German officer was being held prisoner by the *maquis* in Oradour-sur-Glane. Dickmann was convinced it must be Kampfe and received permission to investigate. He took the 120 men of his 3rd Company and drove off, arriving in the sleepy little village early in the afternoon. Dickmann's men raced from house to house, driving their inhabitants into the Champ de Faire. There was no sign of Kampfe or any other German officer. The women and children were herded into the church and the men into barns and garages. Then the shooting began. A total of 648 people died. There were a few lucky survivors, such as three Jewish girls who had managed to stay hidden during the search. When the shooting began, they fled, only to bump straight into an SS private. This man, who has never been identified, gestured for them to run. Dickmann himself never stood trial, being killed in action a few days later.

Exhausted Waffen-SS troops slump in a trench on the Eastern Front. The soldier in the foreground is diligently cleaning his Kar 98k rifle, removing dirt from the bolt area.

TOTENKOPF

Totenkopf returned to the Eastern Front at the start of 1943, in time to join the newly formed I SS-Panzer Korps, and in February was involved in a ferocious battle alongside *Das Reich* in which the Soviet Sixth Army was annihilated. On 26 February the morale of the division took a serious blow when Theodor Eicke was killed; the spotter plane in which he was travelling was shot down by concentrated small arms fire from nearby Soviet troops. SS-Panzergrenadier Regiment 6 was given the commemorative honour title *Theodor Eicke*. Divisional morale was soon improved when in March the *Totenkopf* took part in the victorious recapture of Kharkov and the annihilation of the Soviet 25th Guards Rifle Division.

Totenkopf's next major engagement was in July 1943 when it was thrown into the offensive at Kursk. Part of a massive army of almost one million troops and just under 3,000 tanks, the division provided right flank cover to 4. Panzer Armee. *Totenkopf* made good initial progress, advancing some 20km into the southern part of the salient and smashing the Soviet 52nd Guards Division; and by the end of the second day the division had penetrated some 32km into enemy territory. By 12 July the German spearhead had reached Prokhorovka, where it ran into huge Soviet armoured forces –

PzKpfw VI Ausf B Tiger, schwere SS-Panzer Abteilung 501, 18 December 1944, Ardennes. Tiger '222' is without doubt one of the best-known, if not *the* best-known Tiger II , as the picture showing it passing at Kaiserbarracke with its load of Fallschirmjäger (here re-created in a painting) has been published in almost every book dealing with Panzers of the late World War II. (Osprey Publishing © D. Parker/ R. Volstad)

ABOVE: Winter uniforms, 1943–45. 1: SS-Untersturmführer, 5. SS-Panzer Division *Wiking*. This second lieutenant of Panzergrenadiers wears the SS reversible camouflage/white winter uniform with the white side outermost, and special winter felt boots. The winter cap lined with rabbit fur was widely worn in both the army and Waffen-SS. 2: SS-Schütze, 3. SS-Panzergrenadier Division *Totenkopf*. This machine gunner wears the fur- or fleece-lined field-grey parka. Particular to the Waffen-SS, this garment was of 'pullover' design with an integral fur-lined hood, and was provided with patch breast pockets and slash skirt pockets. 3: SS-Sturmmann. Armed with the deadly *Panzerschreck* anti-tank rocket projector, he wears the heavy winter surcoat of extended length, with enlarged collar and slash hand-warmer pockets. Despite its appearance this clumsy garment was not particularly effective, being made of poor-quality material with a high shoddy content. (Osprey Publishing © Stephen Andrew)

A Waffen-SS anti-tank team in action on the Eastern Front. The low profile of the Pak anti-tank gun was essential to the gun crew's survivability; any weapon system that stood out was an easy target for Soviet gunners.

Totenkopf alone faced the equivalent of four full enemy divisions, and was forced onto the defensive. As the greatest tank battle in history raged around them, *Totenkopf* took heavy punishment, but achieved its primary objective of securing the right flank of the attack. By the time the offensive was discontinued the division had lost almost half its armour and had suffered horrendous casualties.

It had originally been intended that all the divisions forming I SS-Panzer Korps should be transferred to Italy, but a Soviet attack in the Donetz Basin saw *Das Reich* and *Totenkopf* forced back into the line, only *Leibstandarte* being moved briefly to Italy. *Totenkopf* immediately moved south to the area around Stalino, where after heavy fighting the Soviet attack was halted. A new Soviet offensive was launched almost immediately around Kursk, however, and the division was rushed northwards. Thrown into the line on the approaches to Kharkov, the SS held on for a full week under immense pressure before it was decided that the city could not be saved. Nevertheless, *Totenkopf* and *Das Reich* launched localized counter-attacks to cover the withdrawal of German forces from the area. Throughout August and September 1943 the division, along with *Das Reich* and the army's elite *Grossdeutschland* Division, were used as 'fire brigades', rushed from crisis point to crisis point. The arrival of such battle-hardened units often saved the day – if only temporarily. In October *Totenkopf* was involved in a major counter-attack, bringing the Soviet advance near Krivoi-Rog to a halt. This was a vital communications, transport and supply centre for the Wehrmacht and its loss would have been catastrophic. In November the division was further upgraded to the status of a Panzer division, though it was still relatively weak. Nevertheless, during these battles the Soviets lost more than 300 tanks and 5,000 prisoners. Renewed Soviet assaults saw *Totenkopf* once again thrown into the breach, and on 18 November the division began a three-day battle during which it destroyed almost 250 more tanks. After a few days of quiet yet another Soviet assault was launched and once again held. Despite losses of 20 to 25 per cent of its strength in these battles, *Totenkopf* once again blunted a further Soviet attack in the area in December 1943, before being moved to Kirovograd. Acting once again in concert with *Grossdeutschland*, the division was involved in many fiercely fought actions between Kirovograd and the River Bug, covering the withdrawal of other German forces.

In March 1944 *Totenkopf* was moved once again, this time to Balta, where it provided rearguard cover for the withdrawal of Heeresgruppe B into Romania. Further defensive actions in Romania saw the division's strength being worn down; but in May it received several thousand reinforcements transferred in from 16. SS-Panzergrenadier

SS Panzer units advance into Kharkov in 1943. The SS Panzer troops suffered terribly in the actions at Kharkov; *Leibstandarte* Division alone took 4,500 casualties in the early actions of the year.

Totenkopf troops, Eastern Front. The three men in the foreground are carrying the components of a mortar between them, hauling the weight over the endless Russian steppe.

Division *Reichsführer-SS*, and in June, after a brief rest and refit, the division was again up to a strength in excess of 20,000 men.

On 23 June the Soviets launched their major 1944 summer offensive, Operation *Bagration*, which took *Totenkopf* to Grodno in Poland to defend the area against immense pressure from the Soviet Second Tank Army. At odds of ten to one against, the division could do little but delay the inevitable and was gradually pushed westwards. During August, *Totenkopf* teamed up with 5. SS-Panzer Division *Wiking* to defend the approaches to Warsaw. In early September they ejected Soviet units that had entered the city's eastern suburbs, and pushed the enemy back across the Vistula. The reprieve was only temporary, however, and in October *Totenkopf* was forced to withdraw towards Modlin, by now reduced to around 75 per cent of its June strength.

POLIZEI

In January 1943 the SS-*Polizei* Panzergrenadier Division came under Soviet attacks around the south of Lake Ladoga on the Leningrad front; the enemy eventually broke through the German defence lines in February, and forced the SS troops to retreat westwards to new defence positions at Kolpino. These were successfully held, but losses had been severe; at this point elements of the division were withdrawn to Silesia as the nucleus for a re-formed Panzergrenadier division, while the remainder were formed into a smaller Kampfgruppe. During the following month the Dutch volunteers of the Freiwilligen Legion *Niederlande* were assigned to bolster its strength. This Kampfgruppe remained in constant action on the Eastern Front until May 1944, when it was finally disbanded.

In May 1943 the SS-*Polizei* Panzergrenadier Division was sent to the Balkans, where elements took part in anti-partisan operations in northern Greece during the summer and autumn of that year. Troops from the division were recorded by witnesses from the Geheime Feld Polizei to have been involved in atrocities against civilians in the Klissura region during this period. The division remained in Greece until July/August 1944, before going back into the line to face the advancing Red Army.

This PzKpfw IV Ausf G belongs to the *Totenkopf* Division, photographed in Ukraine in 1943. Note the muzzle cover on the cannon and the basic winter paint scheme applied to the tank.

Engaging in house-to-house fighting on the Eastern Front, a Waffen-SS team takes cover in the shattered remnants of a Russian home.

WIKING

The *Wiking* Division, composed in large part of foreign volunteers, had much to prove to the wider SS during 1942–44. At the beginning of 1942, *Wiking* advanced from its positions along the Mius as the German offensive began afresh. That summer it took part in the deepest penetrations of the Russian campaign, the drive on Rostov on the River Don and the attempt to secure the Caucasus oilfields. By the end of 1942 and the onset of another winter *Wiking* had proven itself in combat well enough to warrant upgrading to the status of Panzergrenadier division. It took up positions along the Terek river, deep in the Caucasus. However, after the disaster at Stalingrad in January 1943 and the launch of the Soviet counter-offensive on the southern front *Wiking* was pushed back towards Manych, and was involved in heavy defensive actions around Izym.

In March 1943 a battalion of Estonian volunteers joined the division – SS-Freiwilligen Panzergrenadier Bataillon *Narwa*. The division lost one of its older regiments in May 1943 when *Nordland* was removed to form the cadre for a new Panzergrenadier division of the same name. In October 1943 *Wiking* was upgraded to the status of Panzer division, the first 'non-German' formation to achieve this status. In fact, though it did contain significant numbers of foreign 'Germanic' volunteers, the division still fielded a very large German contingent.

ABOVE: 1: Leutnant, SS-*Polizei* Division, Eastern Front, early 1942. 2: SS-Hauptscharführer of Feldgendarmerie 13. Waffen Gebirgs Division der SS *Handschar*, Balkans, 1944. 3: Waffen-Grenadier, 14 Waffen Grenadier Division der SS, Eastern Front, 1941. 4: Waffen-Sturmbannführer, 20. Waffen Grenadier Division der SS, Baltic coast, 1944. 5: SS-Sturmmann, Britisches Freikorps, 1944–45. (Osprey Publishing © Jeffrey Burn)

The *Wiking* Division ended 1943 in the Ukraine; and in January 1944 the division was encircled in the pocket at Cherkassy along with five other German divisions, faced by 35 Soviet divisions. The pocket was gradually compressed until it measured barely 100 square km; and eventually Hitler, somewhat unusually, was persuaded to allow a break-out attempt. It was *Wiking*, the only armoured division in the pocket and still well equipped, which led the thrust to the south. Once the element of surprise had gone the Soviets launched powerful counter-attacks with heavy armour support. The onset of a snow-storm gave the Germans excellent cover and eventually the break-out force reached the last barrier to safety, a 2m-deep river at Gniloi-Tilkitsch. With no bridge and no ford, the Germans were forced to make a human chain to help non-swimmers across the fast-flowing river. Many were swept away by the icy waters, but many more escaped to safety, thanks to the determination of both the men of *Wiking* and the attached Walloon volunteers of Sturmbrigade *Wallonien*, who provided the rearguard. Of about 55,000 German troops trapped in the pocket, 34,000 escaped.

In March 1944, the *Wiking* Division took part in the advance through the Pripet Marshes towards Kowel, where it saw fierce combat during April. That month the division lost its Estonian volunteers, who transferred en masse to the newly formed 20. Waffen Grenadier Division der SS. In June 1944 the division was withdrawn from the front for rest and refitting in Germany; but it was soon sent eastwards again, joining the German forces around Warsaw in August and helping to drive the Red Army out of the city's eastern suburbs.

A Norwegian volunteer serving with the *Wiking* Division. On his belt are magazine pouches for the MP 40 submachine gun, and a Stielhandgranate 24 grenade is kept at the ready.

NORD

In February 1943, the volunteer Norwegian ski battalion *Norge* was attached to the 6. SS-Gebirgs Division *Nord*. This ski troop element was eventually expanded on paper to brigade status; it suffered heavily in action against Soviet forces around Kaprolat, losing around 50 per cent of its strength before its remnants were redesignated as SS-Panzergrenadier Bataillon (mot.) 506.

From mid-1942 to autumn 1944, the division remained on the virtually static Finnish front as part of 20. Gebirgs Armee, and was involved in numerous defensive actions while holding the line between Kiestinki and Louhi. In summer 1944 the situation on the Eastern Front deteriorated sharply, and Soviet advances along the Baltic coast cut Finland's vital supply lines from Germany. In September the Finnish government concluded a separate armistice with the USSR, and German troops were given two weeks' notice to leave the country. *Nord* provided rearguard cover as the 20. Gebirgs Armee withdrew from Karelia, becoming engaged in skirmishes with the Finnish troops who had long been their allies. This withdrawal into Norway, Operation *Birke*, saw men of the division marching nearly 1,600km between September and November 1944, before being transported south to Oslo by rail. The *Nord* Division had fought for 1,214 consecutive days in the northern sector of the Eastern Front between July 1941 and September 1944, in extremely difficult forest and swamp terrain; in the process it had matured, if not into one of the true elites, then certainly into a far more dependable force than had originally been the case.

Waffen-SS troops engage ground targets with a 2cm Flak 38. Effective range of this weapon was about 2,200m, and it had a practical rate of fire of around 120rpm.

ABOVE: 6. SS-Gebirgs Division *Nord*. From left to right, top to bottom: SS-Hauptsturmführer, c. 1943, SS-Gebirgsjäger, c. 1944; SS-Unterscharführer, 1945; SS-Scharführer, 1943. The ski trooper wears the white/camouflage reversible, padded winter combat dress of parka, overtrousers and mittens over his M1943 field-grey service uniform. (Osprey Publishing © Stephen Andrew)

ABOVE: Three Waffen-SS soldiers on the Eastern Front in 1944. The cuffbands indicate the unit or formation to which they belong: the soldier on the right is a member of the schwere SS-Panzer Abteilung (StuG) 11 *Hermann von Salza*.
(Osprey Publishing © Jeffrey Burn)

The division was subsequently ordered to Denmark. The advance party reached Kolbing in December, although the remainder were still scattered along the length of Norway making their way south. It had been intended that *Nord* be allowed a period of rest and refitting, but almost as soon as the first elements arrived they were ordered to form a new Kampfgruppe *Nord* for commitment to Operation *Nordwind* (North Wind), the German counter-offensive in the Ardennes.

The new battlegroup consisted of the bulk of SS-Gebirgsjäger Regiment 12 *Michael Gaissmair*, along with signals, anti-tank, artillery and pioneer elements. The Kampfgruppe was attached to 361. Volksgrenadier Division in XXXIV Korps; it first went into action on 31 December 1944, surprising US units near Pirmasens before advancing on the town of Wingen. The SS troops broke through the lines held by the US VI Corps and took the town, where they awaited armoured reinforcements from Heeresgruppe G. These were diverted elsewhere, however, and the lack of progress made by German forces flanking the Kampfgruppe left them dangerously exposed. The SS mountain troopers were forced to fight their way back out of Wingen, losing two-thirds of their strength in the process (nevertheless, they did take 400 American prisoners back with them). Operation *Nordwind* was rapidly running out of steam and

MOUNTAIN TROOPS INSIGNIA

Mountain troops insignia consisted of an arm patch and a cap badge. The former was an oval cut from black badge cloth, onto which was machine-embroidered a silver-grey Edelweiss flower with yellow stamens, the whole being enclosed within a silver-grey oval border; this was worn on the upper right sleeve. The cap insignia was similar to that worn on the side of the *Bergmütze* by army mountain troops, but was embroidered rather than in stamped metal. Once again the embroidery was executed in silver-grey yarn on a black base with the stamens in yellow. It was worn on the left side flap of the Bergmütze or M1943 *Einheitsfeldmütze*. The division itself was not authorized to wear a cuffband; however, photos suggest that some personnel used the 'Nord' title as worn by the Allgemeine-SS Oberabschnitt *Nord*. This practice was completely unofficial; the two principal regiments of the division were, however, authorized honour titles.

In June 1942 SS-Infanterie Regiment 6 (later SS-Gebirgsjäger Regiment 11) was authorized the 'Reinhard Heydrich' title, to commemorate the assassinated head of the Sicherheitsdienst. The band was manufactured in machine-embroidered, flat-wire machine-woven and artificial silk (rayon) BeVo machine-woven formats.

In June 1944, SS-Gebirgsjäger Regiment 12 was authorized the honour title '*Michael Gaissmair*' commemorating this Tyrolean rebel leader during the Peasant Wars of the early 16th century. This rare cuffband was manufactured only in BeVo form, of machine-woven artificial silk, the script incorporating the German double-s character.

American forces were going over to the offensive; attacks on *Nord*'s positions were only repulsed with difficulty.

Nord was then transferred to XV Korps near Melch, and tasked with regaining ground that had been lost by 256. Volksgrenadier Division. The wooded terrain was very similar to that in which the division had operated on the Eastern Front, and the SS troops were expert in infiltration techniques and the use of snipers. The Americans suffered heavy casualties and called in armoured support, but the Sherman tanks were also at a severe disadvantage in the snowbound woodland and were easily picked off. *Nord* cut off an entire US unit and eventually forced it to surrender; over 200 US troops were killed and 450 taken prisoner, for a claimed loss of just 26 men by the division. Such victories at this stage in the war were few and far between. *Nord* was then ordered to attack US forces around the Zinsweiler and Rothbach forests. Again infiltrating under cover of darkness without a preparatory artillery barrage, the men of the division made excellent initial progress; but the gradually stiffening resistance slowed their advance and eventually forced the Germans to adopt defensive positions.

The performance of the established divisions of the Waffen-SS left Hitler in no doubt that he had a fanatical elite at his disposal, hence the Waffen-SS would be committed to the 'fire-fighting' role on the worst sectors of both Eastern and Western Fronts. Such was much to their cost, yet even as the old divisions suffered grievous attrition, new formations were taking their place in the Waffen-SS ranks.

NEW BLOOD

In 1942–43, the ranks of the Waffen-SS expanded with the creation of a new generation of battle-hungry divisions. Some of these evolved from smaller units created during the early-war period, while others were created from scratch based on the specific military and political priorities of the SS hierarchy. Whatever the circumstances of their formation, however, they were born at an inauspicious moment in the war. Most were thrown immediately into the cauldron of the Eastern Front, where they began to experience the ghastly attrition that would blight all Waffen-SS formations.

7. SS-FREIWILLIGEN GEBIRGS DIVISION *PRINZ EUGEN*

The formation of the *Prinz Eugen* Division was the culmination of the hopes long held by the recruitment department chief, SS-Obergruppenführer Gottlob Berger, to form an entire SS division from ethnic Germans living outside the Reich. In previous centuries many German-speaking emigrants to the east and south-east had founded communities along the borders of the old Austro-Hungarian Empire and even further afield. Their descendants were seen as a rich seam of potential manpower for the SS, since earlier restrictions on SS recruitment imposed at the insistence of the army applied only to *Reichsdeutsche* (German citizens), and not *Volksdeutsche* (ethnic Germans living outside Germany's borders).

This new division was to be raised primarily from ethnic Germans living in Yugoslavia, mainly in the Serbian Banat, a frontier region heavily colonized by ethnic Germans since the Middle Ages; later the net would be widened, and Romanians and Hungarians of German background were taken in.

The division was officially formed in March 1942; although attempts were made to recruit it entirely from volunteers, and the divisional title specifically identified it as a volunteer formation, the response was disappointing and conscription was quickly introduced – all the region's *Volksdeutsche* males between 17 and 54 years were made liable for service with the division. An initial strength of around 15,000 was reached, though there were still shortages in trained and experienced officers and NCOs.

The senior leadership cadre were almost exclusively German and Austrian, but the shortage of junior leaders was resolved to some degree by transferring ethnic Germans who had been conscripted into the Yugoslavian Army and were at that point still being held in POW camps by the Germans. Ultimately the division reached a full strength of just over 21,000 men. The first divisional commander, Artur Phleps, was an ethnic German from the Transylvanian borderland of Romania, who had previously served in the Austro-Hungarian Army, had commanded Romanian mountain troops, and had also gained more recent experience as a regimental commander in the SS-*Wiking* Division.

The division's mission was planned as the suppression of guerrilla activity in occupied Yugoslavia, where both communist 'Partisan' and royalist 'Chetnik' resistance movements – led by Tito and Mihailovic respectively – were active against the Italian and German occupation forces in the wooded mountain terrain. For such 'police' duties it was not necessary to equip the formation to the standards demanded on the Russian Front, and for this reason much of *Prinz Eugen*'s equipment was obsolescent captured French or Czech material. It did have the addition – unusual for a mountain division – of an armoured element. Even though this one-company 'battalion' had predominantly old French Renault light tanks, given that the opposition were lightly armed partisans this augmentation of its mobile firepower was a definite advantage.

After just over six months of training the division was considered ready for action, and its first operation was against Chetniks on the Serbia/Montenegro borders in

RIGHT: Southern Europe, 1943–44. 1: SS-Obersturmführer, 7. SS-Freiwilligen Gebirgs Division *Prinz Eugen*, Balkans, 1944. 2: SS-Scharführer, SS-Fallschirmjäger Bataillon 500, Balkans, 1944. 3: SS-Sturmmann, Sturmbrigade *Reichsführer-SS*, Corsica, summer 1943. (Osprey Publishing © Jeffrey Burn)

SS soldiers ride in a captured US half-track, with a gun mounted in the back of the vehicle. The Waffen-SS, like all German forces, was not averse to utilizing enemy equipment.

October 1942. These first actions were judged successful, and within two months *Prinz Eugen* was declared to have reached a sufficient level of combat efficiency to be allocated to the order of battle of 12. Armee. It was headquartered in the Zagreb–Karlovac area, and its first major engagement was as part of the German forces committed to Operation *Weiss* (White), an ambitious German–Italian operation which aimed to trap and destroy Tito's forces in Bosnia. The operation was unsuccessful, and the bulk of the partisans escaped destruction by slipping away to the south-east between the sectors of *Prinz Eugen* and the Italian Sixth Army. Nevertheless, the division captured Bihac from the partisans in mid-January 1943, operating in conjunction with other German, Italian and Croatian units; and in late February/early March *Prinz Eugen* took part in further actions around Lapac and Dvar. The division then provided forces to protect the important bauxite mines at Mostar.

In April 1943 the division received an influx of personnel from the disbanded so-called *Einsatzstaffeln*, SS-controlled ethnic German 'self defence' battalions from Croatia (one of which was coincidentally named 'Prinz Eugen'). In May 1943, *Prinz Eugen* was attached to Heeresgruppe E for operations in western Montenegro, taking part in another major anti-partisan sweep by German, Italian and Bulgarian forces, codenamed Operation *Schwarz* (Black). Casualties mounted with every action. During operations along the Dalmatian coast near Dubrovnik, for example, bitter fighting against Tito's communist partisans cost the division over 500 killed and wounded. During this period the divisional commander Artur Phleps was promoted, eventually taking over as commander of V SS-Gebirgs Korps on 21 April, and command of *Prinz Eugen* passed in June to SS-Brigadeführer Ritter von Oberkamp.

After the completion of Operation *Schwarz*, the division was given a brief period of rest, taking over occupation duties around Mostar from Italian forces. When the Italians concluded their separate armistice with the Allies in September 1943 some units of the Italian Second Army in Yugoslavia simply abandoned their equipment to the guerrillas and took ship for Italy, while others actually deserted to the partisans. The latter moved swiftly to seize large quantities of abandoned Italian equipment, which gave their strength a substantial boost. *Prinz Eugen* was then serving under XXV Gebirgs Korps of 2. Panzer Armee, and was involved both in the disarming of remaining Italian troops on the Dalmatian coast and in resisting partisan exploitation of the Italian collapse. Not all Italian units surrendered their arms peacefully; the division captured more than 30,000 Italians at Dubrovnik on 10 September, and took Split only on the 27th, after two weeks of fierce fighting. *Prinz Eugen* then took part in anti-partisan operations on the Peljesac Peninsula and surrounding islands, occupying these for some weeks before returning to anti-partisan duties north-east of Sarajevo and Gorazde in eastern Bosnia in December.

In early January 1944, *Prinz Eugen* operated along with the army's 1. Gebirgs Division in Operation *Waldrusch*; it suffered serious casualties, and was beginning to show the symptoms of a drop in morale. There were almost 1,500 cases of trench foot in the division at this time. From mid-January 1944 the division was in reserve around Split for refitting and further training before returning to the field in March. Shortly after returning to active operations under V SS-Gebirgs Korps the division was reportedly involved in atrocities in Dalmatia which took over 800 civilian lives during anti-partisan actions.

In May 1944 the division took part, alongside army units and SS paratroopers, in Operation *Rösselsprung* (Knight's Leap), the operation which attempted to capture Tito in his headquarters at Drvar. The task of *Prinz Eugen* was to seal the area, seizing partisan supply dumps, railway stations and road crossings to prevent the escape of any partisan forces. Yet forewarned of the attacks, the partisans had prepared strong defensive positions; *Prinz Eugen* ran into bitter resistance almost immediately, and Tito's units even succeeded in mounting local counter-attacks against the SS troops. The partisans also had the advantage of being able to call on Allied air support from Italy, and German units were subjected to constant harrying attacks.

The division captured Ribnik on 27 May; but although the partisans were surrounded, the forest and mountain terrain prevented the German cordons from achieving a real entrapment. The strong and confident partisan forces were liable to appear almost anywhere to mount concerted attacks on German positions – even *Prinz*

Eugen's divisional headquarters came under heavy attack for a while. Several of the basic objectives of the operation were met – considerable casualties were inflicted, supply dumps were captured and the enemy were driven out of the area (albeit temporarily); but Tito himself had escaped just before the operation commenced, and all the Germans found was one of his discarded uniforms. *Prinz Eugen* performed effectively during this period, relentlessly pursuing Tito's elite 1st Proletarian Division through Croatia and into Serbia despite significant casualties, and destroying its ability to undertake any further offensive actions. This series of operations ended in no distinct final battle, but rather in a gradual petering out of confrontations with the partisans in the first week of August.

In the autumn of 1944, as the situation on the Eastern Front became increasingly critical, Bulgaria and Romania deserted the Axis cause and transferred their allegiance, declaring war on Germany. In September 1944, General Phleps flew from Montenegro to his home country of Transylvania on the Romanian/Hungarian frontier in the hope of organizing resistance; he was killed, reportedly when his light aircraft was shot down on 21 September, but alternative accounts have since been published.

With Soviet and Bulgarian forces approaching from the east and Tito's partisans threatening to join up with them, *Prinz Eugen* was committed to Operation *Rubezahl* (Mountain Spirit), smashing its way into partisan forces moving eastwards. The division surrounded and completely destroyed one large force, although Allied air forces again played a part, landing in the surrounded pocket and evacuating partisan wounded.

Enemy attention now turned towards the capture of the Yugoslav capital, Belgrade. *Prinz Eugen* was initially given the task of intercepting lead enemy units approaching Belgrade; but then was almost immediately transferred to the area around Nisch, where it was to play an important role in covering the retreat of over 300,000 German troops of Heeresgruppe E under General–Field Marshal Löhr, who were falling back through Yugoslavia from occupation duty in the Aegean. The division was strung out along a 150km front, in an area of Macedonia infested with partisans, threatened on its right by the Bulgarian Second Army and on its left by the Soviet Fifty–Seventh Army.

Despite the enemy's overwhelming numerical superiority, *Prinz Eugen* held on to its positions in this 'Vardar Corridor' under repeated attacks over a number of weeks. Once again the division suffered significant casualties, and this time it reported numbers of its troops deserting. Under attacks by very strong partisan forces, *Prinz Eugen*'s units

LEFT: Three figures from the *7. SS-Freiwilligen Gebirgs Division Prinz Eugen*, 1943–45. The private (left) in combat dress wears the M1940 reversible SS camouflage smock in its distinctive 'plane tree' pattern, the 'spring/summer' side outwards and a matching first-type helmet cover. The figure in the centre is SS-Obergruppenführer Artur Phleps, former commander of the *Prinz Eugen*, portrayed shortly after his promotion from SS-Gruppenführer to full general's rank and command of V SS-Gebirgs Korps. The final figure is a senior NCO who is shown (speculatively) with the 'Artur Phleps' cufftitle awarded after the commander's death which may have been used.(Osprey Publishing © Stephen Andrew)

River crossings were a frequent part of operational life for the Waffen-SS on the Eastern Front. They had to be performed quickly and efficiently to reduce the time spent exposed on open water.

became fragmented and cut off. In late November the divisional commander, SS-Brigadeführer Kumm, was forced to order his troops to break out; but *Prinz Eugen* had succeeded in its mission of holding back the enemy long enough to allow Löhr's troops to escape. After breaking out, the remnants of the division – now less than 4,000 strong – had to carry out a forced march over four days to reach their designated 'rest' area.

In November 1944 the German cadre remnants of the Albanian 21. SS-Division *Skanderbeg* were ordered incorporated into the division; and one source states that SS-Freiwilligen Gebirgsjäger Regiment 14 was authorized to take the title 'Skanderbeg', though the incorporation seems never in fact to have taken place. Thereafter *Prinz Eugen* fought numerous rearguard actions against both partisans and Soviet units, as the Germans retreated from Yugoslavia and the partisans tried to delay them long enough for the Red Army to overtake and destroy them.

8. SS-KAVALLERIE DIVISION *FLORIAN GEYER*

The origins of the *Florian Geyer* Division stretch back to the very beginning of World War II. In September 1939 the first SS-*Totenkopf* horsed cavalry regiment was formed under the designation SS-*Totenkopf* Reiterstandarte 1, consisting of a staff element and four Reiterschwadron. Commanded by SS-Standartenführer Hermann Fegelein, the regiment was despatched to Poland for 'security' duties following the cease-fire. Further squadrons followed progressively as the regiment was rapidly enlarged, to no fewer than 14 squadrons by May 1940, including specialist support elements and a horse gun battery. (In 1940–41 various types of organization were tried, involving splitting the regiment in two, reuniting it, and finally dividing it once more; Fegelein remained in command of what was in effect a brigade at each stage.)

Headquartered in Warsaw and Lublin and operating in dispersed squadrons among the Polish population, these SS-*Totenkopf* troops soon demonstrated their familiar character: the 4th Squadron was involved in the execution of Jewish civilians at Kutno as early as October 1939. At the start of 1940 the brigade was put under the command of the HSSPf/Ost (East) SS-Gruppenführer Krüger, himself a former inspector of the mounted units of the Allgemeine-SS.

The Eastern Front unleashed enormous destruction upon many of the Waffen-SS divisions. Here we see dead SS soldiers scattered in the snow following heavy fighting around Kharkov in 1943.

During this period the brigade encountered a train of cattle cars carrying deported Jews. The filthy state of the wagons caused officers to worry about the risk of an outbreak of dysentery, a problem that they decided to solve by simply shooting all the Jews. Having insufficient stocks of ammunition they sought to obtain some from nearby army units, who refused outright to supply them. The executions went ahead anyway, carried out by a mixture of SS troopers and German police working under SS orders.

Apart from their participation in such atrocities, the brigade was also suspected of serious looting, to the extent that an investigation was instigated against Fegelein by the Gestapo. The colonel was a personal favourite of Reichsführer Himmler, however, and the investigation came to nothing.

By March 1941 the retitled SS-Kavallerie Regimenter 1 and 2 each had three sabre and five support and service squadrons, with a total strength of about 3,500 men. The two units were formally designated the SS-Kavallerie Brigade only in August 1941, by which time they were already in action on 'mopping-up' duties behind the advancing front of Heeresgruppe Mitte in

Two Dutch SS volunteers attend a lecture. Given the fortunes of the war, many Dutch Waffen-SS volunteers would have doubtless bitterly regretted their decisions by 1944.

Russia. On the opening of Operation *Barbarossa* in June, the cavalry were among a number of former *Totenkopf* units brought together under the authority of the Kommandostab RfSS (rather than the Wehrmacht) to serve behind the frontlines, hunting down Red Army stragglers and taking punitive action against partisans and the civilians suspected of aiding them. In one sweep through the Pripet Marshes the SS troops killed just over 250 enemy combatants but more than 6,500 civilians – a disproportion which would continue to be a feature of the brigade's combat reports. After another operation in early August it was reported that 1,000 partisans and 700 Red Army stragglers had been killed, but the civilian death toll came to well over 14,000, most of them apparently Jewish.

The SS-Kavallerie Brigade came up against rather more serious opposition during the great Soviet counter-attacks of the following winter. In January 1942 it suffered heavy casualties near Rzhev and Gusevo, where around 60 per cent of its personnel were killed in action or died in the harsh conditions. By the end of March the brigade had been reduced to a 700-man battlegroup; the remnants were withdrawn into Poland during April–August 1942, but it was decided to expand this core into a division. A third cavalry regiment was added, and in June 1942 around 9,000 Romanian *Volksdeutsche* were drafted in.

On returning to the front in August 1942 the new SS-Kavallerie Division, now commanded by SS-Brigadeführer 'Willi' Bittrich, was used for more conventional combat duties, operating at first under LIX Korps of 9. Armee of Heeresgruppe Mitte in the Rzhev area, around the Don basin, Golaia and Orel. After a brief rest in November 1942 it came under XXX Korps; in January 1943 it passed to XXXXI Panzer Korps; and in February to 2. Panzer Armee's XXXXVII Panzer Korps, 'Korps Lemelsen'.

Horsed cavalry still had a useful part to play in the vast expanses of Russia, where their high mobility over varied terrain made them valuable for work on the flanks. Withdrawn to 2. Panzer Armee reserve for refitting in March 1943, in June–August the division reverted to anti-partisan operations between the Dniepr and the Pripet Marshes. One of its regiments was detached in April (eventually forming the nucleus for the new 22. SS-Kavallerie Division), but this unit was ordered replaced in August by local recruitment of *Volksdeutsche*, which eventually brought total strength up to about 15,000 men.

In July 1943, the division was attached to Heeresgruppe Süd, and from August saw heavy defensive combat during retreats to the Dniepr and Kirovograd as part of 8.

In this evocative photograph, a Waffen-SS trooper moves along a trench, beneath the barrel of a wrecked T-34 tank, suggestive of the ferocity of the fighting on the Eastern Front.

Russian prisoners captured by the Waffen-SS generally faced a bleak future. Those who were not summarily executed would face the horrors of German labour camps. More than three million Soviet POWs died in German captivity.

Armee and then 1. Panzer Armee; elements remained in the south until early 1944. In October 1943 the formation received the divisional number 8, and its regiments were renumbered. The following March it received the honour title '*Florian Geyer*'. The division was transferred to Croatia in December 1943, fighting partisans until March 1944. During 1944 the record of the movements of dispersed elements of *Florian Geyer* is confused, but at least part of the division saw fierce defensive fighting against the great Soviet offensive of that summer and the collapse of Heeresgruppe Mitte. At the end of the year the division was deployed to Hungary under IX SS Korps as part of the

RIGHT: SS cavalry, 1942–43. 1: SS-Oberscharführer, SS-Kavallerie Division, 1943. This typical SS cavalryman wears the M1940 SS camouflage smock in the so-called 'palm tree' pattern which appears in a number of photographs of this formation; the skirt and wrists have been tucked up inside the elasticated bands for convenience. 2: SS-Rottenführer, 8. SS-Kavallerie Division *Florian Geyer*, 1944. His cuffband bears the divisional title '*Florian Geyer*', authorized in 1944 and officially manufactured in BeVo machine-woven style. His weapon is the Gewehr G43 semi-automatic rifle, but he has only acquired two of the special canvas magazine pouches; a late war 'stick' grenade is thrust into his belt. 3: SS-Obersturmbannführer, SS-Kavallerie Division, 1942–43. This lieutenant colonel's *Schirmmütze*, army-style M1936 service dress and shoulder straps all show the golden-yellow *Waffenfarbe* of the cavalry branch. He wears riding breeches with leather-reinforced inner legs and seat, and officer's riding boots with strapped spurs. The cuffband has the hand-embroidered aluminium wire inscription 'SS-Kavallerie-Division' in Gothic script. (Osprey Publishing © Stephen Andrew)

Budapest garrison, alongside the new 22. SS-Freiwilligen Kavallerie Division *Maria Theresia*. In early November 1944 it took part in a successful counter-attack against Soviet forces advancing on the capital, and recaptured Vesces and Ullo. December found it facing the Soviet IV Guards Mechanized Corps; by Christmas Eve it was in defensive positions on the west bank of the Danube, the 50,000-strong garrison now being surrounded by at least 250,000 Soviet troops.

9. SS-PANZER DIVISION *HOHENSTAUFEN*

The raising of this division was authorized in late 1942, and it was built from drafts of 18-year-old former Hitlerjugend members, up to 70 per cent being conscripts rather than volunteers. These boys were led and trained by a cadre of experienced combat veterans from the *Leibstandarte* Division, the latter initially based at Berlin Lichterfelde. Its first commander was SS-Gruppenführer 'Willi' Bittrich, one of the most able senior combat commanders in the Waffen-SS. Originally designated as a Panzergrenadier (mechanized) division, it was upgraded to full armoured (Panzer) status in October 1943 during the process of formation and training; this brought it a battalion of excellent PzKpfw V Panther tanks in addition to one of PzKpfw IVs. In March 1943 it was given the honour title 'Hohenstaufen', commemorating the renowned dynastic family which had provided German kings and Holy Roman Emperors in the 12th–13th centuries (notably the great Emperor Friedrich II 'Barbarossa', r. 1212–50).

The division spent most of 1943 training and working up in France, initially at Mailly le Camp, the vast, windswept French Army training area east of Paris, where it fell under the operational control of Heeresgruppe D. The new division was to be grouped, as IV SS-Panzer Korps, with another new formation, 16. SS-Panzergrenadier Division *Reichsführer-SS*, and was required to surrender some personnel as cadre for the latter. After various moves around France, in late 1943 *Hohenstaufen* was based in the south near the Mediterranean coast; and in the event it did not serve with *Reichsführer-SS*. Once considered fit for combat service, it would be grouped with its sister formation, 10. SS-Panzer Division *Frundsberg*, to become II SS-Panzer Korps commanded by the veteran armoured general SS-Obergruppenführer Paul Hausser.

On the Eastern Front, 1. Panzer Armee had become encircled by the Soviets in the area around Tarnopol and the Red Army was threatening the Polish border. Hitler decided to commit four fresh divisions to the area in an attempt to break through, two of these being the new II SS-Panzer Korps. With a strength of just under 20,000 men, *Hohenstaufen* moved to Poland in March 1944 to serve under 4. Panzer Armee. From Lvov, it went into action at Tarnopol in the appalling conditions of the Russian spring thaw, which made movement of heavy equipment difficult, and the division suffered

Grenadiers of the 12. SS-Panzer Division *Hitlerjugend* take a moment's rest during the heavy fighting in Normandy in 1944.

heavy casualties. On 5 April, *Hohenstaufen* and *Frundsberg* attacked on the flank of 4. Panzer Armee; the teenage soldiers followed their veteran officers and NCOs in a break-through that smashed a path through the Soviet First Tank Army, and *Hohenstaufen* linked up with the encircled 1. Panzer Armee on 9 April.

The division's initial visit to the Eastern Front was to be short-lived; the landings by the Allied forces in Normandy on 6 June 1944 prompted Hitler to pull II SS-Panzer Korps out of the Ukraine, where it was preparing for a German counter-offensive at Kovel, and send it west. Entraining in Poland on 12 June, the division was joined en route by part of the Panzer regiment which had still been forming up at Mailly-le-Camp. However, *Hohenstaufen* suffered so badly from the attentions of Allied fighter-bombers while in transit to the front that its tanks had to off-load from the rail trucks and move overland, travelling only in the hours of darkness.

The arrival in Normandy of a more or less fresh SS armoured corps led by a general of the calibre of Paul Hausser might have had a significant impact on the campaign if they had gone into the line sooner. However, by the time they were operational on 25 June the Allies, with the advantage of overwhelming air power, already had a strong foothold in Normandy. *Hohenstaufen* was sent into action against British forces involved in the *Epsom* offensive along the River Odon and south-west of Caen on 28 June. On the 29th, while forming up near Noyers, divisional units came under a ferocious combination of heavy artillery fire and shelling from major warships lying offshore. So intense was the fire that the Germans were convinced that they had come under a carpet bombing attack by RAF Lancaster bombers which had been operating in the area. Significant damage was caused, and up to 20 per cent of *Hohenstaufen*'s vehicles were estimated destroyed. (At the end of June, General Bittrich succeeded Hausser in command of II SS-Panzer Korps; the new divisional commander, SS-Oberführer Stadler, would be wounded in late July, and SS-Oberführer Bock would hold temporary command until he returned in October.)

In the fighting which followed the division destroyed some 62 enemy armoured vehicles for the loss of 31 of its own; but replacements would be far easier for the Allies to obtain. As the momentum of the British attack slowed, the Germans went on to the offensive, and after a concentrated artillery and mortar barrage by both 9. and 10. Divisions one of the key objectives was taken – Hill 112, of which General Hausser had said that 'he who holds Hill 112 holds Normandy'. The arrival of II SS-Panzer Korps in the sector was sufficient to bring the British offensive to a halt, but the Allies' massive firepower prevented the German counter-offensive from fully exploiting this success. By 2 July it is estimated that *Hohenstaufen* had lost 81 tanks and 22 self-propelled guns since arriving in the sector (though some of these were lost to mechanical breakdowns rather than enemy action, and were later recovered).

The first week of July was relatively quiet for the division, but on 11 July it was once again thrown into the battle to retain Hill 112. This feature would be fought over so often – lost, retaken and lost again by each side – that it became a desolate no-man's-land, stripped of much of its natural cover. By mid-July the division was located around Bully, between Caen and Evrecy, and went into action again on the 16th against British armoured forces attacking near Gavrus. In fighting around Hill 113 and at Bougy, *Hohenstaufen* knocked out 48 Allied tanks in a day's fighting, for the loss of just five of its own. Casualties overall had been heavy, however, and by the end of this series of actions the division had lost around 50 per cent of its grenadiers and was down to just 38 tanks. *Hohenstaufen* was then fortunate enough to be relieved, and allowed a brief period of respite as part of Panzergruppe West reserve, leaving its sister division *Frundsberg* to hold the line and await reinforcements.

On 18 July a battlegroup from the division was formed to contribute – along with army infantry and elements of *Frundsberg* – to a counter-attack intended to recapture a

RIGHT: Three men of the 9. SS-Panzer Division *Hohenstaufen*, 1943–44 (from left to right): SS-Sturmbannführer, SS-Scharführer, SS-Rottenführer. For his duties in barracks the SS-Sturmbannführer on the divisional staff wears the M1936 style tunic in conjunction with long straight-legged trousers, the outer seams of which are piped in infantry white, and black shoes. Headgear is the regulation white-piped officer's *Schirmmütze*. (Osprey Publishing © Stephen Andrew)

number of villages south of Caen which had been lost to a new British offensive codenamed 'Greenline'. One platoon of *Hohenstaufen* tanks, sent out on a night reconnaissance, found themselves right in the middle of British positions. Taking advantage of the element of surprise, the German tanks blazed away at the startled enemy until their ammunition was almost gone before withdrawing under cover of a smokescreen.

At the beginning of August a breakthrough by General Patton's US Third Army at Avranches and Mortain on the western tip of the beachhead was coupled with a new British offensive, Operation *Bluecoat*, which drove south from Villers-Bocage towards Vire. The British aim was to engage the still powerful German armoured divisions and prevent them from interfering with the American break-out. The weakened units of II SS-Panzer Korps launched yet another counter-attack; on its way to the start line *Hohenstaufen* was once again harried by the Allied fighter-bombers which were now claiming more German tanks destroyed than the ground forces. Despite its losses the division's 72 medium tanks, backed by some 30 heavy PzKpfw VI Tigers, held up the advancing British VIII Corps with over 500 tanks.

As the Germans battled to eliminate the British salient, on 4 August *Hohenstaufen* troops retook the town of Chênedollé with the aid of a battalion of *Nebelwerfer* multi-barrel rocket launchers. Although 39 British tanks were destroyed, fighting continued to rage; by nightfall the town was in British hands once more, and despite renewed attacks they held on to it. During ten days' fighting in this area, the division is reckoned to have cost the British over 5,000 casualties and over 130 tanks; but numbers and firepower told in the end, and on the night of 13/14 August *Hohenstaufen* was forced to begin a withdrawal over the River Orne.

The division withdrew to the north-east, moving from the Argentan area through Trun to Vimoutiers to avoid the closing of the Falaise Pocket. It arrived there on 18 August, but by now at only about one-third of its original establishment – about 5,500 all ranks. The infantry had suffered proportionately far worse, and the two Panzergrenadier regiments were down to a combined strength of just under 500 men. Total divisional casualties in just over eight weeks of combat in Normandy included 5,000 men killed.

In the Falaise Pocket about 60,000 German troops of 19 divisions were trapped between the closing jaws of US Third Army pushing northwards from Argentan, and First Canadian Army driving south from Falaise. When the jaws finally snapped shut at Chambois on 21 August, II SS-Panzer Korps was ordered to strike back towards Falaise and cut a path to allow the trapped German formations to escape. The *Hohenstaufen* units allocated to this attack were by now too weak to penetrate the Allied lines, although some other Waffen-SS units did succeed in making contact with German troops attempting to escape the cauldron.

II SS-Panzer Korps then continued to withdraw to the north-east; while providing the rearguard *Hohenstaufen* saw fierce fighting. The combined tank strength of both *Hohenstaufen* and *Frundsberg* by this point was fewer than 20. The bulk of the division crossed the Seine safely at Duclair, although a few of its personnel were killed by strafing aircraft. The effective survivors of the division were formed into a new Kampfgruppe, moving on to Amiens and from there to Cambrai. Here the battlegroup fought a furious action against US armour, claiming over 40 tanks destroyed before being forced to withdraw northwards (they avoided the attention of enemy fighter-bombers by displaying Allied flags). With the enemy hard on their heels the remnants of *Hohenstaufen* continued northwards through Belgium, passing Mons and Brussels before crossing into Holland, where they arrived in the area north of Arnhem on 7–9 September. Here the division came under Generalfeldmarschall Walter Model's 6. Panzer Armee in Heeresgruppe B.

Arnhem was intended to be simply a stop-off point from which the division – perhaps reduced to fewer than 3,000 men – would entrain for Germany for total refitting, after handing over its remaining armour and artillery to the *Frundsberg* Division. However, on 17 September, just as the division was about to depart, the Allies launched

In the battered streets of Arnhem, an StuH 42 self-propelled gun occupies a carefully selected vantage point. This vehicle belonged to the 9. SS-Panzer Division *Hohenstaufen*.

Operation *Market Garden* into Holland. This combined a cross-country attack by elements of the British Second and US First Armies ('Market') with an airborne assault by the First Allied Airborne Army ('Garden'), with the intention of seizing the bridges over the Waal at Nijmegen and the Lower Rhine at Arnhem.

If the Germans were surprised by the Allied airborne landings, then the Allies were equally surprised to find that they had been dropped into an area occupied by elements of two Waffen-SS armoured divisions; even in their depleted state, together they were still a powerful force with which to oppose lightly armed airborne troops. *Hohenstaufen* vehicles which had been loaded onto rail cars for shipping to Germany were frantically off-loaded again. Most of the division's survivors were brought together in a battlegroup designated Kampfgruppe Harzer, led by SS-Standartenführer Walter Harzer.

Around 9,000 British airborne troops had been landed in the area around Wolfheze, around 11km west of Arnhem on the north bank of the river. The paratroopers who made the dash to seize the north end of the bridge (2nd and part of 3rd Parachute Battalions) numbered around 700 men. An attempt was made to cross the bridge, but heavy German fire forced the paratroopers to concentrate on consolidating their hold on the northern end while awaiting reinforcement, and the southern end remained in German hands. General Bittrich's orders to *Hohenstaufen* were to seize and hold the town and the bridge, and to block the advance of any additional paratroopers from west of the town.

During the battle around Arnhem the division's troops were divided into several smaller Kampfgruppen acting as blocking forces, various elements being spread out from Arnhem itself as far as Neerpelt to the south-west. Some of these included experienced Waffen-SS troops mixed with soldiers pulled in from other commands – some still under training – and even some Kriegsmarine personnel.

While the bulk of the British 1st Airborne Division were trying to make their way along the north bank to Arnhem and the bridge from their dropping zones to the west, stiff German resistance held them up at Oosterbeek just outside the town. The original intention was that the airborne troops would only have to hold the bridge for a day or two before the heavy ground forces punched their way up from the south to relieve them. However, the contested advance of British XXX Corps along the narrow corridor, led by Guards Armoured Division and 43rd (Wessex) Division, became bogged down; and the lightly armed airborne troops came under increasing pressure

LEFT: 10. SS-Panzer Division *Frundsberg*, 1943–44. 1: SS-Brigadeführer of Armoured Troops, 1944. 2: SS-Grenadier, 1943–44. 3: SS-Untersturmführer, SS-Sturmgeschütz Abteilung 10, 1944. The Grenadier wears a combination frequently seen in colder months. The field-grey greatcoat (here without insignia) is worn underneath a camouflage smock – in this case, the first version of the M1942 smock, with horizontal skirt pockets and foliage attachment loops at the shoulders and upper sleeves. (Osprey Publishing © Stephen Andrew)

An injured Waffen-SS soldier holds up his hands in final surrender to US troops in Normandy, 1944. Although Allied firepower came to dominate the Waffen-SS on the Western Front, the British and American forces were still impressed by the defensive tenacity of their opponents.

from the Waffen-SS. Model steadily sent reinforcements to join the encircling German units over the next few days, and in desperate fighting the British perimeters around Oosterbeek and at the bridge itself were continuously constricted.

The force at the bridge finally surrendered on 21 September. On the 24th, through the intervention of *Hohenstaufen*'s medical officer SS-Sturmbannführer Egon Skalka, a truce was arranged which led to the evacuation of over 700 seriously wounded paratroopers; the following day a further 500 were handed over. The Germans had been impressed by the bravery and tenacity shown by the British airborne troops, and British survivors reported their treatment by the Waffen-SS troops as being correct, even 'kind'.

The arrival of a battalion of King Tiger heavy tanks – the army's schwere Panzer Abteilung 503 (Heavy Tank Battalion 503) – finally put paid to any hope of a relief force being able to fight its way through. On 25 September the order was given for the survivors of 1st Airborne Division to withdraw, and those who could made their way back across the Rhine in assault boats crewed by British and Canadian engineers; the evacuation was completed the following day. The British had landed some 9,000 troops at Arnhem, with an additional 3,000 Polish paratroops subsequently dropped in support. It is estimated that about 8,000 of these 12,000 men were either killed or taken prisoner; German casualties numbered just over 3,000.

On 30 September, *Hohenstaufen* was finally withdrawn to Germany for the long delayed refitting. SS-Standartenführer Walter Harzer was decorated with the Knight's Cross in recognition of the performance of his troops – one of 12 awarded to members of the division during the war.

By the next time it was committed to action *Hohenstaufen* had been rebuilt to just under 20,000 men, but not all of these were of impressive quality – the replacements included a large draft of Luftwaffe personnel. The division was still woefully short of armour, vehicles and equipment, with some units recording shortfalls of up to 50 per cent.

On 12 December 1944, the division was moved to the Eiffel region in preparation for the ill-fated Ardennes offensive. *Hohenstaufen* would form part of VI SS-Panzer Armee, along with the *Leibstandarte*, *Das Reich*, and *Hitlerjugend* Panzer Divisions, all under command of SS-Obergruppenführer 'Sepp' Dietrich. The task of the SS-Panzer Armee was to advance on the northern flank to seize Antwerp, the most critical of the Allied supply ports.

Hohenstaufen did not move up to Blankenheim until the offensive opened on 16 December, and was eventually committed to action in the early afternoon of 19 December, as part of II SS-Panzer Korps along with 2. SS-Panzer Division *Das Reich*. It was forced to spend four full days pushing its way along heavily congested roads before reaching the front line. Advancing on the right flank of *Das Reich* towards Poteau, it saw heavy combat when it ran into elements of the US 82nd Airborne Division which succeeded in halting *Hohenstaufen* at Bra. From here it turned south, and moved into the attack at Grand Lalleux, pursuing the Americans as they retreated from the salient at St Vith. On 22 December, at Vielsalm, US troops succeeded in crossing the bridge over the River Salm and partially destroying it to prevent *Hohenstaufen* following. The division finally crossed the Salm on 24 December, and advanced towards Vaux-Chavanne, where it was involved in further heavy combat.

On 3 January 1945, *Hohenstaufen* attacked through Rastadt in an attempt to push the defenders of Bastogne back into an even smaller perimeter. Operating alongside *Leibstandarte* and *Hitlerjugend*, the division made good initial progress; but the Germans were now so seriously weakened that they no longer had the strength, ammunition or fuel to exploit such penetrations. The division gradually retreated towards Dochamps-Lon, fighting several rearguard actions around Salmchateau. By late December, *Hohenstaufen* had only 30 tanks left and some of its Panzergrenadier battalions were reduced to barely company strength. As the offensive crumbled Hitler ordered the withdrawal of his elite Waffen-SS units, which he planned to use for his next insane project: a final offensive in the East. *Hohenstaufen* was withdrawn from the line on 24 January 1945.

10. SS-PANZER DIVISION *FRUNDSBERG*

The order authorizing the creation of this division was signed in December 1942, and the new formation was raised from February 1943, formed from drafts of 18-year-old

1. SS-Panzer Division was supposed to have 16 Flakpanzers with its Panzer regiment in late 1944: eight 3.7cm 'Ostwind' from 10. (Flak) Kompanie of SS-Panzer Regiment 1, and eight quadruple 20mm 'Wirbelwind' from the attached schwere SS-Panzer Abteilung 501, an example of which is seen here. (Osprey Publishing © D. Parker/ R. Volstad)

Reichsdeutsche conscripts around a core of experienced leaders. During its six months' training and working up in France it was initially given the title '*Karl der Grosse*' (i.e. commemorating the 9th-century Emperor Charlemagne); but in October 1943, Hitler signed orders up-grading it to a Panzer division and renaming it *Frundsberg*, the change becoming effective on 20 November. The honour title commemorated Georg von Frundsberg (1473–1528), a famous German commander of Landsknecht mercenaries in the service of Holy Roman Emperors Maximilian I and Charles V.

A river crossing is a delicate business for these Waffen-SS troops in northern Russia. The soldier on the opposite bank appears to have a Soviet PPSh-41 submachine gun.

The division's first year closely paralleled that of the *Hohenstaufen* Division, mostly being taken up by formation and training in various locations in southern and western France under Heeresgruppe D. In October 1943 the formation of a new VII SS-Panzer Korps was ordered, grouping *Frundsberg* together with another new formation, 17. SS-Panzergrenadier Division *Götz von Berlichingen*, for whose nucleus the 10. Division had to surrender part of its artillery and the motorcycle companies from its Panzergrenadier regiments.

In March 1944, as part of II SS-Panzer Korps, the incomplete *Frundsberg* was sent with *Hohenstaufen* to the Eastern Front to counter the great Soviet advance which had steamrollered over Heeresgruppe Mitte and threatened the Polish frontier, trapping

German forces – including *Leibstandarte* and a battlegroup from *Das Reich* – in the area around Tarnopol. Still without the PzKpfw V Panthers of its Panzer regiment's I Abteilung, the division assembled with the rest of II SS-Panzer Korps under Armeegruppe Nordukraine, and went into action for the first time in early April. Fierce fighting achieved a breakthrough at Buczacz on 6 April, and *Frundsberg* linked up with its beleaguered Waffen-SS comrades of 1. Panzer Armee. *Frundsberg* remained in the line, seeing heavy combat on the River Seret (Strypa) and in the Tarnopol-Kovel region. Halted by units of the 1st Ukrainian Front, the division then spent some weeks in static defensive actions on the River Bug. On 12 June, II SS-Panzer Korps was withdrawn from the Russian Front and rushed west to respond to the Normandy landings, its personnel and equipment filling 67 trains.

The division arrived in France on 18 June, but the difficulties of daylight movement under skies ruled by the Allied tactical air forces delayed its arrival at the Normandy front – with a strength of around 13,500 men – until 25 June. Five days later *Frundsberg* was thrown into action to halt the British Second Army's Operation *Epsom*, the attempt to outflank Caen; the division saw intense combat around the strategic Hill 112, suffering heavy casualties.

A British operation codenamed *Jupiter*, tasked with the recapture of high ground around Hill 112, was launched on 10 July and made some initial progress before being driven back by Tigers from the II SS-Panzer Korps heavy tank battalion (schwere SS-Panzer Abteilung 102). The British threw in a further attack and took the summit once again; but at nightfall the British tanks withdrew, leaving the infantry unsupported, to be thrown back yet again by a German counter-attack under cover of darkness. So great was the confusion over which side controlled what ground that at one point the British came under heavy attack by Allied aircraft.

On 15 July, as *Hohenstaufen* was withdrawn into reserve, *Frundsberg* was left to cover the entire sector, and was driven off part of Hill 113, just north of Evrecy, by units of 15th (Scottish) Division. They were brought under heavy fire from Tiger tanks on Hill 112, and the reappearance of *Hohenstaufen* made the British position even more tenuous. Nevertheless, they hung on to the area they had seized on Hill 113 while the Tigers of schwere SS-Panzer Abteilung 102 and a battalion from SS-Panzergrenadier Regiment 21 remained firmly in control of Hill 112, until finally relieved by the army's 271. Infanterie Division. *Frundsberg*, having now lost well over 2,000 men since the beginning of July, was then withdrawn for a brief period of rest.

On 2 August the division was back in action, when a Kampfgruppe successfully held most of Hill 188 against a British attack and destroyed 20 tanks in the process. The next day the remainder of the division arrived, threw back the British units that had established a foothold on Hill 188, and took nearby Hill 301 to form a defence line between the two high points. *Frundsberg* was almost immediately ordered to disengage, and on 6 August the division was committed to an attack on British units north of Chênedollé. They seized two prominent high points, Hills 242 and 224, only to be driven back by shellfire and air attacks.

Moving thereafter to Mortain on the American front, *Frundsberg* was to become the corps reserve for XLVII Panzer Korps. Elements had to be committed to action near Barenton almost immediately, however, to block American probing attacks. Instead of being committed to a counter-offensive, *Frundsberg* found itself being pushed eastwards via Domfront and Fromentel as the Germans pulled back to defend Argentan. By 19 August the division was right in the middle of the Falaise Pocket. It was comparatively fortunate in being one of the formations which did manage to escape over the River Dives before the rapidly narrowing gap at Chambois was finally closed by the US, Canadian and Free Polish armour. The division then retreated north-east to the River Seine, crossing at Oissel between 25 and 27 August by means of two bridges it had seized, fending off attempts by other retreating units to use them until all its own troops had crossed to safety.

From the Seine crossings, *Frundsberg* moved on to the Somme and took up positions between Bray and Peronne. After defensive fighting against the advancing British the division pulled back towards Cambrai, and ultimately into Holland to a rest area between Arnhem and Nijmegen. It had been intended that *Hohenstaufen* be returned to Germany for a full refit, handing over its heavy equipment to *Frundsberg* to make up some of the latter's combat losses; but the arrival of the British 1st Airborne Division on 17 September quickly sent the division back into action. While *Hohenstaufen* was tasked with holding Arnhem town and blocking the advance of the British airborne troops from the west, *Frundsberg* was given the mission of defending the Waal bridge at Nijmegen and blocking the Allied overland attack from the south.

One of the most spectacular incidents at Arnhem bridge involved a *Hohenstaufen* unit temporarily under the command of the *Frundsberg* Division. The armoured reconnaissance battalion SS-Panzer Aufklärungs Abteilung 9, under SS-Hauptsturmführer Gräbner, had already crossed the Arnhem bridge southwards when news of the Allied attacks arrived, and raced to secure the road through Nijmegen. On finding the defence of the Nijmegen bridge well organized, it had returned to Arnhem, and on 18 September it attempted to cross the bridge northwards again and seize the northern end, now held by Lieutnant-Colonel John Frost's 2nd Parachute Battalion. With a mixture of armoured cars, armoured personnel carriers and other light vehicles, Gräbner rushed the bridge, only to be met with a hail of fire from the British paratroopers. Many light armoured vehicles were knocked out by PIATs, and Gräbner himself, leading from the front as always, was among those killed.

SS troops in the Leningrad area attempt to maintain operations in freezing weather. The soldiers had to pay special attention to weapons maintenance, otherwise gun bolts could easily freeze solid.

SS troops ensconced on the southern bank and in brickworks near the southern end of the bridge were able to keep up suppressing fire on British movements on the northern bank. Cut off from reinforcements and running out of ammunition, the survivors of Frost's few hundred paratroopers were forced to surrender on 21 September after three days and four nights of bitter fighting. *Frundsberg* units then moved to their allotted task of supporting the German defences at Nijmegen, and later slowing the advance of the British XXX Corps armour after it crossed the Waal. Considerable casualties were inflicted on both sides during stubborn German defensive fighting. The Free Polish paratroop brigade dropped just south-west of Arnhem on the south bank, and the XXX Corps units who eventually linked up with them, were unable to reach the survivors of 1st Airborne Division at Oosterbeek; these were eventually forced to withdraw over the river by night, leaving their wounded to surrender on 29 September.

As the above examples demonstrate, the Waffen-SS in 1943–44 was being steadily abraded by relentless, intensive combat. In this chapter, and the previous, we have

LEFT: Armoured personnel, 1942–44. Left to right, top to bottom: SS-Hauptsturmführer, SS-Panzer Regiment 2; SS-Hauptsturmführer, SS-Panzer Regiment 5; SS-Unterscharführer, SS-Panzer Regiment 1; SS-Sturmann, SS-Panzer Regiment 3. (Osprey Publishing © Stephen Andrew)

focused on the divisions 1.–10. In the following chapter, we will assess the fate of these units in the last year of the war, but we will also expand the focus to look at the proliferation of foreign units that would fight out the remainder of the war for Nazi Germany, either with glory or ignominy. Before we do so, it is worth a look at the elite with an elite, the special operations units created within the Waffen-SS.

SS SPECIAL OPS

THE SKORZENY COMMANDOS

Well before its take-over of the Abwehr, the SS had been working on the creation of a new unit that would be part of the Ausland-SD, the foreign espionage department of the Sicherheitsdienst or SS Security Service that was involved in military sabotage activities outside of Germany. The officer chosen to lead this new unit was a tough Austrian combat veteran; standing well over 1.8m tall, powerfully built and with a face heavily scarred from duelling during his student days, Otto Skorzeny was certainly an imposing figure by any standards.

His would be the one name that would eventually be directly linked with the special combat units of not just the Waffen-SS but all branches of the armed forces. After the effective dissolution of the Abwehr most of the Brandenburgers – members of the *Brandenburg* special forces unit – volunteered to transfer to Skorzeny's commando organization, the SS-Jagdverbände. He would also ultimately gain responsibility for combat operations by the K-Verbände of the Navy and the Luftwaffe's KG 200. His career offers one of the few examples of the inveterate plotting and empire-building of the SS having a beneficial effect on Germany's war effort, since there can be no doubt that Skorzeny was a highly effective leader who was greatly respected and admired by the men under his command.

Although the Waffen-SS, when on active service in the field, came under the control of the Oberkommando der Wehrmacht, and Skorzeny and many of his troops were Waffen-SS personnel, the direct chain of command for his units was from Amt IV (SD-Ausland) of the RSHA, headed by SS-Obergruppenführer Ernst Kaltenbrunner, who was directly responsible to Reichsführer-SS Heinrich Himmler.

In 1942 the RSHA created its own special unit, closely modelled on the Brandenburgers but manned only by trusted and politically reliable members of the SS. The Austrian-born SS-Hauptsturmführer Otto Skorzeny was appointed to command this new SS-Sonderverband zbV Friedenthal in April 1943. Skorzeny had been recommended by his fellow Austrian SS-Obergruppenführer Kaltenbrunner, who knew Skorzeny personally from pre-war times in Vienna. (Despite their own fervent support of the Nazi cause, Kaltenbrunner and Skorzeny had actually saved the life of the Austrian President Wilhelm Miklas on 12 March 1938, when they prevented his murder by a group of Nazi thugs.)

Otto Skorzeny was born in Vienna on 12 June 1908. On graduating from university with a degree in engineering, he formed his own company. He joined the Austrian Nazi Party whilst still a student, and by the time Austria was annexed by Germany in 1938 he was an active member of the SS. On the outbreak of war Skorzeny volunteered for the Luftwaffe, but at 1.92m he was considered too tall, and at 31 too old, for pilot training. He was posted to the communications branch, but transferred to the SS-VT at the earliest opportunity, and served in the *Leibstandarte* Regiment during the campaign in the West. By the opening of the campaign against the Soviet Union in June 1941 Skorzeny was serving in the *Das Reich* Division. He saw considerable combat, earning the Iron Cross First Class; late in 1941 he took a fragment wound in the head but refused to be evacuated, insisting on staying with his unit until his condition deteriorated to the extent that he had to be shipped back to a hospital in Vienna.

On recovery, he was posted to a staff job in Berlin whilst recuperating. Here he used his time to study commando tactics, and became a keen exponent of the concept of small, highly trained teams operating behind enemy lines. Now, in his new role, he would have plentiful opportunities to put his ideas into practice.

In June 1943, Skorzeny found himself in command of a newly formed unit designated SS-Jäger Bataillon 502, and was given permission to recruit top-quality men not just from within the SS but also from the other armed services. The unit would comprise three companies of German troops and one of foreign volunteers. (In time, as his influence grew, Skorzeny would also have SS-Fallschirmjäger Bataillon 500/600 placed under his command, and would even become involved in developing special weapons units with the Kriegsmarine's K-Verbände and the Luftwaffe's Kampfgeschwader 200.) Soon after being appointed to command the new unit Skorzeny was handed his first mission, which would start him on his climb from relative obscurity to become one of Germany's most famous soldiers.

On 24 July 1943, the Italian dictator Benito Mussolini had been forcibly deposed by his own Fascist Grand Council and placed under arrest. Whatever Mussolini's failings as an ally, Hitler refused to see his fellow dictator humbled and imprisoned, and after considering a number of candidates to lead a rescue mission he personally selected Skorzeny for the task. On 3 September the British landings in Italy began, and on the 8th Marshal Badoglio announced the armistice that had been signed with the Allies five days earlier.

Skorzeny flew to Italy to take command of a mixed group of around 20 Luftwaffe and 50 Waffen-SS troops. Intelligence sources had learned that Mussolini was being held at the Campo Imperatore resort hotel on the Gran Sasso mountain to the north-east of Rome. The only direct route up the mountain was by a funicular railway, which would hardly be suitable for a surprise assault; but aerial reconnaissance revealed that close to the hotel on the plateau there was a level area that looked as if it might possibly be suitable for a glider landing. Skorzeny's force, now just over 100 strong, was split into three groups for the mission: Skorzeny would lead a glider-borne landing on the Gran Sasso, while a second group under the Luftwaffe's Major Mors would seize the funicular railway in the valley to prevent any reinforcements reaching the Italian guard force, and a third group would rescue Mussolini's family from a separate location. In order to conceal their identity the Waffen-SS troops involved in the operation all wore Luftwaffe uniforms.

At just after 1400hrs on 12 September 1943, Skorzeny landed on the Gran Sasso in the first of the gliders; the landing zone was much rougher than anticipated, but the aircraft crash-landed successfully just 15m from the building. A startled Carabinieri guard nearby surrendered immediately, and as the other gliders made their approach Skorzeny stormed into the building, surprising another guard and quickly smashing his radio set. Returning outside and moving around the building, Skorzeny spotted Mussolini at a window and signalled him to stay back. Re-entering the hotel, Skorzeny and his men quickly disarmed a group of guards, ran upstairs, found Mussolini's room and captured the two officers who were guarding him. At this point the whole operation had taken less than five minutes.

The German troops in the following gliders had less luck with their landings, one aircraft being smashed to pieces on the rocks. The Germans then became embroiled in a short firefight with other Carabinieri defending the hotel, but one of the officers who had been guarding Mussolini was persuaded to order the remaining Italians to surrender to avoid further bloodshed. The German detachment tasked with seizing the station for the funicular railway at the base of the mountain had also succeeded, and soon joined Skorzeny on the plateau.

Having achieved his initial goal of securing Mussolini's release, and with the plateau secured, Skorzeny was now faced with the task of moving the dictator to safety in German-held territory. Rather than risk being intercepted while moving overland, it had been planned to fly him out from the nearby Aquila de Abruzzi airfield, or from the foot of the mountain near the funicular railway; in the event, it was decided to take off from the mountain itself. A skilled Luftwaffe pilot, Leutnant Gerlach, succeeded in landing a light Fieseler Storch spotter aircraft on the plateau, but was disconcerted when the giant Skorzeny insisted on joining him and the corpulent Mussolini for the flight off the mountain. With the pilot, Mussolini and Skorzeny crammed inside the tiny, low-powered aircraft barely made it off the plateau, but thanks to Gerlach's skill

ABOVE: Skorzeny commandos, 1943–44. 1: SS-Hauptsturmführer Skorzeny; Italy, September 1943. Otto Skorzeny is seen here as he was photographed soon after the rescue of Mussolini from the Gran Sasso. He wears a Luftwaffe officer's flying branch shoulder straps of his equivalent rank of Hauptmann; at the throat he displays his newly awarded Knight's Cross. 2: SS-Untersturmführer Schwerdt; Italy, 12 September 1943. Schwerdt, one of Skorzeny's officers on the Gran Sasso mission, was photographed standing beside Il Duce. Armed with a Fallschirmjägergewehr 42 (FG 42) automatic rifle, he is wearing a brown belt, black braces, and an intriguing pair of magazine pouches resembling those for the old MP 28 submachine gun. 3: Einheit Stielgau; Ardennes, 17 December 1944. This commando, attempting to misdirect traffic and sow confusion behind American lines during Operation Greif, is disguised as a sergeant of US Army Military Police. To give himself an authentic appearance for his covert role, he wears the M1 helmet with white 'MP' and band, a greatcoat with rank chevrons and an 'MP' brassard, and double-buckle boots. His weapon is a captured Thompson M1928A1 submachine gun, with a triple magazine pouch on a web pistol belt. (Osprey Publishing © Mike Chappell)

it landed safely at Practica di Mare airfield, where Skorzeny and Mussolini boarded a Heinkel He 111 which flew them to an airfield near Vienna.

By any standards the rescue of Mussolini was an audacious operation, brilliantly executed; Skorzeny was promoted to SS-Sturmbannführer (major), and he and Gerlach were both awarded the Knight's Cross. However, although it had been very much a combined operation, under the overall operational command of the Luftwaffe and employing more Luftwaffe than Waffen-SS personnel, it was to be the Waffen-SS element who were hailed as heroes, while the Luftwaffe's contribution was largely ignored. (The previous winter it had been considered whether Skorzeny and his men should be used in a similar operation to kidnap Marshal Petain from Vichy-controlled southern France and move him to the German-occupied area, but in the event this operation had been cancelled.)

Skorzeny and his men were briefly involved in the suppression of the abortive uprising following the bomb attempt on Hitler's life on 20 July 1944. Skorzeny was about to depart Berlin for Vienna when news of the attempt reached him and he was ordered to remain in the capital. His actions that night initially consisted mainly of visiting various commands and advising them not to get involved in what was a highly confused situation, and to remain on the alert in their barracks. After sending a company of his men from their base at Friedenthal to protect the SD headquarters he led others to the headquarters of the Reserve Army, where he met with Major Ernst-Otto Remer of the *Grossdeutschland* Division. Together Skorzeny's and Remer's men occupied the plotters' Bendlerstrasse headquarters to prevent anyone leaving. By this time four of them, including Claus von Stauffenberg, had already been executed (mainly to prevent them being interrogated under torture and forced to reveal the identities of others involved in the conspiracy). Skorzeny put a halt to the executions and arrested the remaining suspects before transferring them to Gestapo custody. Skorzeny then acted as temporary commander at Reserve Army headquarters until the situation was brought under control. This display of loyalty to the regime served to increase even further Skorzeny's standing in the eyes of Hitler.

The attempt on his life destroyed Hitler's already decreasing trust in the army, and plans were put in place to dismantle the 'special forces' character of the Brandenburgers and convert the unit into a conventional combat force; from now on it would be SS-Sturmbannführer Skorzeny who would lead Germany's 'commandos'. His Jäger bataillon was enlarged to become a Jagdverband of six battalions, into which nearly 2,000 men of former Brandenburg units and individual volunteers were transferred.

One of Skorzeny's most able officers at this time was the young SS-Untersturmführer Walter Girg, who in late August 1944 was serving as a platoon commander in 1./ SS-Jäger Bataillon 502. Girg had been tasked with leading a reconnaissance mission deep into enemy territory, to disrupt supply lines and block passes through the Carpathians that would be useful to the advancing Red Army. Having achieved some success in disrupting the enemy advance and also saving some of the ethnic Germans living in the region, Girg disguised himself as a Romanian and took part in the 'celebration' of the Soviet advance. Subsequently, however, he and his men were discovered and taken prisoner near Brasov. After severe beatings the Germans were being lined up to be shot when an artillery barrage distracted the Soviets, and the Germans made a run for it. Girg escaped despite being wounded in the foot while making his getaway, and the information that he and his men had gathered during the course of the operation was instrumental in allowing the Germans to avoid the encirclement of an entire corps. Girg received a well-deserved promotion to SS-Obersturmführer.

Thereafter Girg took command of an armoured unit operating behind enemy lines using captured Soviet tanks. On one occasion, while making his way back to the German lines through Soviet-held territory, Girg was intercepted near Kolberg by German troops who suspected him of being one of the so-called 'Seydlitz' troops (communist-sympathizing German turncoats recruited by the Soviets from among prisoners of war). His captors refused to believe him when he explained his true identity; he was given a summary trial for treason and sentenced to death, and a signal from Skorzeny confirming Girg's true identity arrived only just in time to prevent his execution.

Walter Girg was promoted to SS-Hauptsturmführer, and after Operation *Panzerfaust* (see below) in October 1944 he was awarded the Knight's Cross. Thereafter it was said that even when in disguise during covert operations Girg wore his decoration at all times, hidden under a scarf when necessary. He survived the war, after receiving the Oakleaves to his Knight's Cross.

Skorzeny's next major covert operation was the above-mentioned Operation *Panzerfaust*. The SD had learned that Admiral Miklós Horthy, the Regent of German-allied Hungary, had sent Lieutenant-General Faragho to Moscow to seek a separate peace with the Soviet Union. Skorzeny's objective was to occupy the Hungarian seat of government, on Castle Hill in Budapest; it was hoped that a powerful German show of force would intimidate the Hungarians into remaining loyal to Germany under the leadership of Ferenc Szálasi of the extreme right-wing Arrow-Cross movement. Skorzeny's force would include SS-Jagdverband Mitte, a battalion of SS paratroops, another of Luftwaffe paratroops and a battalion of motorized infantry. Skorzeny was issued with written orders signed by Hitler personally, instructing all military and state agencies to provide whatever support or assistance he requested (this document made Skorzeny temporarily one of the most powerful men in the Reich).

Initially, Skorzeny and some of his staff officers travelled incognito to Budapest posing as civilians. There, it was decided to abduct Horthy's surviving son (also named

Miklós, and party to his father's intentions) as a hostage to ensure the Regent's co-operation. On 15 October, while he was engaged in a meeting with Yugoslav agents, the younger Horthy was seized after a brief gun battle with his Hungarian guards, and was later flown to Germany.

The approaches to Castle Hill were mined and its garrison reinforced as the Hungarians prepared to defy Hitler; at 1300hrs Admiral Horthy issued a proclamation announcing that Hungary had concluded a separate peace treaty with the USSR and that the Hungarian Army at the front should cease fire.

Skorzeny was faced with a possibly difficult and costly assault on the well-defended fortress of Castle Hill. The German reaction to the Hungarian proclamation began with sealing off railway stations and other strategic locations to ensure that German military traffic heading for the front could pass unimpeded. A cordon of Waffen-SS troops was also placed around Castle Hill, drawn from the 22. SS-Freiwilligen Kavallerie Division *Maria Theresia*, which included a number of Hungarian volunteers; the army's Panzer Brigades 109 and 110 also occupied the city, and Skorzeny determined that an assault on the palace precincts would begin at 0600hrs the following day. He rebuffed an attempt to parley by Hungarian forces on Castle Hill, insisting that only a retraction of

1. SS-Panzer Division had 34 Panzer IVs with the 6. and 7. Kompanien of its Panzer Regiment 1 at the beginning of the Ardennes offensive. This Ausf. J belonged to 7. Kompanie. (Osprey Publishing © D. Parker/ R. Volstad)

the national ceasefire was acceptable; at 5pm the order was duly countermanded by the army chief-of-staff, Colonel-General János Vörös.

At 0600hrs on 16 October, Skorzeny led forward a column of Waffen-SS troops supported by a number of giant King Tiger tanks from the army's schwere Panzer Abteilung 503, and by engineers with some tracked, remote-control 'Goliath' demolition crawlers. The German column moved up the hill without challenge and reached the plateau outside the castle; three Hungarian tanks sited there wisely chose not to engage the King Tigers, which then smashed their way through a stone barricade into the castle courtyard.

Skorzeny and his men ran into the castle, and ordered a surprised Hungarian officer to escort them to the general-commandant, who acceded to Skorzeny's demands to surrender the castle and avoid major bloodshed. The entire operation had taken only some 30 minutes and had involved only very limited casualties in minor skirmishing: the Hungarians lost three dead and 15 wounded, and the Germans four dead and 12 wounded. Admiral Horthy officially abdicated at 0815hrs; he slipped out of the castle before it was stormed and surrendered himself to SS-Obergruppenführer Karl von Pfeffer-Wildenbruch, the Austrian commander of IX SS-Gebirgs Korps. Skorzeny was

SdKfz 138/1, SS-Panzergrenadier Regiment 2. Each of the two Panzergrenadier regiments of Panzer Division 44 (a division based on the 1944 organization) was supposed to have a company of six self-propelled infantry guns. (Osprey Publishing © D. Parker/ R. Volstad)

The *Leibstandarte* Division earned the lasting enmity of US forces for its execution of 80 US prisoners of war at Malmédy on 17 December 1944.

The *Leibstandarte* Division earned the lasting enmity of US forces for its execution of 80 US prisoners of war at Malmédy on 17 December 1944.

subsequently ordered to collect Horthy from Pfeffer–Wildenbruch, and personally escorted him back to Germany.

The success of this latest mission brought Skorzeny promotion to Oberstleutnant, and the award of the German Cross in Gold. After the award was made personally by Hitler at the Führerhauptquartier on 22 October, the Führer briefed him on plans for the forthcoming offensive in the Ardennes and discussed what was to be Skorzeny's part in this operation.

Under the code-name Operation *Greif*, Skorzeny was to create – in just five weeks – a force designated Panzer Brigade 150; the designation was based on the intent that the unit would be equipped with substantial numbers of captured Allied armoured vehicles. Skorzeny was to assemble a force dressed in captured US uniforms and riding in captured vehicles; its mission would be to infiltrate Allied lines once these had been disrupted by the initial armoured breakthrough, and advance in the guise of retreating US troops to seize two strategic bridges over the River Meuse. While the bulk of Skorzeny's brigade would be committed to pushing through to capture the designated targets, smaller commando teams of English-speakers, travelling in captured jeeps, would carry out in-depth reconnaissance, posing as US troops as they spread false information, disrupted communications and generally caused as much alarm and confusion as possible. (It is interesting to note that when orders went out requesting English-speaking volunteers, lax German security revealed that they were to work with Skorzeny, yet when the Allied intelligence services became aware of these appeals they failed to grasp their significance.)

Unsurprisingly, in the event nowhere near the required number of vehicles for the planned three battalions became available at the Grafenwöhr training base. The brigade would go into action with just one captured American M4 Sherman tank, backed by German PzKpfw V Panthers and StuG III assault guns modified with thin sheet metal panels to approximate the silhouette of American AFVs, and finished in olive drab paintwork and large white stars. Only four captured American armoured cars and two half-tracks were available, and these too had to be supplemented by disguised German vehicles. Larger numbers of Allied 'softskin' vehicles were scraped together, but not nearly as many serviceable cars and trucks as requested. Suitable captured uniforms and weapons were also in woefully short supply, and only key personnel could be properly equipped.

Quite apart from materiel shortages, it proved impossible to build a unit with the required strength of 3,300 men from specially recruited volunteers in the time available. Skorzeny managed to enlist only about 400 English speakers, of whom only around ten spoke perfect, unaccented English and had a sufficient knowledge of slang to pass themselves off as Americans. Many of the brigade's soldiers were capable of nothing more than issuing basic military commands in English, backed up with suitable profanities. An obvious additional problem was that men – often sailors – recruited solely for their linguistic ability had to be given a crash course in communications, demolitions and all the other necessary combat skills.

Even scaled down to two battalions, Skorzeny's command had to incorporate a company from his SS-Jagdverband Mitte and two from SS-Fallschirmjäger Bataillon 600. Two battalions of Luftwaffe paratroopers, plus army troops from a tank, a tank-destroyer, a reconnaissance and a signals company were also transferred into Panzer Brigade 150, as were artillery gunners, engineers and brigade staff officers. The unit finally numbered around 2,500 men in total, of whom only about 500 were Waffen-SS personnel. They were separated among three battle groups designated Kampfgruppen X, Y and Z (the last two commanded by army officers), and tasked with seizing the Meuse bridges at Amay, Huy and/or Andenne. The jeep-mounted disguised 'commando' teams (Einheit Stielau) were to blow ammunition dumps and unwanted bridges, remove or change Allied road and minefield signs, spread false information, reconnoitre in depth and radio their findings, and also provide spearhead scouts for conventional units.

On 16 December 1944, the three battlegroups of Panzer Brigade 150 went into action in the Ardennes, following immediately behind the lead elements of 1. and 12. SS-Panzer Divisions and 12. Volksgrenadier Division, with the intention of branching out along side roads as these reached various objectives. In fact, initial progress was extremely slow, delayed by very severe traffic congestion on the roads and stiffer enemy

PzKpfw V Ausf. G Panther,
SS-Panzer Regiment 1. 1. and 2.
Kompanien of SS-Panzer
Regiment 1 were equipped with
Panthers as part of Kampfgruppe
Peiper in December 1944: they
could field 37 Panthers at the
beginning of the offensive.
(Osprey Publishing © D. Parker/
R. Volstad)

resistance than expected. It was immediately clear to Skorzeny that capturing the Meuse bridges was completely impossible. On the night of 17/18 December he sought, and was given, approval for the cancellation of that part of Operation *Greif*, and his brigade was reunited and placed at the disposal of I SS-Panzer Korps as a conventional unit.

The brigade's first objective was to seize the key road junction at Malmédy. Earlier intelligence proved outdated, and when Kampfgruppen X and Y launched their attacks on 21 December they ran into unexpectedly strong resistance backed up by heavy artillery fire. The battered Kampfgruppe Y was forced to withdraw almost immediately, and although Kampfgruppe X (led by SS-Hauptsturmführer von Fölkersam, the former Brandenburger who had distinguished himself at Maikop) persisted for several hours it too was eventually forced to pull back, von Fölkersam himself being badly wounded. While making his way to the headquarters of 1. SS-Panzer Division to report, Skorzeny was hit in the head by artillery splinters and almost blinded. Regardless of doctors insisting that he be evacuated he refused to leave his men until he was summoned to the Führerhauptquartier to give his report on Operation *Greif*. Despite the failure of the operation, Hitler was pleased with Skorzeny's performance and awarded him the Honour Roll Clasp of the German Army.

Panzer Brigade 150 remained with the *Leibstandarte* Division until 28 December, when it was withdrawn from the front for transfer back to Grafenwöhr. There it was officially disbanded, and the surviving non-SS troops returned to their original units.

Whilst the bulk of Panzer Brigade 150 failed to achieve their objectives, some of Skorzeny's commando teams did succeed in carrying out their designated tasks. One of the teams reached the bridge at Huy, and managed to divert a US armoured column onto a long and pointless detour away from the frontline. Other teams succeeded in blocking roads and causing general confusion; one even managed to persuade an American unit busy setting up defensive positions to retreat in order to avoid being cut off by fictitious German movements on their flanks. So great was the American paranoia over the actions of these commandos that many US troops were arrested by their own side on suspicion of being 'German spies', and some firefights broke out between different groups of US soldiers.

The fate of those members of Skorzeny's Einheit Stielau who were captured is exemplified by one such three-man team – Unteroffizier Pernass, Oberfähnrich Billing and Gefreiter Schmidt. Stopped by a US Military Police

The attempt to use SS troops in US uniforms in the Ardennes offensive ended disastrously for many Waffen-SS soldiers – this man is about to be executed by firing squad as a spy.

checkpoint and unable to give the correct password, they were immediately arrested. Since they were wearing American uniforms, and were in possession of fake identity documents and large sums in US currency, they were tried by court-martial as spies; all were found guilty, and executed by firing squad on 23 December 1944. (It also seems that significant numbers of German soldiers were captured wearing – simply for the sake of warmth – such items as American field jackets, greatcoats and winter overboots in conjunction with their own uniforms. In the atmosphere of 'spy mania' created by Einheit Stielau's real and rumoured activities, they often paid for this booty with their lives.)

During the final months of the war, Skorzeny was ordered to form a defensive bridgehead at Schwedt on the River Oder, a few kilometres west of Königsberg. He travelled eastwards from Friedenthal (still using some of the captured American jeeps), and on arrival at Schwedt he found that in addition to his own Jagdverband he would have to face the might of the Red Army with a battalion of pioneers and three grossly under-strength battalions of elderly reservists.

Kampfgruppe X at Malmédy, 21 December 1944. The Panthers modified to represent M10s for Panzerbrigade 150 were painted in olive drab and displayed thickly ringed white stars on the front armoured plate and on both sides of the turret. Like all vehicles 'modified' for Panzerbrigade 150, the Panther/M10 displayed a yellow triangle at the rear. (Osprey Publishing © D. Parker/ R. Volstad)

At this time the roads were clogged with civilian refugees fleeing the advancing Soviets, as well as considerable numbers of soldiers from fragmented units trying to make their way westwards. Sending his reconnaissance platoons over onto the east bank of the Oder, he ordered his troops to set up positions on the exit roads from Königsberg and escort both civilian and military personnel safely to Kolberg. Here, military personnel were assembled at the local barracks and those who were fit for combat were assigned to Skorzeny's Jagdverband. Though the quality of many of these odds and ends was distinctly variable Skorzeny was happy to have the additional resources. Reinforcements in the form of a regiment of Reichsarbeitsdienst (RAD; Reich Labour Corps) troops and a battalion of Volkssturm from Hamburg also arrived, and were put to work straight away helping the pioneers construct defensive fortifications.

The arrival of SS paratroopers, three batteries of Luftwaffe Flak and three companies of surplus Luftwaffe personnel gave Skorzeny a significant boost, as did the discovery of

ABOVE: Preparation for attack by Kampfgruppe X, at Ligneuville, on 21 December. SS-Hauptsturmführer von Foelkersoam (centre), the commander of Kampfgruppe X, consults with an Oberleutnant Deier (left) and an unnamed 'Special Guide' dressed entirely as a US soldier. (Osprey Publishing © D. Parker/ R. Volstad)

German POWs look distinctly humbled in the presence of US armour. Even after the Malmédy massacre, however, the Waffen-SS prisoners could expect more humane treatment in Western Europe than on the Eastern Front.

a factory nearby with a stock of 7.5cm anti-tank guns. An outer perimeter was established on the eastern bank of the Oder, and part of Skorzeny's force was despatched to help defend Königsberg. Other reinforcements that gradually filtered through to Skorzeny included a newly raised and inexperienced battalion from Fallschirmpanzer Korps *Hermann Göring* and, albeit temporarily, an assault gun detachment sent by Reichsführer-SS Himmler; but there was little chance of Skorzeny being able to hold back the Red Army. Soon advancing Soviet units had penetrated Königsberg's defensive rings, and although the troops sent by Skorzeny made a spirited attempt to hold open the links between that city and the bridgehead at Kolberg, Königsberg had been surrounded by late January 1945. (The German defenders were only finally forced to surrender on 9 April.)

Skorzeny's troops continued to defend their bridgehead robustly, launching several local counter-attacks with temporary success, but in the event Skorzeny himself would not see the final events at Kolberg unfold, since he was ordered to return to Berlin on 28 February. There he received orders to transfer the staff element of his Jagdverband to the so-called 'Alpenfestung', the mythical 'Alpine Redoubt'. During a conversation with Hitler in late March, he learned that he was to be awarded the Oakleaves to his Knight's Cross to reward his performance on the Oder front; the award was officially conferred on 9 April. Skorzeny took no further part in any major military operations, and surrendered to US troops on 20 May 1945.

Skorzeny's reputation led to his immediate arrest, and he was subjected to interrogation over several months regarding his wartime activities, both real and imaginary. When he was taken to Nuremberg as a witness during the trials Allied paranoia over his reputation was reflected in wild rumours of a rescue attempt, leading to increased security precautions. Skorzeny's status changed from witness to accused in July 1947, when he was charged with war crimes in relation to the Ardennes offensive, but all these charges were soon dropped. His captivity now rested solely on his being a former officer in the Waffen-SS, a category subject to immediate arrest.

After the war, the most influential leader of Germany's special-forces troops spent three years in prison awaiting 'de-Nazification'; he was a victim of his own reputation, but all war-crimes charges against him had been dropped for lack of evidence. Never formally released from captivity, Skorzeny was helped to escape on 27 July 1948 (allegedly, by some of his former troops masquerading as US MPs!), and made his way to Spain. The mystique surrounding him gave birth to wild rumours of his being behind the so-called 'Odessa' movement which helped suspected SS war criminals to escape, involvement in training Arab military forces in their struggle against Israel, and the elimination of former SS men who were prepared to give evidence against those wanted by the Allies.

This trooper, captured by soldiers of the US 82nd Airborne Division, illustrates the extreme youth of many of the Waffen-SS soldiers by the late years of the war.

ABOVE: Skorzeny commandos, 1944–45. 1: SS-Obersturmbannführer Skorzeny; Schwedt bridgehead, February 1945. A photo taken on the Oder front shows Skorzeny looking somewhat haggard, and without his distinctive moustache; in the last week of December 1944 he had suffered another head wound from a shell fragment. 2: SS-Oberscharführer, SS-Jagdverband Mitte; Budapest, October 1944. Photos show that nothing distinguished the men of this unit from any other Waffen-SS infantry – indeed, apart from the M1942 'raw edge' steel helmet without insignia, this senior NCO has a distinctly early-war look. He is armed with the MP 40, and carries a Panzerfaust 60. 3: SS-Hauptsturmführer Walter Girg, SS-Jagdverband Mitte; Budapest, October 1944. This swashbuckling captain, renowned for daring operations behind Soviet lines, would be decorated with the Knight's Cross after Operation *Panzerfaust*. (Osprey Publishing © Mike Chappell)

In 1970 Skorzeny was diagnosed with a cancerous tumour on the spine. The operation for its removal left him paralysed below the waist, but by sheer strength of will he had learned to walk again within six months. The surgery had only delayed the inevitable however, and on 6 July 1975 he finally succumbed to the disease.

SS PARATROOPERS

The origins of the SS-Fallschirmjäger Bataillon lay in the disciplinary processes within the Waffen-SS, and the concept of *Bewährungsschützen* – 'disciplinary soldiers' or B-Soldaten. These were men who had committed offences serious enough to warrant trial by court-martial (as opposed to minor offences dealt with within the unit), and who in many cases had been sentenced either to long periods of imprisonment or, in extreme cases, to death. Such sentences were usually carried out at the SS penal camp at Danzig-Matzkau.

In August 1943, Himmler issued an order that up to 600 of these men were to be transferred to a new paratroop unit and given the opportunity to redeem themselves in combat – this despite his having been advised that only a small proportion of them were considered suitable for training as paratroopers. It was originally intended that the new

Tank '204' was one of the six Waffen-SS Tigers which succeeded in reaching the La Gleize area during the Ardennes offensive. In position in an orchard at the edge of the village, it covered the north-east approaches. Painted in the 'ambush scheme' (as were all the 15 Tigers possessed by schwere SS-Panzer Abteilung 501 on the eve of the offensive), it showed the corps insignia on the left front armour. (Osprey Publishing © D. Parker/ R. Volstad)

unit would be used primarily on anti-partisan operations, and indeed the unit's first title was SS-Fallschirm Banden-Jäger Bataillon (SS Parachute Partisan-Hunter Battalion). However, by the time of the official announcement of the formation of the unit, on 6 September 1943, the title had changed to simply SS-Fallschirmjäger Bataillon.

The men allocated to the battalion were sent to the Luftwaffe's Paratroop School No. 3 at Mataruška Banja to begin their jump training. Not all the personnel were military prisoners; a cadre of regular Waffen-SS combat veterans were also transferred into the unit, some of whom were decidedly unhappy to find themselves serving alongside convicts. The fact that many of the disciplinary cases were indeed unsuitable was confirmed when around 100 of them were returned to the SS authorities, either as being physically unfit or, in some cases, having being caught selling equipment (including weapons) on the black market. After completing their training at the Hungarian airborne base at Papa, to which Fallschirmschule III had relocated, the remaining men of the SS Paratroop Battalion were allocated to anti-partisan duties in Yugoslavia, and during this period the unit was officially renamed as SS-Fallschirmjäger Bataillon 500.

The unit's first real test came during Operation *Maibaum* (Maytree) in April–May 1944 when, under the command of SS-Hauptsturmführer Kurt Rybka, it assisted V SS-Gebirgs Korps in an operation intended to destroy Tito's III Partisan Corps near Srebrenica in Bosnia. Partisan units attempting to advance into western Serbia were halted by the SS troops and suffered heavy losses.

Almost immediately afterwards the unit began preparing for their next operation, as the Germans prepared to follow up their success with an attack on Tito's own headquarters at Drvar. The plan envisaged various army and Waffen-SS units converging on the area from north, south, east and west, whilst SS-Fallschirmjäger Bataillon 500 parachuted directly into Drvar. A total of some 280 men, divided into three groups, were to parachute into the immediate area of Tito's headquarters in the hills to the west of Drvar, and attempt to capture the partisan leader. At the same time a further six groups were to land by glider, with subsidiary targets including the capture of the British, American and Soviet military missions with the partisans and also the radio station at Drvar.

The operation began in the early morning of 25 May 1944 and almost immediately hit serious problems. Many Fallschirmjäger were injured during landing on the rocky slopes, and the glider-borne element was particularly unlucky, one entire squad being killed when their glider crashed. Rybka himself was seriously wounded by grenade fragments; his troops eventually secured the cave in which Tito's headquarters had been located and the immediate surroundings, but all that they captured was his new dress uniform.

Waffen-SS troops of the *Leibstandarte* Division march along an Italian road in the summer of 1943. The division was briefly deployed to Italy following the Italian armistice with the Allies.

Strong partisan forces were still in the area, and the SS-Fallschirmjäger found themselves under increasing pressure as their adversaries attempted to recapture the lost ground. Casualties were heavy, but the paratroopers got some support from Stuka dive-bombers and some airdropped ammunition resupply. By the following day troops of 7. SS-Freiwilligen Gebirgs Division *Prinz Eugen* were arriving, and the partisan forces were finally forced to withdraw. The survivors of SS-Fallschirmjäger Bataillon 500 remained in the area, carrying out numerous anti-partisan sweeps along with mountain troops from *Prinz Eugen* before, in June, the battered battalion was withdrawn to Ljubljana for rest and recuperation. Around 850 men from the battalion had taken part in the action at Drvar, of whom only about 250 remained in the ranks.

Command passed to SS-Hauptsturmführer Siegfried Milius and work began on rebuilding the unit. Reinforcements arrived, in the shape of men who had been left out of battle, fresh volunteers and more probationary troops. The problems involved in allocating too many men with bad disciplinary records to what should have been an elite combat unit had been appreciated, and only the 'best' of the B-Soldaten were now posted in. (Others who were considered 'redeemable' would join Skorzeny's Jagdverband, and the worst of what remained would be sent to the infamous SS-Sonderkommando Dirlewanger (see next chapter). The battalion was subsequently sent to Gotenhafen in East Prussia, from where it had been planned to use the SS-Fallschirmjäger in an operation to the Aaland Islands to block the Gulf of Bothnia. The operation was cancelled, and instead the paratroopers found themselves attached to III (germanisches) SS-Panzer Korps under SS-Obergruppenführer Felix Steiner on the

ABOVE: SS paratroops, seen in the uniforms from the late war period. 1: SS-Jäger, SS-Fallschirmjäger Bataillon 500; Bucharest, October 1944. Parading after the successful Operation *Panzerfaust*, this man is identifiable only by his Waffen-SS belt buckle. He wears the Luftwaffe paratroop helmet without insignia; the Luftwaffe second-type jump smock in splinter camouflage pattern, again without insignia; field-grey jump trousers, and front-lacing jump boots. For parade his equipment is reduced to the belt and two sets of triple rifle ammunition pouches, and he presents arms with the Mauser 98k rifle. 2: SS-Sturmmann, SS-Fallschirmjäger Bataillon 500; Memel bend, Baltic front, July 1944. This senior private MG 42 gunner also closely resembles an air force paratrooper; he is identifiable to his service only by his buckle, and by the fact that the field-grey collar of his M1943 tunic is turned outside his jump smock, exposing the collar patches of service and rank. As the gun 'No.1' he has a holstered Walther P 38 pistol for self-protection. 3: SS-Oberscharführer, SS-Fallschirmjäger Bataillon 600; Eastern Front, November 1944. This figure is based on a photo of the decorated senior NCO Walter Hummel wearing M1936-style service dress, complete with the enlisted ranks' service cap with infantry-white piping. (Osprey Publishing © Mike Chappell)

ABOVE: This plate recreates the appearance of a three-man mortar team from SS-Fallschirmjäger Bataillon 500 on the Baltic front in summer 1944. The 8cm schwere Granatwerfer 34 fired 3.5kg high-explosive or smoke projectiles out to ranges of about 2,500m, and a practised crew could average some 15 rounds per minute – if the available ammunition held out. (Osprey Publishing © Mike Chappell)

Narva front, where some albeit temporary success was achieved in halting several Soviet advances. The battalion was sent to Lithuania in July 1944, and attached to a Kampfgruppe from the elite Panzer Korps *Grossdeutschland* for an operation to relieve the city of Vilnius. The German force succeeded in penetrating Soviet-held territory, reaching Vilnius and thereafter escorting thousands of cut-off German troops back to the relative safety of German-held territory. Though the battalion suffered only minor losses during this operation, subsequent heavy fighting south-west of Vilnius saw the approximately 260 men who then remained with the battalion reduced to only about 70 survivors. These were transferred to Sakiai, where the unit was to receive around 100 much-needed replacements.

At the end of August 1944 the remnants of the battalion were moved first to East Prussia and then on to Austria, where they were placed at the disposal of Otto Skorzeny. Skorzeny employed them during Operation *Panzerfaust* in Budapest on 15 October, when the SS paratroopers took part in the successful occupation of Castle Hill in Budapest; they infiltrated passages under the castle, and from these into the War and Interior ministries.

On 1 October SS-Fallschirmjäger Bataillon 500 had been officially disbanded, and its survivors became the nucleus of a new unit, SS-Fallschirmjäger Bataillon 600.

The reason for the change was that the '500' number series was typically used for probationary units, and Himmler had decided that he no longer wished the unit to be 'tainted' with the implication of second-rate character. Indeed, the percentage of disciplinary cases within the battalion had decreased by now from around 70 per cent to 30 per cent, and even these were considered the most promising of the potential material. Recruits were by now mostly regular personnel rather than military convicts, including men from the army and Kriegsmarine as well as the Waffen-SS, and by November unit strength was back up to just under 700 men.

The battalion's association with Skorzeny was made permanent on 10 November, when SS-Fallschirmjäger Bataillon 600 was formally absorbed into the SS-Jagdverbände. At the end of January 1945 the unit formed part of Skorzeny's force for the defensive bridgehead at Schwedt on the Oder; the paratroopers were positioned in the Königsberg area, operating with SS-Jagdverband Mitte around Grabow. There, on 4 February, its 3. Kompanie was completely overrun by the Soviets, suffering heavy casualties; the survivors took part in efforts to retake the city a few days later, but after some initial progress the battered German formations were once again forced out of Königsberg. The battalion's defensive positions around Grabow came under repeated attack by Soviet armour, and many tanks fell victim to the *Panzerfäuste* of the SS paratroopers.

It was decided that SS-Fallschirmjäger Bataillon 600 and SS-Jagdverband Mitte were to be temporarily merged to form an SS regiment, which would be held as the reserve for Skorzeny's Schwedt bridgehead. Shortly afterwards, however, Hitler decided that the defenders of the bridgehead could be withdrawn. SS-Fallschirmjäger Bataillon 600 was then moved southwards to another east-bank bridgehead at Zehenden to the south-west of Königsberg. Here, on 6 March, in its merged form with Jagdverband Mitte, the battalion joined a number of other smaller Waffen-SS units in a new SS-Kampfgruppe Solar, which came under the control of the newly formed Division zbV 610 (Special Duties Division 610) – by now, of course, the term 'division' was purely nominal.

On the evening of the same day a stray Soviet artillery shell hit an explosive charge on the bridge over the Oder near Alt-Cüstrinchen which had been prepared for demolition. The bridge was destroyed, effectively cutting off the SS-Fallschirmjäger on the east bank as the Red Army approached. The next two weeks passed quietly enough, but on 25 March a new Soviet offensive began. For two days the SS troops held out against overwhelmingly superior opposition, but on the third day, after sustaining huge losses, they were forced to withdraw. Due to the loss of the bridge the troops were forced to swim the Oder, many being lost to drowning or enemy fire.

In the weeks that followed, the battalion was yet again reinforced and brought up to a respectable strength of well over 800 men. In mid-April 1945 the unit was absorbed into a new SS-Kampfgruppe Harzer, in which it temporarily became part of SS-*Polizei* Panzergrenadier Regiment 7, assigned to the bridgehead around Eberswalde north-east of Berlin. This was intended to threaten the flank of the advancing Soviets, but the Red Army's advance was so fast and powerful that the proposed attack was cancelled. In late April the battalion found itself assigned to XXXVI Panzer Korps in the defence of the area around Prenzlau, among German units by now at only around 10 per cent of their nominal strength.

The battalion was pushed back to positions west of Fürstenwerder and then to Neubrandenburg, where on 28 April it was involved in heavy defensive fighting before withdrawing west in an effort to avoid Soviet captivity. The remnants of the unit were under constant attack as they withdrew westwards; in one engagement with Soviet horsed cavalry at Neuruppin, the 400 or so SS-Fallschirmjäger who engaged the enemy suffered more than 50 per cent losses. The survivors, numbering fewer than 200 men, surrendered to US forces at Hagenow on 2 May 1945.

The SS special forces, and the prestigious Waffen-SS divisions described in this chapter, can give the false impression that all the Waffen-SS was an elite. Yet as the next chapter will demonstrate, during the late war years other Waffen-SS formations emerged which would have short, and far from auspicious, war records.

DIVERSIFICATION AND DESTRUCTION

LEFT: The Warsaw ghetto uprising in 1943 saw SS and security forces put down the revolt in the most brutal fashion. The fate of captives such as these was typically either summary execution or death in the concentration camps.

Already acknowledged in the previous chapter, the years 1941–44 saw a radical change in the nature of the Waffen-SS. In 1941 the battlefield prowess of the original SS divisions on the Russian Front prompted their expansion. Limited in his ability to compete with the other three armed services for German (*Reichsdeutsche*) conscripts, Himmler, at first redesignated and retrained security personnel of the Totenkopfstandarte as combat troops. The constant need for recruits, both to replace battle casualties and to police the enormous areas coming under German occupation, then led Himmler and his recruitment chief, SS-Obergruppenführer Gottlob Berger, to explore two main sources of manpower outside the borders of the Reich. The first were non-German but acceptably 'Germanic' volunteers from the occupied countries of North-West Europe, who initially proved themselves in the ranks of the *Wiking* Division in 1941 (see previous chapter). The Waffen-SS continued to recruit there; the survivors of the original regimental-size volunteer 'legions' of 1941–42 were later rebuilt into brigades in 1943; and finally into (at least nominal) divisions in 1944, although this involved adding recruits from various other more or less arbitrary sources. The second source of manpower after racially 'Germanic' volunteers was a range of '*Volksdeutsche*' – men of distant German descent, from communities in the border provinces of the old Austro-Hungarian Empire. Units raised both from Germanic and *Volksdeutsche* recruits were normally designated SS-Freiwilligen (SS Volunteer), and in many cases they were given national emblems on the right hand collar patch – although in practice many wore the standard SS-runes.

Distinct from the Waffen-SS divisions, which served at the front under the command of army higher formations, Himmler retained under his own control SS combat units designated Kommandostab *Reichsführer-SS*. Deployed behind the frontlines in Russia in 1941–42 on 'anti-partisan' duties, this force consisted of one cavalry and two motorized infantry brigades; the former later evolved into the 8. SS-Kavallerie Division *Florian Geyer*. The infantry brigades initially consisted of former Totenkopfstandarten redesignated as 'SS infantry regiments': 1. SS-Infanterie Brigade (mot.) with SS-Infanterie Regiments 8 and 10, and 2. SS-Infanterie Brigade (mot.) with SS-Infanterie Regiments 4 and 14. These brigades were used as a pool of replacements for the frontline divisions; and it was under their control that the first foreign SS volunteer legions were introduced to active service.

In April 1941 some 2,500 Dutch and Flemish-Belgian volunteers were formed into Freiwilligen Standarte Nord-West (Volunteer Regiment North-West). By early autumn the Freikorps *Danmark* and Freiwilligen Legion *Norwegen* were raised in Scandinavia. The Nord-West Regiment was divided into the Freiwilligen Legion *Flandern* and Freiwilligen Legion *Niederlande* in September. After training, the *Flandern* and *Niederlande* Legions joined the 2. SS-Infanterie Brigade (mot.) behind the Leningrad

front in midwinter 1941/42, followed in February 1942 by the Norwegian Legion. In May 1942 the Freikorps *Danmark* arrived at the front and was temporarily attached to the 3. SS-Division *Totenkopf*; subsequently the 1. SS-Infanterie Brigade (mot.) took over the Norwegian and Danish legions.

Croatian recruits swear allegiance to the Waffen-SS. The loyalty of these soldiers was decidedly shaky – some 2,000 men of the *Handschar* Division deserted in September 1944 alone.

Reviewing this sudden influx of foreign personnel, the first question is why on earth, within weeks of seeing their own countries overrun by the German armed forces, should hundreds of volunteers from Norway, Denmark, Holland and Belgium flock to join the ranks of the Waffen-SS? Austrians and Czechs were already being absorbed into the SS prior to 1940, both countries having had fairly extensive Nazi parties of their own before their almost bloodless take-overs. In addition, substantial parts of the populations of both countries were essentially 'German', had seen the effects of Hitler's economic miracle, and wanted to take part in the 'great adventure'.

But why others – particularly before the invasion of Russia gave an excuse to anyone who was anti-communist – should have wanted to join up remains even today something of a mystery. What is fascinating is that many are proud of the fact, even after being vilified by their fellow countrymen following their release from internment camp or prison.

Inevitably, some were politically inspired, just as were the Italian blackshirts who continued to fight in SS units after the overthrow of Mussolini and Italy's surrender in

1943. It must be remembered that extreme right-wing, anti-Semitic and anti-communist parties were not restricted to Germany, Austria, Spain and Italy in the 1920s and 30s, and even the United Kingdom had its share of similarly minded fanatics in Oswald Moseley's blackshirt fascist movement.

Politics were only part of the answer, however. Another part was, strangely, the fact of occupation itself. Many men, recognizing the sheer military virtuosity of the German armed forces and the ineffectual resistance of their own, were keen to join such a magnificent fighting machine once the opportunity arose – an opportunity which the chief Waffen-SS recruiting officer, Gottlob Berger, was eager to exploit because it expanded his own and Himmler's empire without treading on the toes of the army. Most people in the occupied countries – to begin with, at least – were also impressed by the smart turn-out and correct behaviour of the occupying forces. Finally, it must be admitted that, like many farm labourers in Germany itself, many enlisted in the Waffen-SS for the same reason that for decades had drawn others into the French Foreign Legion: for adventure, glamour and travel, or to escape from problems at home (it should be noted rather ironically that quite a few Waffen-SS men found sanctuary from post-war prosecution in the Legion).

Most of the early Western European foreign volunteers eventually found themselves in either the *Wiking* or *Nordland* Divisions, where they discovered that things were not quite as rosy as they had been painted. Their officers were predominantly German, and unfortunately for those like Steiner who were trying to create something like a pan-European precursor of the North Atlantic Treaty Organization (NATO), the new recruits from the occupied countries quickly found that they were regarded as second-class citizens in the Waffen-SS. This was partly because they swore a slightly different

LEFT: 'Nordic' volunteers, 1941–44. 1: SS-Sturmmann, Finnischen Freiwilligen Bataillon der Waffen-SS, autumn 1941. 2: Legions-Unterscharführer, Freiwilligen Legion *Norwegen*, summer 1942. 3: SS-Rottenführer, Britisches Freikorps, 1944. Probably the smallest of all national contingents, the BFC was never more than about 30 strong. This tawdry little group were enlisted in British and Commonwealth military and merchant marine prison camps in January–October 1943, in return for alcohol, access to prostitutes and very limited freedom. Ill-disciplined, and in some cases of very low intelligence, they were more trouble than they were worth, and even their propaganda value was minimal. A section were trained as combat engineers; and a handful of men were briefly attached to the reconnaissance battalion of the 11. Division *Nordland* near Angermünde in March 1945. They were rejected (reportedly by the corps commander SS-Obergruppenführer Felix Steiner, in person), and wandered pointlessly until they were captured or gave themselves up. Only one or possibly two British citizens did fight with *Nordland* in Berlin. The captured BFC survivors were tried, and served prison sentences suitable to their individual guilt. Despite its tiny size, an effort was clearly made to provide this squalid gang with a full set of special insignia; original examples do not survive, but a few clear wartime photographs confirm their use. This corporal wears M1942 uniform with a single-button M1943 field cap. His right hand collar patch shows three left-facing heraldic 'lions' (leopards) passant guardant. A Union flag armshield is worn above a machine-embroidered cuffband bearing the Gothic-lettered English language title 'British Free Corps'. The BFC were issued P 38 pistols, but no ammunition. 4: SS-Hauptscharführer, Ersatzkompanie, Freikorps *Danmark*, autumn 1941. (Osprey Publishing © Stephen Andrew)

oath, partly because their mastery of the German language was often insufficient, leading to misunderstandings, and partly because many German SS officers *did* regard them as second class and resented their own appointment to command them.

This resulted in many of the volunteers feeling they were being victimized, for example by being given extra duties or docked pay for imaginary transgressions while the German soldiers alongside whom they were soon to be fighting got away scot free with similar offences. Felix Steiner did everything he could to counteract this situation, even to the issuance of standing written instructions, but it did not really improve until the new 'European Germanic' formations went into combat in Russia. Then the German attitude began to change drastically as the men proved themselves in combat, the *Wiking* Division in particular ending the war with as fine a combat record as any.

With the expansion of German operations into Greece and Yugoslavia in 1941, and with Operation *Barbarossa* from June of the same year, a new well of SS manpower began to be tapped, in the form of blatantly non-Germanic recruits from the Balkans, Baltic States and occupied Soviet Union. Such formations were designated Waffen

SS forces in France advance forward on a half-track to meet the Allied advance. Such vehicular movements became extremely vulnerable to Allied air attacks.

Divisionen der SS (Armed Divisions of the SS) in 1944, to distance them from the original *Reichsdeutsche* of the plain 'SS Divisions' and the racially acceptable 'SS Volunteers'; apart from their German cadres, these units were forbidden to display the SS-runes. Of uneven combat value, some of them were limited to 'anti-partisan' duties in the rear areas. The year 1943 also saw a second series of armoured divisions (9., 10. and 12.) raised from ever younger *Reichsdeutsche* conscripts, led by cadres of veteran officers and NCOs posted from the senior divisions.

Given the change in ethnic composition, the period 1942 to 1944 was a critical one in the history of the Waffen-SS, as reflected in the divisional histories outlined below. From a strategic perspective, however, the years were also important because the tide of the war inevitably turned against the SS and the Wehrmacht. With the German defeat at Stalingrad in the winter of 1942/43, and the subsequent failure of the Kursk offensive in July–August 1943, the Nazi war machine began a grinding, bloody retreat back to the Reich. During the increasingly feverish defence, the combat record of the Waffen-SS became far patchier, as divisions old and new replaced the fight for victory with the fight for pure survival. Drafts of bewildered German airmen and sailors for whom there were no longer aircraft, ships or fuel might find themselves transferred at the stroke of a pen into the Waffen-SS, and thrust into gaps in the Eastern Front after the sketchiest preparation. Training school and depot personnel would be assembled around worn-down battlegroups into 'paper' SS divisions with minimal armament and transport. The retreating frontline caught up with sinister gangs of German criminals and foreign renegades redesignated as combat divisions, who sometimes met a richly deserved fate at the hands of the avenging Red Army.

Units quoted from fragmentary official documents as components of late-war formations may never actually have been formed, or may have served dispersed without ever being assembled under effective divisional command. The battlefield value of these units was wildly

Fanatical to the end. Eichstall, 1945 – the body of an SS trooper hangs from a tree, the man being hanged by his own comrades when he attempted to surrender to Allied forces.

uneven; but, remarkably, a few of them fought on stubbornly amid the ruins until the very last hours of the Third Reich.

In this chapter, we focus on the ethnic expansion of the SS, and in so doing take our story up to the final destruction of the Waffen-SS in 1945, both morally (if it had any moral standing in the first place) and tactically. First, however, we will look at the fates of those premier divisions we studied in previous chapters.

LEIBSTANDARTE

In February 1945, the *Leibstandarte* Division moved to Hungary to take part in Operation *Frühlingserwachen* (Spring Awakening), whose objectives were both to recapture Budapest and retake the vital Hungarian oilfields. Here the *Leibstandarte* would operate as part of 6. SS-Panzer Armee under its old divisional commander, 'Sepp' Dietrich.

The spring thaw had turned the roads east of Lake Balaton into a sea of mud, and off-road the marshy terrain was even worse. A preliminary artillery bombardment followed by a delay in launching the advance only served to forewarn the enemy. On the morning of the attack, 6 March, no artillery bombardment was provided; and in a vain attempt to maintain an element of surprise, some troops were dropped off as much as 18km from the start point of their attack, leaving them already exhausted by the time they got there. *Leibstandarte*'s tanks began to bog down almost immediately, some sinking as deep as the turret ring. Despite all these difficulties the men of the division attacked with their customary aggression, but progress was painfully slow; only 3km were covered on the first day. By 11 March the SS had taken the towns of Simontornya and Azora and were holding off determined counter-attacks. Although exhausted, they pressed on and crossed the Sio Canal; and despite the slow movement of most of the German force, the LSSAH reconnaissance battalion under Joachim Peiper actually penetrated 72km into enemy territory, almost two-thirds of the way to Budapest.

Any hope that the bulk of the German force could fight its way forward to support him was dashed by a massive Soviet counter-attack; although the Germans held fast, their Hungarian allies disintegrated on their flank. The SS troops were pulled back to regroup around Stuhlweissenburg on the main route to Vienna. Fortunately for the *Leibstandarte*, the same appalling conditions that had hampered the German advance now slowed the Red Army, allowing the remnants of the division to make a relatively orderly retreat covered by successful rearguard actions.

The failure of the offensive, and false rumours from senior army commanders that the SS troops had showed a lack of determination, enraged Hitler. Accusing the Waffen-SS troops of cowardice, he ordered them to remove their distinctive unit cuffbands as a

Waffen-SS soldiers in the Ardennes, 1944/45. The Waffen-SS placed a greater emphasis on saturation firepower than the army, delivered via weapons such as the MG 42 seen here.

punishment. Despite apocryphal tales of Dietrich and his officers sending back their cuffbands to Hitler in a chamber pot, the truth is that Dietrich simply refused to pass on the order. (Though such an order would have been taken as a great insult, these units had in fact already been ordered to remove their cuffbands as a security measure to prevent Soviet intelligence identifying the units opposing them.)

During late March 1945 isolated Kampfgruppen from the division were still fighting determined rearguard actions while slowly retreating towards Wiener Neustadt. By the beginning of April the *Leibstandarte* had been reduced to two small combat groups holding the line between that city and Vienna, where they successfully held off several powerful attacks before disengaging. By now the entire division numbered less than 1,600 officers and men and just 16 tanks – less than ten per cent of its normal strength. Gradually forced back through Austria in the closing weeks of the war, by mid-April its remnants were in the area around Mariazell. When the war ended on 8 May, those who had survived immediately headed west to surrender to US forces and avoid the fate of less fortunate Waffen-SS troops who were captured by the vengeful Red Army.

The *Leibstandarte* had evolved from parade troops treated with some scorn by the armed forces, to one of the most highly regarded combat formations Germany possessed. Given its reputation for holding fast in even the most dire straits, it was said of it that 'Every unit wants to have the *Leibstandarte* by its side. Its self-discipline, eagerness and

An SS Panzer commander keeps a vigilant watch during movements through France in 1944. Standing in the open hatch gave excellent all-round visibility, but made the commander a good target for snipers.

enthusiasm, unshakable calm in crisis situations and sheer toughness are examples to us all.' Despite the tarnishing of the reputations of many Waffen-SS units by atrocities, there can be no doubt that in terms of sheer combat effectiveness the *Leibstandarte SS Adolf Hitler* was one of the best German formations of the war. By way of testimony to that fact, a total of 52 soldiers from this division were decorated with the Knight's Cross.

DAS REICH

Still not yet back up to full strength in the spring of 1945, the division was thrown into the last desperate attack in the East in Operation *Frühlingserwachen*. As described above under LSSAH, the attack stalled almost immediately in the deep mud of the spring thaw, and was halted by Soviet counter-attacks within just ten days. *Das Reich* was forced onto the retreat, and by April was defending vital bridges over the Danube in Vienna. House-to-house fighting followed as the Red Army pressed into the suburbs of the Austrian capital, and by 9 April *Das Reich* units were concentrated around the Florisdorfer bridge. Over the next few days the remnants of the division withdrew towards Dresden, the few remaining tanks providing rearguard cover; on reaching that city, with fuel and ammunition all but exhausted, the Panzers were destroyed.

While elements of *Deutschland* succeeded in surrendering to US forces, part of the regiment was still in action around Prague, and most of this force were lost in action against Red Army units and Czech partisans while trying to fight their way westwards. *Der Führer* spent the last days of the war in a mission to rescue German civilians from Prague. Forcing his way into the city, the regimental commander, Otto Weidinger, gathered together a disparate group of civilians, female auxiliaries and wounded soldiers, and led them out again to the relative safety of US captivity at Rokicyany in Bohemia. Most of those who went into US captivity survived, but those who fell into Soviet or Czech hands mostly died – either shot out of hand, or perishing during long years in Soviet labour camps. A total of 72 soldiers from this division were decorated with the Knight's Cross, the largest number of such awards to any SS formation.

TOTENKOPF

After a brief respite from frontline duty, on 1 January 1945 *Totenkopf* was thrown into action, once again with *Wiking*, in an abortive attempt to break the enemy encirclement of Budapest. Fierce resistance halted the SS divisions after ten days; a renewed attack a week later initially made far better progress, but enemy resistance stiffened once again. Eventually major counter-attacks pushed the SS troops back to the forest of Bakony near Lake Balaton, where they dug in.

March 1945 saw *Totenkopf* take part in Operation *Frühlingserwachen*, the last major German offensive on the Eastern Front in which *Leibstandarte*, *Das Reich*, *Totenkopf* and *Hohenstaufen* attempted to advance their heavy armour over hopelessly inappropriate terrain. After advancing around 30km the division ground to a halt, and the enraged Hitler called off the offensive. Enemy counter-attacks soon drove the weakened *Totenkopf* back to the very gates of Vienna. Through late March and into April the division fended off Soviet probing attacks, but no longer had the strength to resist the overwhelming enemy forces, and Vienna fell on 13 April. By the end of the month the division could count only about 1,000 combat-worthy troops and just six tanks. On 9 May it surrendered to elements of the US Army, who accepted *Totenkopf*'s surrender on the condition that it disarmed the guards at nearby Mauthausen concentration camp. The division carried out this apt request, at which point the Americans reneged on the agreement and handed over the survivors to the Soviets. It is unsurprising that only a small number of these soldiers who wore the death's-head on their collar survived Soviet captivity. A total of 46 soldiers from this division were decorated with the Knight's Cross.

POLIZEI

In late 1944, the *Polizei* Division joined other German units reinforcing the southern sector of the front around Belgrade, Yugoslavia. It once again suffered heavy losses, and by September 1944 was down to around half its strength. The division was pushed back into Slovakia in January 1945, from where it was transferred north into Pomerania and then on to Danzig. During these final defensive battles it did successfully hold back the Red Army at Turnu Severin, thus allowing the army's 1. Gebirgs Division to escape destruction. Caught in the encirclement of Danzig, the division was fortunate to be evacuated by sea to Swinemünde. After a brief period of rest near Stettin, the remnants of the division fought their way over the Elbe to surrender to US forces at Wittenberg-Lenzen.

LEFT: Eastern Front, 1945. 1: SS-Hauptscharführer, 31. SS-Freiwilligen Grenadier Division; Austria, March 1945. 2: SS-Untersturmführer, SS- und Polizei Fusilier Abteilung 35; Niesse front, April 1945. 3: SS-Scharführer, schwere SS-Panzer Abteilung 502; Oder front, March 1945. The three SS heavy tank units equipped with the PzKpfw VI Tiger I, and later the Tiger II (Königstiger), originated in a heavy company formed within each of the Panzer regiments of the 1. *Leibstandarte*, 2. *Das Reich* and 3. *Totenkopf* Divisions in winter 1942/43. In early 1944 the remnants of these formed the nucleus of, respectively, schwere SS-Panzer Abteilungen 101, 102 & 103, which were detached from the divisions and employed as assets of I & II SS-Panzer Korps. After heavy losses in Normandy the three units were retitled schwere SS-Panzer Abteilungen 501, 502 & 503 in autumn 1944, and completed re-equiped with the Tiger II Ausf B Königstiger before being sent to the Eastern Front. This battalion was finally destroyed in the Halbe Pocket in late April 1945. (Osprey Publishing © Stephen Andrew)

The SS-*Polizei* Division was never an elite force; but from its origins as, effectively, a second-rate reserve unit, it matured into a reasonably effective fighting division. A total of 19 soldiers of the division were decorated with the Knight's Cross.

WIKING

SS troops man a trench with a tripod-mounted MG 34, near the Westwall in 1945. With the weapon in this configuration, the soldiers would be able to deliver fire out to 2,000m.

In December 1944, *Wiking* was sent south to attempt to break through to the encircled city of Budapest, but was thrown back by the Soviets and forced onto the defensive throughout January and February of 1945. March saw the division take part in the ill-fated offensive around Lake Balaton in the atrocious mud of the spring thaw; and by the second half of the month *Wiking* was on the retreat as the Red Army launched yet another counter-attack. The division was driven back into Austria, receiving a number of Hungarian troops to bolster its dwindling strength in mid-April. In May the remnants

of the *Wiking* Division were forced to surrender to the Red Army in Czechoslovakia. A total of 54 soldiers from this division were decorated with the Knight's Cross, testimony to the essential solidity of this most famous of Waffen-SS formations.

NORD

In February 1945, *Nord* was transferred once again, returning to XXXIV Korps to be used in an attempt to recapture Trier on the Moselle river. In this case the opposition was the US 10th Armored Division, and the weakened SS units found the going impossibly hard. At the beginning of March a mixture of SS mountain troopers and Volksgrenadiers were tenaciously resisting the US advance after having failed to retake Trier. On 3 March, the division was allocated to LXXXII Korps under Generalmajor Hahn and committed to an attack on positions held by the US 302nd Infantry (94th Infantry Division) near Lampaden. Just before midnight elements of SS-Gebirgsjäger Regiment 12 infiltrated on the northern flank of the attack and SS-Gebirgsjäger Regiment 11 on the southern flank. In heavy and confused fighting they took a number of positions, but the Americans were able to bring up sufficient reserves to hold the line. So confused did the situation become that the *Reinhard Heydrich* (11th) and *Michael Gaissmair* (12th) Regiments attacked each other during the night of 6 March, each believing the other to be the enemy.

Nord was thereafter ordered to form defensive positions along the River Moselle, behind which the other battered German divisions in the area could withdraw. However, the immediate American follow-up, in overwhelming superiority, forced the division gradually back along the Moselle towards the Rhine. The *Michael Gaissmair* regiment was fragmented into small groups which withdrew towards the River Nahe; one group crossed successfully after finding a bridge whose American guards were reportedly drunk on liberated wine, but the majority were intercepted and taken prisoner before reaching the river. Other elements of the division even managed to halt the American advance near Koblenz; but the remnants of *Nord* – by now reduced to about 25 per cent of its former strength – were then ordered to withdraw over the Rhine, and were safely on the east bank by 18 March. The survivors were thrown into the line again along the River Lahn, but were almost immediately shattered by a major US armoured attack on 27 March. The original *Nord* Division had effectively ceased to exist, but reinforcements from the divisional replacement battalion were still being sent from its base in Austria to join units at the front. Several of these groups of soldiers were in action until the very end of the war, while retreating ever deeper into Germany; most were destroyed or surrendered piecemeal to US units in the closing days of the war.

That the division had long put behind it the poor performance of its original soldiers four years before is illustrated by the fact that five of its members were decorated with the Knight's Cross of the Iron Cross.

PRINZ EUGEN

In mid-January 1945, the Germans in Croatia attempted to drive off the partisan forces which were harrying them by launching Operation *Frühlingssturm* (Spring Storm). Operating under XXXIV Korps, *Prinz Eugen* seized the town of Nemeci and formed a bridgehead at Buzot; a second phase, *Wehrwolf*, lasted from 4 February until the end of that month, after which the division was transferred to Heeresgruppe E reserve. It was soon in action again, against powerful partisan forces encircling German units in the town of Zenica north of Sarajevo; before long *Prinz Eugen* pushed the enemy back and relieved the town.

The tempo of operations now became desperate as the enemy pressed in all around the retreating German forces, and *Prinz Eugen* fought with notable determination. No sooner had the division relieved Zenica when elements were detached and sent to the south of Sarajevo to relieve a Croatian infantry division which had been trapped by partisans. There then followed a remarkable episode when, in order to relieve yet

An Waffen-SS MG 34 team. The soldier on the right has two ammunition boxes, each containing 250 rounds of 7.92mm ammunition for the machine gun.

another cut-off German Army unit, the entire division scaled Mount Igman, moving through deep snow drifts. *Prinz Eugen* emerged behind the partisan units, not only relieving their army comrades but pursuing the enemy into the mountains. When the partisans regrouped on a high peak a vicious battle ensued, with the summit changing hands several times before the rate of casualties on both sides persuaded them that this exposed peak – lacking any sort of cover, and where every shell burst caused many casualties – was no longer worth contesting. The army unit relieved in Sarajevo ran into yet another partisan ambush, and once more *Prinz Eugen* came to the rescue.

Over the following days the division provided rearguard cover for withdrawing German units making their way north-west towards Austria. At Brod the bridge over the River Sava had already been captured by strong partisan forces; but *Prinz Eugen* pioneers successfully ferried the entire mixed army/Waffen-SS force across the river in assault boats, though at the cost of abandoning all heavy equipment.

As the Third Reich finally collapsed in April/May 1945 German units were determined not to fall into the hands of the vengeful partisans, and for this reason fighting continued in this area even after the German surrender on 8 May. Eventually, an agreement was reached with the enemy that *Prinz Eugen* would surrender its arms in return for safe passage to the Austrian border. Unsurprisingly, this agreement was not honoured, and the division was forced to put in a counter-attack four days after the war had officially ended.

On 12 May the division discharged its troops, leaving each man to try to make his own way to safety, and some groups succeeded in reaching Austrian soil. Those still in enemy territory finally surrendered at Cilli in Slovenia on 16 May, fully eight days after the war in Europe had ended. The treatment meted out to them by the partisans was predictably brutal, and not many survived.

The form of warfare in which the *Prinz Eugen* Division was involved was perhaps uniquely ugly, and the formation was reportedly guilty of many atrocities. Occupied Yugoslavia was the arena for merciless guerrilla warfare, but not simply between the Germans and their allies on one hand and unified patriots on the other. The communist and Chetnik resistance movements were divided by mutual hatreds; the communists devoted great energy to fighting the royalists, and there were instances of Chetniks joining forces with the occupiers to fight the partisans. This internal war was often pursued as ruthlessly as SS anti-guerrilla operations (a fact that should not surprise us, in the aftermath of the Balkan wars of the 1990s), and claimed perhaps as many lives as Axis security operations. Nevertheless, there can be no denying that the SS-led anti-partisan sweeps nearly always involved barbarous reprisals against local civilians in areas of anti-German activity. In this kind of warfare neither side expected or offered any quarter, and all the participant forces committed atrocities. In the last months of the war *Prinz Eugen* units showed themselves capable of courageous fighting against odds, and six members of the division were decorated with the Knight's Cross; but the stain of its atrocities against civilians cannot be avoided.

FLORIAN GEYER

Cut off and with dwindling supplies in Budapest in early 1945, *Florian Geyer* fought on in an ever-shrinking perimeter; the area occupied by *Florian Geyer* by the final stages of the defence of Budapest was barely one kilometre square. The remnants staged a desperate break-out attempt on 11/12 February 1945, but were caught by the Soviets and annihilated. Barely 800 German survivors, including just 170 men from the two SS cavalry divisions, reached the safety of German lines, and were subsequently absorbed into the 37. SS-Kavallerie Division. The *Florian Geyer*'s last commander, Joachim Rumohr, committed suicide after being wounded during the break-out attempt.

Although the division did see considerable frontline combat against regular Soviet forces, and 23 of its members were decorated with the Knight's Cross, much of its career was spent on operations against partisans, and there is no doubt that it was responsible for the deaths of many thousands of civilians.

HOHENSTAUFEN

After the briefest rest, the *Hohenstaufen* Division moved to Hungary at the beginning of March 1945, serving under II SS-Panzer Korps of Dietrich's VI SS-Panzer Armee in Operation *Frühlingserwachen*. By now *Hohenstaufen*'s personnel losses had largely been made up, in numbers at least (drafts of replacements now even included Ukrainian conscripts who were unable to speak German); but it was still well understrength in armour and artillery. The spring thaw came early in 1945, and the ground, expected to be iron-hard for the SS heavy armour, was a slushy bog. As the date of the offensive approached, Hitler's paranoid fear that the Soviets would discover his plans had forbidden reconnaissance patrols being sent out lest this forewarn the enemy. He had also forbidden the approach of large numbers of vehicles towards the start lines, thus leaving huge numbers of men to march up to 18km through boggy terrain to reach their jumping-off points. The troops were cold, wet and exhausted before the battle even began; and in fact Soviet intelligence had been aware of German intentions long before the attack opened on 6 March.

Almost immediately the advance began to bog down in the unseasonably soft ground. The equipment, leadership and professionalism of the Red Army had improved exponentially since the heady days of the German advance into Russia in 1941; now

ABOVE: Camouflage clothing, 1944–45. 1: SS-Schütze, 38. SS-Grenadier Division *Nibelungen*; Upper Bavaria, May 1945. 2: SS-Rottenführer, 32. SS-Freiwilligen Grenadier Division *30 Januar*; '9th Army Pocket', April 1945. 3: SS-Funker, SS-Freiwilligen Sturmbrigade *Langemarck*; Zhitomir, Russia, January 1944. There was little uniformity in the appearance of Waffen-SS units in spring 1945. Even where camouflage clothing was available in store, it often went unissued in the chaotic final weeks, and many SS troops fought their last battles in field-grey or in their camouflaged padded winter jackets. (Osprey Publishing © Stephen Andrew)

The goal for many Waffen-SS divisions was to surrender to the Americans or British, rather than the Russians. Here troops of the *Leibstandarte* Division surrender to US soldiers in Aachen, 1945.

the weakened Waffen-SS divisions struggled to make headway against a very powerful and determined enemy. The Soviets launched a massive counter-attack on 16 March, and in little more than a week the German front lines had been torn apart, with the Red Army punching through gaps up to 97km wide. Abandoning hundreds of tanks and heavy vehicles that had bogged down in the mud, the Germans were forced onto the retreat into Austria, to the very gates of Vienna.

By now *Hohenstaufen* had almost ceased to exist as a cohesive entity, being reduced to a number of small independent battlegroups fighting rearguard actions as they slowly retreated into Austria. Remarkably, however, despite having been torn to pieces in the disastrous Lake Balaton offensive, by late April the division had once again received sufficient replacements to bring it almost up to strength – though largely with virtually untrained personnel, including 17-year-olds barely out of school.

Although Hitler committed suicide on 30 April, and Berlin surrendered on 2 May, the beginning of that month found the division in new positions on the River Elbe, intent on preventing US troops from crossing it eastwards. This river was in fact the agreed demarcation line between Soviet troops advancing from the east and US troops approaching from the west. Not surprisingly, *Hohenstaufen*'s commander was intent on getting his men onto the western bank when hostilities ceased; their future if they were taken prisoner by the Soviets would be extremely bleak. Tentative contact was established with the approaching Americans; on 7 May the German surrender document was signed, including among its conditions that the surrender would only be accepted of German units that were on the western side of the demarcation line on 8 May – any attempting to cross after that date would be handed over to the Soviets. SS-Brigadeführer Stadler was determined that his men would go into captivity as a disciplined military unit; accordingly, after Stadler had reported to the American HQ his divisional units marched past in review – much to the astonishment of GIs accustomed to disheartened and bedraggled prisoners only too happy that their war was over. Along with its sister formation, *Frundsberg*, the *Hohenstaufen* division had truly earned its first-class combat reputation.

FRUNDSBERG

On 18 November 1944 the *Frundsberg* Division, by this time reduced to a battlegroup after its losses in Normandy and at Arnhem, was withdrawn to Aachen in Germany for rest and refit. During December its strength was built up once again to around 15,500 men – about 75 per cent of establishment. In December 1944/January 1945 it saw action around Linnich and Geilenkirchen, and Jülich north-east of Aachen. In January it was committed along the upper reaches of the Rhine as part of Heeresgruppe Niederrhein, and was earmarked for use in the reserve forces for Operation *Nordwind*. Mid-January saw *Frundsberg* cross the Rhine and attack in the direction of Gambsheim. Anticipating stiff resistance, the division moved very cautiously, not realizing that the US units facing them had made a tactical withdrawal. On 24 January *Frundsberg* crossed the Moder River and captured the high ground commanding the area between Hagenau and Kaltenhaus. Despite being at near full strength after its recent refit, the division met such fierce resistance that its advance faltered, and the following day orders arrived withdrawing it from the line for immediate transfer to the Eastern Front. Luckily, it had not suffered any significant level of casualties during its brief participation in *Nordwind*.

On 10 February 1945, the division arrived at the front as the situation became ever more critical. It was committed to a German counter-offensive codenamed Operation *Sonnenwende* (Solstice) on 16 February as part of III SS-Panzer Korps, and for a month saw heavy combat around Stargard and Furstenwalde, before being pulled back across the Oder into Stettin for a brief respite. It then joined Heeresgruppe 'Weichsel' as part of the army group reserve.

At the end of March the divisional commander, General Heinz Harmel, was recalled from the front for hospital treatment in Berlin. Around this time *Frundsberg* was

ordered to move to the Dresden area, but while still en route was diverted back to the front to counter a Soviet breakthrough on the Oder front.

In mid-April, *Frundsberg* was encircled by Soviet forces near Spremberg. The division was fragmented, but despite its perilous position, orders were received from the Führerhauptquartier for *Frundsberg* to close the gap in the German lines by immediately attacking. Harmel realized that carrying out these orders would be suicidal; he decided instead to break out of the encirclement and move towards German forces massed to the south of Berlin. The break-out was achieved, but only at the cost of further fragmentation of the remnants of the division. Some did manage to re-form and take up defensive positions north-west of Dresden. Harmel's refusal to obey the insane order to attack at Spremberg led to his being ordered to report to Generalfeldmarschall Schörner, a fanatical Nazi, who relieved Harmel of his command. (In the circumstances this was a light punishment – at that stage of the war others had been executed for lesser 'crimes'.)

Under 4. Panzer Armee of Heeresgruppe Mitte, the remnants of the division were led by SS-Obersturmbannführer Franz Roestel in the last few vain fights against the advancing Russians, but to no avail. They fell back to the Elbe, crossing near Dresden and heading south. After claiming a few Soviet T-34 tanks on 7 May the last few Panzers of the *Frundsberg* Division were blown up by their crews, who then attempted to head west and avoid capture by the Soviets. Only a handful reached the relative safety of US captivity, the majority of the survivors surrendering to the Red Army at Teplitz-Schonau.

Thirteen soldiers from *Frundsberg* were decorated with the Knight's Cross. Despite its relatively brief combat career, it earned its reputation as one of the best of the Waffen-SS Divisions, fighting with great élan in the attack and stubborn fortitude in defence. The bonds forged during war have survived to this day; a thriving Old Comrades association still meets regularly, and until his death in 2000 Heinz Harmel remained a father-figure to his men, taking an intense interest in the welfare of every surviving soldier of his division.

LEFT: France, 1944. 1: SS-Unterscharführer, 12. SS-Panzer Division *Hitlerjugend*. The reversible second-pattern helmet cover and M1942 second-pattern smock have slightly contrasting 'summer' sides exposed, the first in sharp-edged so-called 'oakleaf' and the second in 'burred edge' pattern. 2: SS-Kanonier, SS-Sturmgeschütz Abteilung 12. This young artillery private wears the jacket of the field-grey 'special' uniform; his personally acquired trousers are made up from Italian Army camouflage material – quite widely seen in Normandy. 3: SS-Rottenführer, 17. SS-Panzergrenadier Division *Götz von Berlichingen*. This junior NCO of either SS-Panzergrenadier Regiment 37 or 38 is represented as he might have appeared after the remaining Kampfgruppe of this division was pulled out to eastern France for refitting. Despite regulations, photographs show that the old M1940 'Schiffschen' field cap was often still worn alongside its 'universal' M1943 peaked replacement (even by the teenagers of the newly raised *Hitlerjugend*). (Osprey Publishing © Stephen Andrew)

By the time the first ten Waffen-SS divisions had been raised in 1943 it was clear that there had already been a watering-down of the elite quality of the Waffen-SS combat units. Of the first five divisions, only 4. SS-*Polizei* Division was of relatively low quality, the others being generally regarded as first-rate combat formations, and accorded the grudging respect (for their fighting qualities, at least) of not only the Wehrmacht but even their opponents. Of the next five formations, only *Hohenstaufen* and *Frundsberg* could be considered as first class. Not only did these two Panzer divisions fight with considerable skill and determination against often overwhelming enemy forces; on occasions, such as the battle of Arnhem, they even showed themselves capable of a degree of chivalry towards their enemies. *Nord*, an extremely poor-quality organization in its earliest days, did improve substantially, but never reached the levels of combat efficiency attained by the premier Waffen-SS divisions. Both *Prinz Eugen* and *Florian Geyer* spent much of their short careers on brutal 'anti-partisan' operations, and were implicated in appalling atrocities. Both suffered crippling losses when faced by hardened

An SS Tiger, for the Allies one of the most feared weapon systems of the war. Note the *Zimmerit* non-magnetic coating applied to the vehicle's exterior, to prevent the enemy attaching magnetic mines.

Red Army combat units; their remnants fought hard at the end, but they had little alternative, given their predictable fate if captured.

This was a pattern set to continue and deteriorate as Himmler strove to expand his SS empire. Of the remaining Waffen-SS divisions still to be covered, the truly elite units were to be the exception rather than the rule. Many were mediocre at best, and several were utterly without merit. It would be impossible to cover each of the Waffen-SS divisions in detail – by the end of the war, there were no fewer than 38 divisions plus various volunteer legions. Some scarcely existed on anything more than paper, while others fought to the death on the Reich's shrinking borders. A representative sample, however, will show clearly how the fortunes of war had reshaped the nature of Hitler's elite.

NEW GERMAN FORMATIONS

Alongside the foreign Waffen-SS divisions, which ranged from Dutchmen to Cossacks, the later years of World War II also saw the establishment (and destruction) of many other German Waffen-SS divisions.

HITLERJUGEND

One of the most famous, and prestigious, was the 12. SS-Panzer Division *Hitlerjugend*. Individual voluntary enlistment by members of the Hitler Youth (Hitlerjugend) organization had been encouraged by the Waffen-SS, but in early 1943 the Hitler Youth's National Leader, Artur Axmann, suggested to Himmler that a complete division be formed from Hitler Youth boys born in 1926. Hitler approved the plan, and recruiting chief SS-Gruppenführer Berger even proposed himself as the commander. Himmler sensibly preferred a combat veteran with close links to the Hitler Youth, SS-Standartenführer Fritz Witt, a 35-year-old regimental commander in the *Leibstandarte SS Adolf Hitler* and holder of the Knight's Cross with Oakleaves; Witt became Germany's second youngest general (after the 31-year-old Luftwaffe Generalmajor Adolf Galland) when promoted to SS-Brigadeführer on 1 July 1943.

In May 1943 the first 8,000 17-year-olds reported for two months' preparatory instruction; and by 1 September, 16,000 youths were forming the units of the *Hitlerjugend* Division at Belgian training areas. The cadre of battle-proven officers and NCOs came mainly from the *Leibstandarte*, but a number of army officers were also posted in. Initially a Panzergrenadier division, the formation was numbered '12th' and up-rated to a Panzer division in October, with a complete regiment of 218 PzKpfw IV and PzKpfw V tanks. Even when the cadre were included the average age was only

ABOVE: Three soldiers of the *Hitlerjugend* Division, one clutching a *Panzerschreck* anti-tank weapon, are watched over by an SS-Unterscharführer of the schwere SS-Panzer Abteilung 501 (left). (Osprey Publishing © Jeffrey Burn)

18 years; and it is interesting to note that rations of sweets – candy – were allocated instead of cigarettes.

Once declared ready for active service, the division moved in April 1944 to northern France, under I SS-Panzer Korps. When Allied troops landed in Normandy on 6 June 1944, *Hitlerjugend* was ordered forward, and after a night march it was the first SS

THE *HITLERJUGEND* DIVISION COUNTER-ATTACKS NEAR CAEN, NORMANDY, JUNE 1944

On the morning of 7 June, the day after the landing of Commonwealth and US troops, elements of the 12. SS-Panzer Division *Hitlerjugend* were concentrated just to the west of Caen. Canadian armour was pushing south from the invasion beaches when the *Hitlerjugend* sprang an ambush and launched a frantic counter-attack. Panzer IVs from the II Abteilung (Battalion) of the division's Panzer Regiment, along with Panzergrenadiers, captured the villages of Authie and Franqueville on their first rush, the Allies being taken completely by surprise. Pushing on further north, the elated troops felt they were on the point of breaking through to the sea, but a dangerously exposed flank caused them to be pulled back. (Osprey Publishing © Elizabeth Sharp)

A Danish SS volunteer in action. Himmler quite readily accepted the Danes into SS service, believing them to be of nearly the same 'Aryan' stock as the Germans.

formation into action on 7 June. A battlegroup under the CO of SS-Panzergrenadier Regiment 25, Kurt Meyer, and including a battalion of PzKpfw IV tanks, drove back the Canadian 27th Armoured Brigade on Caen-Carpiquet airfield, and in their first action the young soldiers claimed 28 Allied tanks destroyed for the loss of only six men. The pattern was repeated for the next month; the teenage soldiers followed their seasoned officers in a series of highly effective attacks on British and Canadian forces around Caen. One result of their inexperience and fanaticism was high losses: the *Hitlerjugend* took more than 60 per cent casualties in four weeks. Another was violations of the Geneva Convention: some 64 Canadian and British prisoners had been murdered by 16 June (atrocities for which Kurt Meyer later served nine years of a life sentence). Fritz Witt was killed by naval gunfire on 16 June, and command passed to the 33-year-old 'Panzermeyer', who led the division in almost continual fighting against great odds until the survivors were withdrawn to the Potigny area on 11 July.

A week later they were back in the line, facing the British Operation *Goodwood* in Normandy on 18–20 July. Early August found I SS-Panzer Korps divided, with the *Leibstandarte* sent west to Avranches, while the *Hitlerjugend* held the northern edge of the 'Falaise Pocket' in which the Allies sought to trap some 90,000 Germans. Fiercely resisting the 4th Canadian and 1st Polish Armoured Divisions, Meyer fought with great determination although facing overwhelming artillery and under skies ruled by Allied aircraft. The *Hitlerjugend* avoided encirclement, but of the troops in the pocket only some 30,000 escaped; Meyer was wounded while holding Hill 159 against 3rd Canadian Infantry Division with some 500 Panzergrenadiers. About 3,500 survivors fell back to the Belgian border; by early September, when it reached the River Meuse, Meyer had been captured and the 12. SS-Panzer Division numbered only some 600 fit men and no tanks.

Rebuilt and refitted, in December 1944 the division took part in the Ardennes offensive under 6. SS-Panzer Armee. Divided into four Kampfgruppen for attacks along the Elsenborn Ridge, the division made little progress and was redeployed; by 1 January 1945 it formed part of the ring around besieged Bastogne, but by the 18th all the forces committed had been obliged to withdraw.

An SS officer passes the sign to Malmédy during the Ardennes offensive. The 'Battle of the Bulge' was essentially a fruitless waste of resources when the Waffen-SS could least afford it.

After the abandonment of the 'Battle of the Bulge', *Hitlerjugend* was sent with *Leibstandarte* to Hungary to take part in Operation *Frühlingserwachen*, the offensive around Lake Balaton. In early February the division fought in the successful preliminary destruction of a Russian bridgehead on the River Gran; and on 6 March the main offensive opened. A combination of atrocious terrain and stubborn resistance brought this to a premature halt. The I SS-Panzer Korps was forced into a fighting retreat to the north-west, and by 13 April had been driven out of Vienna; on that date the total strength of the *Hitlerjugend* – including men in hospital or detached – was just over 7,730, but its fighting strength was far fewer. The priority was now to move westwards towards the advancing US Army so as to avoid capture by the Soviets; and on 8 May 1945 some hundreds of survivors of the 12. SS-Panzer Division *Hitlerjugend* (and one remaining tank) surrendered to the US 65th Infantry Division near Enns in Austria.

REICHSFUHRER-SS

Pandering to Himmler's considerable vanity, another late-war German SS formation was 16. SS-Panzergrenadier Division *Reichsführer-SS*. Back in May 1941, troops from Himmler's Kommandostab *Reichsführer-SS* (RfSS) formed a new elite 'escort' unit, the Begleit Bataillon RfSS. After the opening of the Russian campaign it was employed with the rest of this command on anti-partisan duty. In February 1943 it was decided to upgrade the battalion to brigade status, and at this time it was renamed as 'Sturmbrigade *Reichsführer-SS*' (Assault Brigade *Reichsführer-SS*). Before leaving the front the unit is believed to have operated alongside troops commanded by the notorious Oskar Dirlewanger during an anti-partisan operation near Minsk, Operation *Kottbus*, in March 1943.

Shortly thereafter the embryo brigade was moved to the Mediterranean island of Corsica, and during the summer Himmler took steps to enlarge it to divisional status. In September it was on stand-by for use against the Italians should they decide to resist the German occupation following the unilateral Italian armistice. On 3 October, Hitler approved the formation of the division; the Sturmbrigade provided the nucleus, with various SS training and replacement units, a draft from the 9. Division *Hohenstaufen*, and a considerable number of Hungarian *Volksdeutsche*. During the last quarter of 1943 and early 1944 the new 16. Division was forming up and training in Slovenia and at Baden south of Vienna, reaching a strength of just under 13,000 by the end of the year.

RIGHT: *Reichsführer-SS* and *Horst Wessel* Divisions, 1944. 1: SS-Unterscharführer, 18. SS-Panzergrenadier Division Horst Wessel; Poland, summer 1944. 2: SS-Panzergrenadier, 16. SS-Panzergrenadier Division *Reichsführer-SS*; Italy, summer 1944. 3: SS-Gruppenführer, 16. SS-Panzergrenadier Division Reichsführer-SS; summer 1944. This last figure is based upon photos of SS-Gruppenführer Max Simon, the divisional commander until the end of October 1944, in everyday service dress. (Osprey Publishing © Stephen Andrew)

In late January 1944 the Anglo-US landings around Anzio and Nettuno on the west coast of Italy led to parts of both Panzergrenadier regiments and the Panzerjäger unit being rushed to this front, seeing combat under 14. Armee until 9 March. A battalion from the division may also have been involved in anti-partisan operations on the Eastern Front in early 1944. At the same time, much of the division was allocated to Operation *Margarethe*, the German plan for the occupation of Hungary, whose Axis leadership was wavering. These elements – reinforced by a newly re-formed Begleit Bataillon RfSS, and an SS-Panzergrenadier *Lehr* Regiment from the Prosetschnitz training school – left Baden in March 1944 for occupation duties around Debrecen. By April the detached units from Italy rejoined; some men were transferred to the 3. SS-Panzer Division *Totenkopf*, and replaced by local recruitment. However, the 16. Division was very soon on its way back to Italy, where it was reported in May.

Throughout June and July 1944 the division, as part of LXXV Korps, resisted the British Eighth Army's advance in Liguria, making a fighting retreat via Siena and Pisa

The crew of a *Nordland* Division SdKfz 251 half-track lie dead around their vehicle on the streets of Berlin in 1945. On the Eastern Front, the Waffen-SS men typically fought to the death, expecting little mercy from the Soviet troops.

to Carrara in August. Later operations were under XIV Panzer Korps, and I Fallschirm Korps, part of 10. Armee.

Attrition steadily reduced Himmler's namesake division in strength. By the end of 1944 some 3,000 casualties had lowered divisional strength to just below 14,000. Under attacks by Italian partisans the division also reverted to its former standards of behaviour: men from SS-Panzer Aufklärungs Abteilung 16 executed 560 civilian men, women and children at Sant'Anna di Stazzema on 12 August. Later that month troops thought to be from the division killed a further 370 civilians at Bardene San Terenzo; and SS-Panzer Aufklärungs Abteilung 16 killed perhaps 1,670 during 29 August–3 September and on 1 October, in villages around Marzabotto.

In January 1945 the division moved from the Apennine mountains north-east to the area south of Lake Commachio; it then entrained at Ferrara (minus its anti-tank battalion) for transfer back to Hungary during February. There it came under 6. SS-Panzer Armee for Operation *Frühlingserwachen*, in which it had no more success than any of the other formations committed to this ill-planned attack.

During late March and April, under XXII Gebirgs Korps of 2. Panzer Armee, the division – still about 13,000 strong on paper, but with far fewer men in the line – was pushed back steadily westwards into southern Austria. The remnants surrendered in early May to British forces west of Graz, and to US troops around Klagenfurt and Radstadt.

GÖTZ VON BERLICHINGEN

Another Waffen-SS division formed in 1943 was the 17. SS-Panzergrenadier Division *Götz von Berlichingen*. This division, like the 16th, was ordered into being by Hitler on 3 October 1943. Over the next eight months the manpower and equipment were brought together at various bases in western France, the HQ being at Thouars south of Le Mans. Personnel included transfers from the 10. and 16. Divisions, training and replacement units, and *Volksdeutsche* from the Balkans and Italy.

Committed as part of LXXXIV Korps, 7. Armee, following the Allied invasion of Normandy on 6 June 1944, the division faced the same problems as many others as it struggled to reach the front, hampered by enemy aircraft and by shortages of transport and fuel. The first unit to see action was the armoured reconnaissance battalion, which engaged troops of the British 7th Armoured Division near Trévières on 10 June, while the bulk of the division was stranded around Vers by fuel shortage.

When these elements reached Périers south-west of Carentan late on 11 June, they met up with the much weakened Fallschirmjäger Regiment 6, which had withdrawn from Carentan under pressure from the US 101st Airborne Division. The paratroopers of Fallschirmjäger Regiment 6 were placed under the command of *Götz von Berlichingen*;

there was considerable animosity between Fallschirmjäger Regiment 6's Oberst von der Heydte and the 17. Division's SS-Oberführer Ostendorff (who would try unsuccessfully to have von der Heydte court-martialled). Short of ammunition, and without the promised air support, Ostendorff launched an attack on Carentan on 13 June, headed by SS-Panzergrenadier Regiment 37 and the StuG IV assault guns of the Panzer Abteilung, supported by the attached paratroopers. Boggy and restricted terrain slowed the advance; the US paratroopers resisted stoutly, and after some hours received tank support from 2nd Armored Division. The attack failed with SS losses of some 460 men and 20 assault guns.

Fighting continued south of Carentan, and by the end of June casualties would climb to just over 1,000, including SS-Oberführer Ostendorff wounded; replacements included low-quality drafts from two 'East battalions'. In early and mid-July, Regiment 37 suffered particularly heavy losses. By 25 July, Operation *Cobra* – the US armoured break-out from the Normandy beachhead, west of St Lô – found the division's capability rated only '4th Class'. Pulling out from a threatened encirclement in the Roncey area on 28–31 July, the remnants of both 2. SS-Panzer Division *Das Reich* and *Götz von Berlichingen* were trapped on narrow roads by Allied fighter-bombers and US armour; the division lost its last assault guns and hundreds of men.

On 1 August the infantry survivors were retitled as a battlegroup, under SS-Obersturmbannführer Jakob Fick. Grouped with *Das Reich*, it was allocated to the doomed Avranches counter-offensive of 7 August; and on the 24th of the month it was disbanded after falling back to the Seine. On 15 August the other remnants were ordered to the Saarland, for rebuilding near Metz. There the infantry regiments received the remnants of the so-called SS-Panzer Brigades 49 and 51 – in truth, ex-coastal defence troops from Denmark; some 50 junior officers arrived straight from the Metz academy.

Götz von Berlichingen were under XIII SS-Panzer Korps in the second half of September,

A soldier of the *Frundsberg* Panzer Division prepares 15cm rockets for the Panzerwerfer 42 weapon in the background. The half-track vehicle mounted a ten-tube launcher system, and usually carried enough rockets for two salvos.

holding off US attacks around Dornot south of Metz, where the Americans had established bridgeheads over the River Moselle. Despite stiff resistance the bridgeheads were slowly expanded; the division was then committed to the defence of Metz itself during October, with fighting dispersed in various sectors. On 7 November, the division was ordered out of Metz; but two days later a major American assault was launched, which virtually destroyed the defenders, including SS-Panzergrenadier Regiment 38.

During December the rest of the division, with a combat strength of about 3,500 and 20 armoured vehicles, retreated towards Saarbrücken and the Westwall defences. There *Götz von Berlichingen* received drafts of East European *Volksdeutsche*, but also a strong SS-Panzergrenadier *Lehr* Regiment from the Prosetschnitz school. Additional reinforcements included a company of excellent PzKpfw V Panthers from the Wehrmacht's 21. Panzer Division, and even a handful of colossal Jagdtiger self-propelled guns.

On the last day of 1944 the division, under XIII SS-Korps south of Zweibrücken, took part in Operation *Nordwind* – the attack in southern Alsace, which the Germans hoped had been stripped of American troops rushed north to stem the Ardennes offensive. The 17. Division's initial attack was against elements of the US 44th and 100th Infantry Divisions; at a feature known as Schlietzen Hill the inexperience of the rebuilt battalions caused heavy casualties. The offensive made little progress; on 6 January 1945 the division began to withdraw towards Lothringen, and on the 9th the latest commander, SS-Standartenführer Linger, was taken prisoner and an army colonel had to take temporary command.

In February and March 1945, the division fought in the Westwall around Rimlingen. US troops broke through on 18 March, forcing *Götz von Berlichingen* on to the retreat once again. On 22 March it abandoned its vehicles and withdrew across the Rhine; on the same day yet another divisional commander – SS-Standartenführer Fritz Klingenberg – was listed as missing, believed killed. In early April the division was resisting the US 63rd and 100th Infantry and 10th Armored Divisions on the Jagst and Kocher rivers; by 21 April it was fighting in the hopeless defence of Nuremberg. Retreating southwards via Munich, *Götz von Berlichingen* eventually crossed the Danube, and the remnants surrendered to US troops near the Achensee on 7 May 1945.

Götz von Berlichingen was the only Waffen-SS division to spend its entire combat career on the Western Front rather than being exposed to the brutalizing conditions of Russia, and its reputation was relatively unsullied by allegations of atrocity. Ironically, there is some evidence that troops from this division themselves became victims of war crimes: the remains of about 200 of its men, apparently shot by Allied troops and buried in a mass grave, were discovered in the mid-1970s.

HORST WESSEL

Ethnic Germans became an increasingly fruitful source of manpower for the burgeoning SS, and 18. SS–Freiwilligen Panzergrenadier Division *Horst Wessel* is a case in point. By 1943 many of the personnel of 1. SS-Infanterie Brigade (mot.) were *Volksdeutsche*. In December 1943, when it was serving as part of XXXV Korps, 9. Armee, it was decided to use the brigade as the nucleus for a new Panzergrenadier division.

Hitler wanted this to be formed with volunteers from the SA and to be named after the SA 'martyr' Horst Wessel. While the title was adopted, and (to a limited extent) the SA's *Kampfrune* symbol, the actual recruits would include very few SA men, among whom volunteers for military service were already channelled to certain Wehrmacht units. Given the extreme hostility between the SA and SS following the latter's bloody purge of the former on 30 June 1934, it is unsurprising that there should have been little enthusiasm among SA men for joining the SS, or among SS men for displaying the SA emblem.

An alternative source of manpower was the ethnic Germans of Hungary. From February 1943 Himmler had persuaded the regime of the Regent, Admiral Horthy, that *Volksdeutsche* should be permitted to volunteer for the Waffen-SS; more than 50,000 such volunteers would ultimately serve with the *Prinz Eugen, Nordland, Reichsführer-SS* and *Florian Geyer* divisions. From April 1944 voluntary service was replaced by actual conscription, making nonsense of the new 18. Division's 'Freiwilligen' title. The division was formed and trained in separated locations in northern Croatia and Hungary, its staff and non-infantry units being based on those from 1. SS-Infanterie Brigade (mot.), with assault guns from the *Nord* Division.

Completion of the *Horst Wessel* on paper would not be achieved until November 1944, but detachments would see combat much earlier. In the second half of March units from the division were deployed in Hungary together with *Florian Geyer* and *Reichsführer-SS* during Operation *Margarethe*, as insurance against the wavering of the Horthy regime. Some elements were detached for anti-partisan duty in Croatia in April–June 1944.

RIGHT: Eastern Front, 1944–45. 1: SS-Hauptsturmführer, winter clothing. This captain is shown wearing a fairly typical set of late-war winter clothing. Over his M1936-style tunic and M1943 trousers, worn with canvas gaiters and ankle boots, he has an early example of the jacket of the M1943 reversible, padded winter clothing. Insignia worn on the front flap varied; sometimes both the metal eagle and death's-head from the service cap were pinned on, but often only the latter. 2: SS-Flak Kanonier, winter clothing. He wears the reversible, padded winter suit, complete with mittens, with the 'autumn' camouflage pattern showing. He carries a magazine of 2cm cannon shells, and has a P 38 pistol as a personal sidearm. 3: SS-Oberscharführer, SS-Fallschirmjäger Bataillon 500; Lithuania, summer 1944. Field-grey Fallschirmjäger trousers are worn with front-lacing jump boots. This warrant officer is armed with the new selective fire Sturmgewehr 44, and has spare magazines in the large smock pockets. He also carries two M1924 'stick' grenades, and the very potent Panzerfaust 60 anti-tank weapon. (Osprey Publishing © Stephen Andrew)

Budapest, 1945. A soldier of the *Florian Geyer* Division watches anxiously from a trench; the division was entirely destroyed in the action in Hungary.

Schäfer helped free a number of German divisions from the 'Brody Pocket'. In August the Kampfgruppe fought south of Lvov; it suffered heavy casualties in combat against both the Red Army and partisans, and had to be reinforced temporarily with a French battalion from SS-Sturmbrigade *Frankreich*. A battalion group, apparently from this Kampfgruppe, also took part in the suppression of the Slovak uprising at the end of August. During the crisis of summer 1944 following the Soviet breakthrough against Army Group Centre, a divisional battlegroup built around SS-Panzergrenadier Regiment 40 was sent to Galicia, and in July this Kampfgruppe uprising at the end of August.

During November 1944 the rest of the division was transferred to Hungary, under LVII Panzer Korps, 6. Armee. It was heavily engaged in the fighting around Budapest, and in December the battlegroup from Galicia rejoined it. At the end of the year *Horst Wessel* became part of Panzer Korps *Feldherrnhalle* of 8. Armee; it escaped encirclement, moving east and north via Jaszbereny into Slovakia and Moravia. Here it carried out anti-partisan operations while briefly refitting in February 1945. In March the division was fighting in south-east Silesia under Army Group Schörner; encircled in a tiny pocket at Oberglogau, it managed to fight its way out and reach German lines nearly 24km west.

After a brief rest the remnants were withdrawn to Neustadt. *Horst Wessel*'s last battlegroup fought around Breslau under 17. Armee in April; they finally surrendered to the Red Army near Hirschberg on 8 May, only a handful of escapees managing to reach American captivity.

As we can see from the example of *Horst Wessel*, the notion of a 'pure' German Waffen-SS division was becoming increasingly uncommon in Himmler's army by the mid years of the war.

FOREIGN DIVISIONS – THE WEST

It is an striking fact that the Waffen-SS recruited significant numbers of men from the citizens of occupied nations in Europe. We have already reflected on the possible reasons for doing do, but the fact remains that Germany was not the only place in which national socialist sympathies flourished. Scandinavia proved to be an especially good recruiting ground, 11. SS-Freiwilligen Panzergrenadier Division *Nordland* being an important example.

NORDLAND

The origins of the *Nordland* Division can be traced to January 1943, when Himmler and Gottlob Berger reshaped the northern European element in the Waffen-SS. After the initial surge of volunteers, slower recruiting made it difficult to keep the individual national legions up to strength. It was planned to bring them together to create a division, and to twin it with 5. SS-Panzer Division *Wiking* in a new 'Germanic Armoured Corps' – III (germanisches) SS-Panzer Korps. The formation of the new 11. Division was put in hand in March–July 1943 at the Gräfenwöhr training area; the nucleus was the existing *Nordland* Regiment transferred from the *Wiking* Division, and the Freiwilligen Legion *Norwegen* and Freikorps *Danmark*. Originally it was intended to include a third regiment based on the Freiwilligen Legion *Niederlande*, but later that the Dutch should form a separate *Nederland* Brigade within III (germanisches) SS-Panzer Korps. The divisional commander, SS-Brigadeführer Fritz von Scholz, was the former commander of the *Nordland* Regiment.

Since many of the personnel were combat veterans, training was completed by August 1943. The *Nordland* Division was sent into action that September in northern Croatia, to help counter Tito's communist partisans. Following the Italian armistice of that month, it also helped to disarm the Italian 57th 'Lombardia' Division. In late November the division left Croatia for the northern Russian Front, assigned to 18. Armee; at this point it numbered just under 11,500 men.

ABOVE: *Nordland* Division, Russian Front, 1944–45. 1: SS-Untersturmführer, SS-Panzer Artillerie Regiment 11. 2: SS-Unterscharführer, SS-Panzergrenadier Regiment 24 *Danmark*. 3: SS-Rottenführer, SS-Panzer Abteilung (Sturmgeschütz) 11 *Hermann von Salza*. The *Nordland*, as a Panzergrenadier division, was entitled to a tank battalion, but in most such divisions by 1944 this was in fact equipped with self-propelled armoured assault guns. (Osprey Publishing © Stephen Andrew)

On 14 January 1944 the Oranienbaum sector on the Gulf of Finland was struck by the Soviet Second Shock Army, outnumbering the defending German forces by four to one. The first German units to feel the brunt of the attack crumpled almost immediately,

A recruitment poster for the Waffen-SS Ski Jäger Battailon. The battalion formed part of the 6. Waffen-SS Gebirgs Division *Nord*.

leaving *Nordland* in a precarious position. The division held on tenaciously, and elements of the *Norge* Regiment even launched counter-attacks; but after two days' heavy fighting the division withdrew to new positions, to which they clung alongside the *Nederland* Brigade and remnants of two Luftwaffe divisions. On 25 January Soviet attacks almost destroyed I Bataillon of the *Danmark* Regiment; the division continued a fighting retreat westwards, reaching the River Luga. On the evening of 30 January, under continuing pressure, all German troops were pulled back and the bridges were blown; however, the Red Army had already crossed further south. After two days of heavy combat, *Nordland* was forced to abandon its positions along the Luga and retreat to the Narva line.

Between February and August 1944 the units of III (germanisches) SS-Panzer Korps managed to hold the area around Narva despite repeated attempts to dislodge them. When the first assaults failed the Soviets unleashed a massed bombardment over several days before once again attempting to storm the German positions, the main weight now falling on the *Nederland* Brigade. After several days the Dutch were forced to withdraw from the foremost positions, but were then reinforced by elements of *Nordland*. Once again the line was held, and by now the enemy offensive had begun to lose momentum. During a period of static warfare the hardest-hit units of *Nordland* – I Bataillon of both the *Norge* and *Danmark* Regiments – returned to Germany for rebuilding.

On 22 June 1944 the Red Army launched its massive offensive against the German Army Group Centre – Operation *Bagration* – which ripped a gap in the Eastern Front almost 400km wide, through which huge Soviet formations poured westwards. The Baltic front to the north was now in danger of being completely cut off, and in late July all German forces were withdrawn from the Narva bridgehead to the 'Tannenberg' defence line. There too heavy assaults were repulsed, but at huge cost, including the *Nordland* Division's commander, SS-Brigadeführer von Scholz, killed during a bombardment.

In mid-September, the German forces in Estonia were ordered to withdraw into Latvia in the face of yet another offensive; and by 23 September, *Nordland* had taken up positions south-east of Riga. For the next two weeks the division took part in defensive fighting against overwhelming odds. On 6 October, Heeresgruppe Nord, including *Nordland*, was withdrawn into Kurland (Kurzeme), Latvia's westernmost region; on the 12th, the division took up new positions in the south of the 'pocket'; and on the 13th the last bridges over the River Daugaua were blown and Riga was abandoned to the Soviets. Throughout October, determined attacks on the pocket were held off, at heavy cost, but the last two months of 1944 passed relatively quietly.

On 20 January 1945 the Red Army attacked once more, and *Danmark* was all but annihilated. It was decided to evacuate the greatly weakened division by sea for refitting in Germany. Embarking at Libau, *Nordland* sailed on 28 January; arriving in Pomerania, it was allocated to the new 11. Panzer Armee in Army Group Steiner. In mid-February III (germanisches) SS-Panzer Korps attempted Operation *Sonnenwende* to the north-west against the flank of Zhukov's 1st White Russian Front near Arnswalde. Conceived by Guderian, this operation was originally planned on a much larger front, but was scaled down on Hitler's orders into little more than a localized counter-attack. *Nordland*'s attack was a complete success, driving the enemy back as far as Lake Ihna, relieving the

Norwegian Waffen-SS volunteers manually haul an anti-tank gun into position. Between 1940 and 1945, approximately 15,000 Norwegians served in the German Army and Waffen-SS.

garrison of Arnswalde and allowing the evacuation of civilians. Inevitably, however, after the initial shock Soviet resistance stiffened; SS-Obergruppenführer Felix Steiner eventually ordered a withdrawal, and by 28 February *Nordland* had fallen back to the area around Stargard and Stettin on the River Oder. (By this time the I Bataillon of both Norge and Danmark regiments had left the division, serving thereafter with the 5. SS-Panzer Division *Wiking*.)

On 1 March 1945, the Red Army launched the greatest artillery bombardment yet seen. The German defenders could do little more than attempt to slow the flood of enemy tanks that followed, and within a week *Nordland* had been pushed back to Altdamm, the last German bridgehead on the east bank of the Oder; on 14 March the remnants were pulled back across the river and into the town itself. Over the next few days they fought on in the rubble, but on 19 March *Nordland* was pulled out of the line and sent west for a few days' rest and refitting in the Schwedt-Angermünde area, about 65km north-east of Berlin. The last drafts of replacements included former Luftwaffe and Kriegsmarine personnel.

The final Russian offensive opened on 16 April. *Nordland* was holding an area east of Berlin as part of LVI Panzer Korps; by the 18th, it had been pushed back into the suburbs and was declared part of the garrison. Small, fragmented battlegroups fell back through Mahlsdorf, Biesdorf and Neukölln to Tempelhof airfield; even in these last desperate days the *Hermann von Salza* battalion launched a counter-attack which held up the Soviets in the Treptow area. However, when the division was ordered to attack on 25 April the commander, SS-Brigadeführer Ziegler, refused to sacrifice any more of his men in futile actions. He was removed from command and replaced by SS-Brigadeführer Dr Gustav Krukenberg – who brought with him some 300 Frenchmen of the so-called 33. Waffen Grenadier Division der SS *Charlemagne*. By 1 May a few score survivors were clinging to the rubble around the Chancellery. Krukenberg

LEFT: Dutch volunteers, 1941–45. 1: Legions-Schütze, Freiwilligen Legion *Niederlande*, 1941–42. This private wears a greatcoat on which collar patches have been applied (although not used by the army, collar patches on SS greatcoats were relatively common). The right patch shows the vertical version of the so-called 'wolf hook' rune. On the left sleeve is the early Dutch national colours patch, worn just above the '*Legion Niederlande*' (German spelling) cuffband – a rather crudely lettered, locally made example, which omits the 'Frw.' prefix. 2: Legions-Unterscharführer, Freiwilligen Legion *Niederlande*, spring 1943. This junior NCO in walking-out dress wears the M1941 tunic and the peaked service cap for non-commissioned ranks, with white infantry piping. 3: SS-Oberschütze, 23. SS-Freiwilligen Panzergrenadier Division *Nederland*, 1944–45. The M1940 field cap was still seen in the last year of the war. On the M1942 tunic this senior private displays the later horizontal form of *Wolfsangel*. 4: SS-Sturmmann, 23. SS-Freiwilligen Panzergrenadier Division *Nederland*, 1945. He displays the divisional cuffband with the final, Waffen-SS-pattern Dutch arm shield. The black shoulder straps are piped artillery red, and he wears the army Flak Battle Badge. A separate Flak Abteilung often disappeared from divisional orders of battle during 1944; there was a policy of gathering these as corps assets, and some divisions seem to have retained only a Flak company, sometimes grouped with the Panzerjäger unit. (Osprey Publishing © Stephen Andrew)

Danish Waffen-SS recruits look cheerful during a physical exercise session. Six thousand Danes became Waffen-SS soldiers, helping Himmler flesh out his ranks when the Wehrmacht had a near-monopoly over German recruitment.

authorized them to attempt to break out, but only a handful succeeded, most being killed or captured in the final days of resistance.

Twenty-seven soldiers of the *Nordland* Division were decorated with the Knight's Cross of the Iron Cross.

Although the *Nordland* Division was ostensibly from Scandinavia, by the end of the war its ranks came from across Europe as far east as Latvia and Finland. It even included a tiny British contingent, the British Free Corps. Perhaps 20 members of this tiny propaganda unit are believed to have been attached briefly to the division's reconnaissance battalion – SS-Panzer Aufklärungs Abteilung 11 – in March 1945 while it was out of the line in the Angermünde area south of Stettin. A cuffband with the legend 'British Free Corps' (English spelling) in machine-embroidered Gothic script was photographed being worn.

FREIWILLIGE LEGION *NIEDERLANDE*

Being considered a true 'Germanic' people, the Dutch were welcomed as volunteers in the Waffen-SS as early as spring 1941. A retired chief of staff of the Dutch armed forces, Luitenant-Generaal H.A. Seyffardt, was appointed to head the Freiwilligen Legion *Niederlande*. Recruitment was slow, especially among officers, but eventually three battalions were formed and despatched to the Leningrad sector of the Eastern Front in January 1942.

From March they served under 2. SS-Infanterie Brigade (mot.), and earned a dependable reputation during the Wehrmacht's horrendous first winter in Russia. In March the unit was praised for successfully attacking Soviet bunker systems. In June it captured the village of Mal Sawoschye, with some 3,000 prisoners – among them General Andrei Vlassov, who later commanded an entire army of anti-Soviet volunteers. The Legion remained on the Leningrad front throughout 1942, fighting alongside the legions from Norway and Belgium as well as Latvian SS units. Back in Holland the Legion's commander, General Seyffardt, was assassinated by the Dutch resistance in February 1943.

In April 1943 the Legion was withdrawn from the front for upgrading to regimental status, but lost 1,700 men as cadre for the *Nordland* Division. In May the unit's title changed to SS-Freiwilligen Panzergrenadier Brigade *Nederland*, later adding the number '4'. In September the brigade was transferred to Croatia for anti-partisan duty; and in November its regiments received their honour titles.

In January 1944, about 5,500 strong, the brigade was back on the Leningrad sector of the Russian Front, just in time for the great Soviet breakthrough. Pushed back steadily westwards to the Narva line between the Gulf of Finland and Lake Peipus by the end of February, *Nederland* continued to fight with great spirit throughout the battles of the spring and summer. The brigade held on to its positions doggedly until the Soviet summer offensive of late June completely unhinged the whole Russian Front, and deep penetrations in Lithuania to the south threatened to cut off the German forces in Latvia and Estonia. Under the massive attacks of late July the brigade made a brief stand at a feature called Orphanage Hill with elements of *Nordland* and *Langemarck*; two days later they were pushed back, after costing the Red Army more than 100 tanks, but suffering huge casualties. During August, the *De Ruiter* regiment of *Nederland* suffered the same fate; a few hundred replacements were received, but these were mostly former Kriegsmarine sailors of limited combat value. The brigade was pushed back ever further south-westwards through Estonia; and by October 1944 the exhausted remnant of *Nederland* was around Libau in Kurland.

In December the decision was taken to upgrade the brigade to divisional status – 23. SS-Freiwilligen Panzergrenadier Division *Nederland* – taking the vacant number of the disbanded *Kama* (see below). The Dutch survivors were evacuated from the Kurland Pocket by sea to Stettin (with further heavy loss of life in the sinking of the transport ship *Moira*). After forming in Pomerania in January–February 1945, the 23. Division *Nederland*, with only about 2,200 combatants, was sent back into action around Stargard and Stettin. In the closing weeks of the war *Nederland* moved south along the Oder front and fought on the eastern approaches to Berlin, taking heavy casualties around Fürstenwalde. In early May survivors managed to surrender to US units near Magdeburg.

BELGIAN UNITS

The Netherlands' neighbour Belgium also had thriving nationalist movements; the Rexists in French-speaking Wallonia, and the Vlaamsch Nationaal Verbond in Flanders, had been sympathetic to Germany, and the Flemish-speaking element of the Belgian population were considered as racially 'Germanic'. In December 1940 a Dutch/ Belgian Flemish regiment, entitled *Westland*, became part of the new 5. SS-Division *Wiking*; and in April 1941 a further Flemish-speaking volunteer regiment was formed under the title Freiwilligen Standarte *Nordwest*. After the German invasion of Russia in June 1941 the Dutch and Belgian-Flemish elements of this unit were separated into two new national regiments, the Freiwilligen Legion *Niederlande* and Freiwilligen Legion *Flandern*.

The collaborationist leader of the Flemish National League, Staf de Clercq, addresses Flemish men volunteering for German service. The volunteers eventually reached sufficient levels to form the 27. SS-Freiwilligen Grenadier Division *Langemarck* (flamische Nr.1).

LEFT: Dutch and French volunteers. 1: SS-Oberscharführer, SS-Pionier Kompanie 33; Berlin, April 1945. 2: Grenadier, 33. Waffen Grenadier Division der SS *Charlemagne*; Pomerania, February 1945. 3: SS-Unterscharführer, Landstorm *Nederland*; Holland, autumn 1944. (Osprey Publishing © Stephen Andrew)

Despite the willingness of many Flemings to enlist, *Flandern* suffered from the same problems that were to dog many foreign SS units. There was a gulf between the propaganda of the recruiters and the actual conditions of service. The former stressed national identity, exaggerated the degree of independence that would be enjoyed, and at first made such promises as the retention of former Belgian Army ranks, and even that service would be limited to local policing duties. Once in uniform the recruits found these promises to be worthless; they were harshly treated by German officers and NCOs, and morale plunged. Himmler had to intervene personally to improve this culture; but in November 1941 the Legion, about 1,100 strong (of whom 14 officers and 950 men were Flemish), was judged combat ready and was sent to join the 2. SS-Infanterie Brigade (mot.) in the Novgorod area of the northern Russian Front.

Between December 1941 and June 1942 the unit saw repeated heavy action around Volkhov – often in concert with the Spanish 'Blue Division' – and earned a good reputation, at a high cost in casualties.

Pulled out in June for brief rest and refitting at the Heidelager Training Area, east of Debica in Poland, and Milovice, Czechoslovakia, it returned to the Leningrad front in August, now under the command of Major Konrad Schellong, transferred from the *Wiking* Division. For the rest of the year and into spring 1943 the unit was frequently in action alongside Dutch, Norwegian and Latvian volunteers, and despite successive batches of replacements it was worn away by combat attrition.

In April 1943 the survivors were withdrawn to Debica and Milovice; and the following month the Legion was ordered expanded into the 2,200-strong SS-Freiwilligen Sturmbrigade *Langemarck* (SS Volunteer Assault Brigade *Langemarck*). Main units were two infantry battalions plus a Panzerjäger Kompanie, Sturmgeschütz Kompanie and Flak Kompanie. Posted back to the rear areas of the Eastern Front, it spent some six months working up before being declared combat ready in December 1943.

That month and the next the Sturmbrigade saw heavy fighting around Berdichev and Zhitomir, being reduced to about 400 men while covering the withdrawal of the 1. SS-Division *Leibstandarte Adolf Hitler*. In February 1944 the brigade was attached to a Kampfgruppe of *Das Reich* Division, finally falling back after suffering up to 75 per cent losses. During April–July 1944 the brigade was rested and rebuilt in Poland and Bohemia. In the face of the great Soviet summer offensive, Operation *Bagration*, a battlegroup from the brigade – Kampfgruppe Rehmann – was sent to the Narva front west of Leningrad. They fought on 25–29 July alongside the *Nederland* and *Wallonien* brigades and elements of the 11. SS-Division *Nordland* in the defence of Orphanage Hill, from which only 37 men of the unit survived unwounded, and where a young anti-tank gunner named Remi Schrijnen earned the Knight's Cross for sustained heroism. The survivors were evacuated by sea back to Germany.

ABOVE: Belgian divisions, 1945. 1: SS-Unterscharführer, 28. SS-Freiwilligen Grenadier Division *Wallonien*; Pomerania, spring 1945. 2: SS-Sturmmann, Panzerjäger Kompanie, 28. SS-Freiwilligen Grenadier Division *Wallonien*; Pomerania, spring 1945. 3: SS-Schütze, 27. SS-Freiwilligen Grenadier Division *Langemarck*; Altdamm bridgehead, March 1945 – on his right collar is the 'Trifos' three-legged sunwheel swastika; on his left sleeve, the German-made version of the national armshield with a black lion on a yellow ground, above the *Langemarck* cuffband. (Osprey Publishing © Stephen Andrew)

At Soltau on 18 October 1944 the brigade was upgraded to divisional status (27. SS-Freiwilligen Grenadier Division *Langemarck*), its roughly 3,000 men being reinforced with drafts from the Luftwaffe and Kriegsmarine, the Flemish Allgemeine-SS and Labour Service, the Vlaamse Waach militia, Flemish conscript workers, and others who had chosen to leave Belgium as the British liberation army rolled forward. Even with this additional manpower, however, Langemarck was well under strength. It had been planned that the division would take part in the December 1944 Ardennes offensive for propaganda purposes; but the advance had already begun to falter before it could be committed, and the division returned to the Eastern Front.

By the end of January 1945 Langemarck was located around Stettin, and saw action at Stargard and Altdamm through February and March. Reduced to a battalion-strength battlegroup, it was forced back over the River Oder on 20 March, resting briefly around Schwedt and re-arming as tank-hunters. Between 3 and 10 May the remnants of the division surrendered to the British in Mecklenburg.

Unlike their Flemish fellow-countrymen, the Walloons of the French-speaking Belgian provinces were not at first considered sufficiently 'Germanic' for SS service. After the invasion of the USSR volunteers were accepted for the German Army, however; the leader of the Walloon nationalist Christus Rex party, Léon Degrelle, successfully encouraged the formation of a volunteer battalion. Initially about 1,200 strong, the recruits left for Polish training camps in August 1942, and were soon designated (Wallonische) Infanterie Bataillon Nr.373. Although offered a commission in view of his leadership of the Rexist party, Degrelle chose to serve as a private soldier. After completing its training the unit was committed to anti-partisan duties in Poland in November 1941–February 1942; it was then attached to the 100. Jäger Division. By May 1942, Degrelle had risen through the NCO ranks, been commissioned Leutnant and awarded both classes of the Iron Cross.

After a brief period with the 68. Infanterie Division, the battalion joined the 97. Jäger Division on the southern sector of the Russian Front, seeing fierce combat along the River Don and later in the Caucasus during the deep advances of summer 1942; by December strength had been reduced to less than 200 men. However, Belgian replacements restored the unit to about 1,600 strong by May 1943; and the following month it was transferred from the army to the Waffen-SS and expanded into an assault brigade.

In September 1943, the men of the SS-Sturmbrigade *Wallonien* were in action in the Dnieper Bend alongside the *Wiking* Division; and in November they were among the 56,000 troops cut off in the Cherkassy (Korsun) Pocket. Fighting was extremely intense, and the Walloons were reduced from about 2,000 to some 630 men by February 1944. The brigade played a leading part in the break-out of that month, but lost over a third of its remaining strength. The commander was among those killed, and SS-Standartenführer Léon Degrelle – awarded the Knight's Cross on 20 February – appears to have replaced him at this date; he would continue to command until the end of the war.

After the briefest withdrawal to Germany, in April 1944 the rebuilt brigade was sent to help bolster the Narva front in the far north. The fierce defensive battles of that summer involved so many foreign volunteer units that Narva has been dubbed the 'Battle of the European SS'. In August *Wallonien* fought stubbornly as they were gradually pushed back from the 'Tannenberg Line', to Kambi, Dorpat and Noela to the Parna–Keerdu line. On 27 August, Degrelle was awarded the Oakleaves to the Knight's Cross; and a few days later SS-Obergruppenführer Steiner, commanding III (germanisches) SS-Panzerkorps, decorated 200 men of his brigade with the Iron Cross.

In September–November 1944 the brigade refitted in Hanover and Brunswick, and was raised on paper to divisional status as 28. SS-Freiwilligen Grenadier Division *Wallonien*. Although it received some armour, and the same kind of influx of motley replacements as *Langemarck*, it too remained far below true divisional strength, and had only about 4,000 combatants when, late in January 1945, it was posted to the Oder front in Pomerania. In February, under 11. Panzer Armee, it saw fierce defensive fighting around Stargard and Stettin, launching counter-attacks at Streelow, Arnswalde and in the Linden Hills. Some 1,200 survivors were forced back to the Altdamm bridgehead on 8 March; after its evacuation they were briefly rested and inadequately resupplied around Schwedt in the last week of the month. After holding part of the 'Randow–Bruch' defensive line in April, a battalion-strength remnant succeeded in withdrawing into Schleswig-Holstein in early May; others surrendered further south, at Schwerin and Brandenburg. On 8 May, Degrelle – condemned to death in absentia by a Belgian court – made good his escape and flew to Spain, where he lived openly until his death in 2000.

ITALIAN UNITS

Given its fascist heritage, Italy seemed another obvious choice for Waffen-SS manpower. Following the Allied invasion of Sicily in July 1943, King Victor Emmanuel of Italy dismissed the fascist government and ordered the arrest of Benito Mussolini. By the time the Allies landed on the mainland on 3 September the new government of General Badoglio had already secretly agreed an armistice, which was declared on 8 September. The substantial German forces in Italy immediately moved to disarm the Italian Army and occupy all key points. On 12 September, commandos led by Otto Skorzeny made their daring glider landing at the mountaintop hotel on

the Gran Sasso where Mussolini was held, and spirited him off to Berlin. Hitler persuaded him to announce a new Fascist regime, the Italian Socialist Republic (RSI), based in German-occupied northern Italy.

On 24 September 1943, Himmler announced the creation of an Italian SS Legion, though not yet as a tactical unit of the Waffen-SS. By December some 15,000 men had reportedly come forward; some were genuine fascist volunteers, but others former inmates of prison and labour camps released to serve the German cause. During October about 3,000 were sent to the Munsingen training grounds in Germany and to an officer training school at Ferrara; during the winter some 8,600 all ranks were apparently under instruction, including a battalion trained at Debica in Poland which took that town's name. Many RSI units were being formed, changes of title were frequent, and the sources are confused over the manpower of those specifically intended for the SS. Training did not proceed smoothly, and a number of well-motivated volunteer officers resigned over mistreatment of the Italians by German personnel.

The Waffen-SS recruiters used a variety of stirring images in an attempt to lure foreign volunteers to the cause. The poster here was used in Italy following the armistice in 1943.

The so-called 1. Italienische Freiwilligen Sturmbrigade/1a Brigata d'Assalto (1st Assault Brigade, Italian Armed Militia), first saw action against communist partisans in early 1944, with its two battalions named *Debica* and *Vendetta*. These would later become respectively I & II Bataillon, Waffen Grenadier Regiment der SS 81; and *Debica* would later still be retitled SS–Fusilier Bataillon 29. In March both battalions were sent to fight against the Anglo-US landing forces at Anzio/Nettuno, split into dispersed companies deployed alongside German units – whose commanders later gave them favourable reports. They took heavy losses, *Vendetta* suffering 340 casualties from 650 while fighting with 16. SS-Division units against the US 3rd

LEFT: Italian volunteers, 1944–45. 1: Waffen-Sturmbannführer, Legione SS Italiana, January 1944. 2: Schütze, 1. Italienische Freiwilligen Sturmbrigade; Nettuno front, April 1944. 3: Waffen-Scharführer, 29. Waffen Grenadier Division der SS (italienische Nr.1); northern Italy, April 1945 (Osprey Publishing © Stephen Andrew)

SPANISCHE-FREIWILLIGEN KOMPANIE DER SS 101

This very small unit was the last remnant of the Spanish volunteer *División Azul*, which earned a high reputation on the Russian Front between October 1941 and November 1943 as the Wehrmacht's 250. Infanterie Division. After General Franco withdrew the division under Allied diplomatic pressure, a 1,500-strong 'Blue Legion' fought on until March 1944 on the Narva front. The Blue Legion itself was then withdrawn, but a couple of hundred diehard anti-communists insisted on remaining, passing on to the Waffen-SS order of battle as SS-Freiwilligen Kompanie 101 (spanische) – when formed in June 1944 it was originally named after its barracks, at Stablack near Königsberg. Even at that stage some 150 new volunteers from Spain made their way to German recruiting offices, allowing the raising of Kompanie 102 at Stablack by March 1945. According to the Waffen-SS veterans' magazine *Die Freiwillige*, the Spanish companies were dispersed. Commanded by Captain Miguel Ezquerra Sanchez, Kompanie 101 fought in the retreat through Pomerania in early 1945 attached to the *Wallonien* Division. Ultimately Captain Ezquerra's unit, at least, was attached to the *Nordland* Division, and fought in the final defensive battles in Berlin. The few survivors of those captured by the Soviets were not released until 1954; Ezquerra himself had managed to escape from his captors and, remarkably, succeeded in making his way back to Spain. No special insignia were authorized, but the armshield worn by the Blue Division continued in use, probably on the left upper sleeve: a gold-edged heraldic shield with red/broad yellow/red horizontal stripes, below gold lettering 'ESPAÑA', all on a black background.

Infantry Division in April. In recognition of their performance, on 3 May Himmler declared these Italian troops to be fully integrated into the Waffen-SS.

The Italian SS troops spent the second half of 1944 dispersed for anti-partisan duties all over northern Italy. In September, following the absorption of other RSI units, they were collectively retitled as 9. Waffen Grenadier Brigade der SS (italienische Nr.1), but this unification was in name only and individual units continued to fight dispersed, entirely on anti-partisan operations. In the last weeks of the war the brigade was officially upgraded as the 29. Waffen Grenadier Division, taking the vacant number of the former Kaminski Brigade. On 30 April 1945, the *Debica* Bataillon was fortunate enough to surrender to US forces at Gorgonzola; the rest of the Italian SS were forced to surrender to partisans in early May, and many were reportedly executed more or less out of hand.

33. WAFFEN GRENADIER DIVISION DER SS *CHARLEMAGNE* (FRANZÖZISCHE NR.1)

France was also not immune to the siren calls of Waffen-SS recruiters. Following the German invasion of the USSR in June 1941, right-wing factions in occupied France called for the creation of a volunteer French legion to fight in the East. Some 5,800 of about 13,000 applicants were initially accepted, and the first batch left for training at Debica, Poland, in September 1941. Commanded by Colonel Roger Labonne, this Légion des Volontaires Français contre le Bolchévisme (LVF) was attached to the German Army as a two-battalion infantry regiment, which saw immediate combat when it arrived with 7. Infanterie Division on the Moscow front in November. The LVF lost about half its strength by February 1942, although some 1,400 replacements from France had brought it up to three battalions. Pulled out of the line in March, the remaining two battalions (I and III) were used for dispersed anti-partisan operations throughout 1942 and 1943, occasionally suffering significant casualties. In June 1943 the II Bataillon was re-raised, Colonel Edgar Puaud was appointed CO, and the unit was brought together under 286th Security Division.

Meanwhile, continued signs of French willingness to enlist in pro-German units led Himmler to explore the possibility of taking French volunteers into the Waffen-SS. By January 1943 a recruiting office had been set up in Paris; in July the Vichy government authorized enlistments; and in November, the first batches of French officers and NCOs entered the Bad Tölz and Posen training schools. This decision heralded the absorption of the LVF as the Französische SS-Freiwilligen Grenadier Regiment; the official date is variously reported, but the unit was in action against Soviet partisans in January–February 1944.

When the Red Army launched its June 1944 offensive the regiment distinguished itself in furious defensive fighting. Withdrawn into Bohemia in July for rest and refitting, it was renamed Waffen Grenadier Brigade der SS *Charlemagne* (französische Nr.1), and subsequently deployed alongside the 18. SS-Division *Horst Wessel*. During August the unit took further heavy punishment in the Carpathian Mountains of Hungary, losing more than 80 per cent of its officers killed and 790 rankers dead or wounded. (One source gives September 1944 as the date of the LVF's official disbandment, but this may have been a retrospective announcement.)

Rebuilt at Wildflecken, the retitled Waffen Grenadier Brigade *Charlemagne* received replacements from several sources, including men of the Milice and other collaborators who had been obliged to leave France ahead of the Allied and Free French liberation forces. In February 1945 it received its final change of title, to the 33. Waffen Grenadier Division der SS *Charlemagne* (französische Nr.1); this did not reflect an expansion to true divisional size, however, since it had only some 7,500 men.

In mid-February the division was despatched to Hammerstein, Pomerania, where it was struck by a massive Soviet assault and almost at once fragmented into three main elements. One battlegroup, under the divisional commander SS-Brigadeführer Dr Gustav Krukenberg, fought its way to the Baltic coast and was fortunate enough to be shipped to Denmark, whence it transferred to Neustrelitz in Mecklenburg. During

The bottom of the barrel. Two German boys, recruited into the Waffen-SS in the dying days of World War II, make sorry-looking prisoners between two US military policemen. The *Hitlerjugend* Division came to incorporate 16- and 17-year-old boys.

March the other units were driven by the Red Army from successive positions near Hammerstein, Körlin and Kolberg. About 3,200 survivors and replacements seem to have gathered at Neustrelitz and Wildflecken at the end of March.

In April 1945 the divisional commander gave these Frenchmen the choice of being released from their oath, and about 800 drifted away or were allocated to construction units. Krukenberg led the remainder to take part in the defence of Berlin, as Kampfgruppe *Charlemagne*, attached to the 11. SS-Division *Nordland*; identified units were Kampfbataillon 58, and SS-Bataillon Fenet under the former CO of Regiment 57. Reportedly, Kampfbataillon 58 withdrew westwards in time to surrender with some

RIGHT: *Handschar* Division, Balkans, 1944–45. 1: Waffen-Untersturmführer, autumn 1944. 2: Waffen-Gebirgsjäger. 3: SS-Hauptsturmführer. Note how figure 2 wears an M1942 first-pattern camouflage smock over his M1943 field uniform, the collar patches the only visible insignia. The field-grey fez is one of the shorter models of the range of styles produced. [Osprey Publishing © Stephen Andrew]

other elements to British forces at Bad Kleinen and Wismar. In the last few days of the war Fenet's handful of survivors proved themselves adept tank-killers in the shattered streets of the capital, the last 30-odd men surrendering near the Potsdamer rail station.

EASTERN EUROPE AND THE SOVIET UNION

Given the horrors unleashed on Eastern Europe, as well the Nazis' racial perspectives on the East, it is scarcely conceivable that the Waffen-SS ranks would come to be filled with tens of thousands of citizens from these territories. The Baltic States, Croatia, Ukraine, Russia and others nations yielded many willing volunteers, their recruitment often fuelled by personal experience of communist persecution or Eastern brands of anti-Semitism. The units thus formed were often unleashed within their own nations, 'anti-partisan' duties becoming a label behind which the most appalling atrocities were committed.

The diversifying ethnicity of the Waffen-SS is perfectly demonstrated by 13. Waffen Gebirgs Division der SS *Handschar* (kroatische Nr.1). The idea of creating a volunteer division of Muslims from Croatian possessions in the now fragmented Yugoslavia was first raised by Himmler in late 1942; Hitler favoured the idea, but authorization for its raising was not given until February 1943. The intention was to harness the historical enmities between different communities to serve German ends. The communist partisans under Tito, who were proving so troublesome to the Italian and German occupiers, were predominantly from the traditionally Orthodox Christian population of Serbia. There was a historical hostility between the Serbs and the roughly 40 per cent Muslim population of the often-disputed province of Bosnia-Herzegovina.

Despite obstruction by Ante Pavelic's Croatian regime, recruitment began in March 1943. The SS made use of the pro-Nazi Muslim religious leader, the Grand Mufti of Jerusalem, to encourage the cause of fighting the 'Jewish-Bolshevik menace'. Initial efforts brought in almost 8,000 volunteers, but this flow soon slackened. Stern measures were taken against Croatian obstruction; the numbers were bulked out by transfers of Muslims from the ranks of the Croatian forces, and the Germans soon resorted to blatant conscription. Leadership was provided by (predominantly) *Volksdeutsche* and some Muslim officers of the Croatian Army, and by a *Reichsdeutsche* and *Volksdeutsche* cadre transferred from the *Prinz Eugen* Division.

The Muslim troops were unique within the SS in being permitted to have their own religious teachers (imams) serving with them. Chaplains served in the German Army and Kriegsmarine (but not in the Luftwaffe); Waffen-SS troops were not formally forbidden to hold religious beliefs, but the officially approved status was '*Gottglaubige*' or 'believer in God', as opposed to declared membership of a specific faith.

In July 1943 it was decided that the division should be formed at a safe distance from local distractions, around Le Puy in central France. This move was unpopular, and not only with the openly resentful conscripts; many of the volunteers had reportedly been tricked into enlisting and had no wish to become part of the Waffen-SS. Morale was further damaged by the contemptuous attitude shown towards these 'Mujos' by German and *Volksdeutsche* cadres. This culminated on 16 September 1944 in a mutiny at Villefranche-sur-Rouergue by about 1,000 men, who killed a number of officers and NCOs before being disarmed by better-disciplined units. Ringleaders were executed, some 250 were sent to concentration camps, and more than 500 others into forced labour with the Todt Organization.

The elements of the division were moved progressively to training areas in Silesia, and in January 1944 its strength was listed as 21,065 all ranks. By mid-February it had

A parade of Croatian troops from the *Handschar* Division. Special dispensation was given for the wearing of the traditional Muslim fez. A special collar patch was introduced showing a hand holding a scimitar (*Handschar*) and a small swastika.

returned to northern Bosnia, based around Brcko on the River Sava; and in March it was serving against Tito's partisans as part of V SS-Gebirgs Korps alongside the *Prinz Eugen* Division. Not long after its arrival *Handschar* lost one of its battalions, transferred to provide a cadre for the Albanian 21. SS-Division *Skanderbeg*. Manpower was swiftly made up by local recruitment; but only a month later the division had to provide yet another large cadre for 23. Division *Kama*, and in June over 1,300 men were transferred.

From March to September 1944 *Handschar* continued anti-partisan operations, committing many atrocities. By the latter month the general withdrawal of German forces from the Aegean and Balkans had begun, as a consequence of the defection of Bulgaria and Romania from the Axis; and *Handschar* suffered 2,000-plus desertions in September alone. (Returns for 20 September still give a paper strength of 18,520, of whom 6,015 were German.) Things came to a head in October when a large part of the division's supposedly elite *Begleitkompanie* ('escort company') deserted. The furious Himmler ordered all Bosnians whose loyalty was suspect to be disarmed and assigned to labour duties.

In mid-October *Handschar* became a regimental battlegroup; some sources state that it had roughly equal numbers of Germans/*Volksdeutsche* and loyal Muslim volunteers, others that there were few if any Bosnians remaining. The unit was led by SS-Sturmbannführer Hans Hanke of Regiment 28; in November–December by SS-Standartenführer Helmuth Raithel; and again by SS-Obersturmbannführer Hanke from January 1945. By November the unit was in action against Red Army advances in southern Hungary and in the Danube bridgeheads in northern Yugoslavia, retreating into the so-called 'Margarethe-Stellung' (Margaret Redoubt) between the River Drava and Lake Balaton. In December the *Handschar* battlegroup was near Barcs on the Drava, under LXVIII Korps of 2. Panzer Armee.

This sector was relatively static until late March 1945, when a renewed Soviet offensive pushed the Germans out of the Margarethe-Stellung. The battlegroup retreated westwards into the Austrian mountains, moving north past Klagenfurt; and

RIGHT: Eastern volunteers, 1944–45. 1: Waffen-Sturmbannführer, 21. Waffen Gebirgs Division der SS Skanderbeg, summer 1944. This reconstruction shows a *Reichsdeutsche* member of the staff wearing the M1943 *Einheitsfeldmütze*, the crown piped in aluminium for officers, and with the SS mountain troops' Edelweiss side badge. 2: SS-Oberscharführer, 22. SS-Freiwilligen Kavallerie Division, spring 1944. This Hungarian senior NCO wears a casual field uniform plausible for training in the first half of 1944. The NCO's peaked service cap is piped in cavalry yellow, as are the shoulder straps of his M1943 tunic; cloth-reinforced late-production riding breeches are worn with long riding boots. 3: Waffen-Gebirgsjäger, 23. Waffen Gebirgs Division der SS *Kama*. One of the small number of mountain riflemen actually enlisted for this projected second Muslim mountain division, he wears the M1943 field tunic with plain patches on both collars. Mountain trousers, Styrian gaiters and cleated mountain boots are worn, and conventional belt equipment is carried. This Kosovar recruit displays the rarest pattern of fez associated with the *Handschar* Division, also believed to have been worn within *Skanderbeg*; of conical shape, it follows the traditional Albanian form – the Kosovo area had a large population of ethnic Albanians. (Osprey Publishing © Stephen Andrew)

in early May the survivors surrendered to British troops south of St Veit. Given *Handschar*'s reputation, they were lucky to fall into British rather than Soviet or Yugoslav hands (although there is an unconfirmed report that some were handed over to Tito's forces and subsequently executed).

The raising of a second 'Croatian' anti-partisan division – 23. Waffen Gebirgs Division der SS *Kama* (kroatische Nr.2) – was ordered in June 1944, but the division never attained the status even of a single formed unit. Its manpower was to be Bosnian Muslim with a German cadre, and some 1,350 men from the *Handschar* Division provided a nucleus. In order to avoid interference by partisans while forming up, it was based in a part of Hungary predominantly occupied by ethnic Germans. However, *Kama* never received enough men to create any of its units, and its training area lay in the path of the Soviet advance. It became clear that the division would be unable to complete formation, and in September it was ordered disbanded. The troops on hand were reallocated, the cadre back to Kampfgruppe Hanke of the *Handschar* and others to the planned 31. SS-Freiwilligen Grenadier Division of Volksdeutsche.

Nearby Albania yielded the 21. Waffen Gebirgs Division der SS *Skanderbeg* (albanische Nr.1). From 1939 until 1943 Albania was occupied by the Italians; but communist partisans led by Enver Hoxha enjoyed virtual free rein in the countryside. When Italy surrendered in September 1943, Italian occupation troops in Albania surrendered to the partisans, and German troops immediately moved to occupy the country.

In April 1944 authority was given for the raising of a Muslim SS division to combat the communist partisans. Initial recruitment was from the ethnic Albanian population around Kosovo, and a nucleus from the *Handschar* Division was provided. Recruitment was slow, and many of those who came forward were judged unsuitable. By June the strength was only around 6,000; but troops were committed to Operation *Draufgänger* (Daredevil) against Tito's partisans in Montenegro in July 1944. Following this, *Skanderbeg* was tasked with guarding the chromium mines near Kosovo; but within weeks the area had been overrun by partisans, and many Albanians deserted – a single regiment is reported to have lost over 1,000, and Heeresgruppe E claimed that the unit had absolutely 'no military value'. At the beginning of October 1944 its strength was listed as just over 4,900, of whom fewer than 1,500 (only a third of them Albanians) were fit for combat. In desperation, drafts of unemployed Kriegsmarine personnel were brought in to make up the numbers.

On 1 November 1944 the division was officially disbanded. Its cadre were transferred to the *Prinz Eugen* Division as Kampfgruppe *Skanderbeg*, and took part in that division's successful rearguard actions against Tito's partisans in December 1944–January 1945. Most of the former Navy men ended up in the 32. SS-Freiwilligen Grenadier Division *30 Januar*.

Following the overthrown of Horthy's government in Hungary in 1944, the Hungarians were instructed to provide the manpower for two Waffen-SS divisions. The first – 25. Waffen-Grenadier Division der SS *Hunyadi* (ungarische Nr.1) – began to form in November, from almost 17,000 Hungarian soldiers of the Honved 13th Division and including a ski battalion. By January 1945 over 20,000 men had been assembled at the Neuhammer training grounds in Germany, but were desperately short of weapons, vehicles and other supplies. In February the Red Army was approaching Neuhammer; the division was rapidly evacuated, apart from a Kampfgruppe – this rearguard was annihilated. By April 1945 *Hunyadi* had withdrawn into Austria where, on 3 May, it was finally involved in serious (if brief) combat, against US Third Army forces. The Hungarians knocked out five Shermans but suffered heavy casualties, surrendering on 4–5 May near the Attersee. The 26. Waffen Grenadier Division der SS (ungarische Nr.2) was authorized at the same time as *Hunyadi*, but by the end of 1944 only about 3,000 Hungarian troops had been taken on strength, with a further 5,000 civilian conscripts. By January 1945 the 'paper' numbers had risen to around 13,000, of whom some 10,000 conscripts were still without uniforms or weapons. The new division was to be equipped and trained at Sieddratz, Poland, where Hungarians came under sporadic attack by Polish partisans

Muslim troops of the 13. Waffen Gebirgs Division der SS *Handschar*, instantly recognizable through their distinctive fez headgear, decorated with a Nazi eagle surmounting a death's head.

RIGHT: Latvian and Estonian volunteers, 1944–45. 1: Waffen-Sturmmann, 19. Waffen Grenadier Division der SS, winter 1944–45. 2: Waffen-Hauptsturmführer, Waffen Grenadier Regiment der SS 45, March 1944. 3: Waffen-Scharführer, 20. Waffen Grenadier Division der SS, autumn 1944. The Estonian volunteer captain in the centre displays the first-pattern Estonian collar emblem – a white metal mailed arm, sword and 'E' – presented to the regiment by the Estonian town of Tartu in February 1944 and sewn onto their previously plain black right collar patches. (Osprey Publishing © Stephen Andrew)

in mid-January while scavenging for food. On 14 January, barely a week after some heavy weapons were issued, these were confiscated by 9. Armee for use against the Soviet winter offensive. The approach of the Red Army forced the division to retreat westwards to the River Oder, losing some 2,500 casualties along the way. In February 1945 the remainder joined their compatriots of the *Hunyadi* at the Neuhammer training grounds, but were forced to withdraw with them into Austria; this division also contributed men to the doomed rearguard. Men of the division surrendered to US troops at the Attersee on 3–5 May.

Looking further afield to the Soviet territories, the Baltic States produced both Latvian and Estonia divisions. Latvia was one of the three Baltic states forcibly annexed to the USSR in June 1940, having enjoyed only 20 years of independence after a long history of German and Russian domination. Soviet repression was so harsh that the German invasion of summer 1941 was seen as liberation. The Germans raised a number of Schutzmannschaften ('Schuma') units of para-military police in Latvia, as in the other occupied Eastern territories, and a number of Latvian volunteers were also accepted into the Wehrmacht. Schuma battalions were sent into the line on the Leningrad front from October 1941, later attached to the 2. SS-Infanterie Brigade (mot.) of the Kommandostab RfSS.

The record is confused by Himmler's decision in February 1943 that in Latvia's case the term 'SS Volunteer Legion' would not apply to a single tactical unit, but should embrace all Latvians in German service. It was within this umbrella designation that a 'Latvian SS Volunteer Division' – the 15. Waffen Grenadier Division der SS (lettische Nr.1) – was authorized in February, drawing upon fresh recruits, Latvians serving with the Wehrmacht, and drafts from other SS-controlled units. These did not include the original Schuma battalions already at the front, who formed a separate brigade (see 19. Division, below).

The flow of volunteers was limited by muddled efforts and mutual suspicion between German and Latvian authorities; as usual, contradictory promises were made over the degree of national independence the force was to be given. Conscription was adopted as early as March 1943; in May, the Latvian General Rudolf Bangerskis was appointed to the rank of SS-Gruppenführer and made Inspector General of the Latvian SS Legion; and late in the year increased Latvian control over recruitment led to improved results. Forming up and training continued during March–November 1943, and by the end of the year the division had attained a strength of some 20,000 men.

In November 1943 the division was in reserve on the northern Russian Front under 16. Armee. In January 1944, Regiment 34 and part of Regiment 33 were attached to Wehrmacht units, taking heavy casualties around Novosokolniki during the Soviet offensive which broke the German encirclement of Leningrad. By mid-February the rest of the division were around Belebelka on the west bank of the River Radja; they fought rearguard actions during withdrawal to the 'Panther Redoubt' on the River Velikaya, where the division was reunited.

By mid-March the 15. and 19. Divisions together formed VI SS-Freiwilligen Korps under 18. Armee, holding a front of nearly 35km along the Velikaya, only 32–64km east of the Latvian border. A number of Russian assaults were held off at heavy cost; a Soviet bridgehead in the 15. Division's sector of the west bank was at first contained. Costly fighting continued until mid-April, when both Latvian divisions were transferred to 16. Armee in the Bardovo/Kudever area about 32km east of Opochka.

Defensive fighting continued throughout May, the Latvians being inspired by the fear that their homeland would once again be occupied by the Soviets. In concert with Operation *Bagration* against Heeresgruppe Mitte, on 10 July a massive attack pushed the whole of Heeresgruppe Nord westwards, and the survivors of the 15. Division fell back into Latvia nine days later fragmented into various battlegroups, some of which suffered over 96 per cent casualties – Regiment 32 was almost completely annihilated. In July some survivors were transferred into the 19. Division, and the others were withdrawn to the Sophienwalde/Konitz area of Prussia as cadres for rebuilding the 15. Division.

By the end of September 1944 the division had been restored to just under 17,000 men. Morale suffered badly when, on 13 October, the Latvian capital Riga fell; from now on the hope of saving their homeland faded, but the Latvians were still willing to fight. In December 1944 the division received personnel from a number of disbanded Latvian police battalions.

The Soviet advance into East Prussia in January 1945 sent the re-formed division back into the front line near Nakel under 3. Panzer Armee. Driven back, some troops shipped out through Danzig, where others remained to be captured by the Red Army in March. During February most of the infantry made a fighting retreat, broken up into battlegroups. In late March the 8,000-odd survivors were ordered to Mecklenberg for refitting and 'fortress construction', and were unable to join their sister division in Kurland as originally intended. Most surrendered in separate groups to US and Canadian forces near Schwerin on 2–3 May. Kampfgruppe Janums skirted south through the eastern suburbs of Berlin, fighting several actions before most reached American captivity at Güterglück on 27 April; SS-Fusilier Bataillon 15 became separated and fought in Berlin until overrun on 3 May. The 19. Waffen Grenadier Division der SS (lettische Nr.2), the second SS division to be raised from Latvian volunteers, was in late 1944 pushed westwards into the Kurzeme region – the 'Kurland Pocket' – with the survivors of more than 30 other divisions. Here it remained trapped for the rest of the war, fighting in five major defensive battles in the Dobele sector under VI SS Korps as

part of 16. Armee. Its units were around Saldus when Army Group Kurland surrendered on 8 May 1945.

Like her neighbour Latvia, Estonia enjoyed only a brief inter-war independence before being forcibly incorporated into the Soviet Union in June 1940. After a year of Soviet persecution Estonians saw the German invasion of June–August 1941 as a liberation, and it was enthusiastically aided by local guerrillas. Enough Estonians came forward in 1941–43 to allow the raising of three 'East Battalions' to serve with the Wehrmacht, and the SS & Police authorities raised 11 Schuma auxiliary battalions. Astutely, on the first anniversary of the German liberation of the capital, Tallinn, a call was made for volunteers to serve against the common enemy in an Estonian SS Legion. Many Estonian former soldiers preferred the German Army and were suspicious of the SS, but the formation of a three-battalion regimental group began at the Heidelager Training Area, east of Debica in Poland in November 1942.

Once trained, I Bataillon of the Legion was detached in April 1943 and sent to join the *Wiking* Division. This unit, renamed SS-Freiwilligen Panzergrenadier Bataillon *Narwa*, distinguished itself as III Bataillon of the *Westland* Regiment; it would not return

Alongside the Waffen-SS, paratroopers were another elite revered by Hitler. Here we see two paras (centre and right) advance by the side of a wrecked Soviet tank in January 1945, one of them clutching a *Panzerfaust* anti-tank weapon.

to the Estonian formation until July 1944 (when it formed the core of the new Fusilier or infantry reconnaissance battalion).

Conscription from February 1943, and drafts from 1. SS-Infanterie Brigade (mot.), increased the strength of the Legion to just over 5,000 by that September; but in May it had already been ordered expanded to a two-regiment brigade. In October the incomplete 3rd Estonian SS Volunteer Brigade was sent to fight partisans in the Nevel area. In December the brigade went into the 16. Armee's frontline at Staraya Russa, and in January 1944 it was driven back by the Red Army's northern offensive. Meanwhile, the brigade's official expansion to a division – 20. Waffen Grenadier Division der SS (estnische Nr.1) – had been ordered on 24 January 1944. In practice this process, carried out while the brigade was in the front line, took until April 1944 to complete even nominally; it required ever more searching conscription, and the German Army's Estonian 658th–660th 'East Battalions' were transferred en bloc into the new SS division.

Red Army pressure on the Narva defences on the old Estonian/Russian frontier threatened the horrific prospect of renewed Soviet occupation, and Estonian enlistments increased sharply (at this time six border guard regiments were also raised). Between February and August 1944 the understrength division put up a stubborn resistance against huge odds on this narrow front, between the Gulf of Finland and Lake Peipus. Army Detachment *Narva* (formerly LIV Korps) also included the 11. SS-Division *Nordland* and 4. SS-Brigade *Nederland*; they would be joined in August by the Belgian 5. *Wallonien* and 6. *Langemarck* brigades. The Estonians held a front north of Narva city until Soviet advances to the south of them obliged a withdrawal westwards in August, followed by confused fighting in dispersed battlegroups. These fought around Tartu on the Emajogi River in southern Estonia in September, but on the 23rd, with the capital Tallinn lost, all German forces were ordered to retreat into Latvia.

The much weakened 20. Division was withdrawn to Germany, and in October–November 1944 was rested at Neuhammer in Silesia, where it was hastily rebuilt with men from the Estonian border guard regiments. In mid-January 1945 the renewed Soviet offensive crossed the Vistula and reached the Oder a week later. The division spent the rest of the war under 17. Armee and 1. Panzer Armee of Army Group Centre. Despite the loss of their homeland they fought well on the Oder front, where divisional units including Regiment 45 formed one battlegroup; another, Kampfgruppe Rehfeldt, included Regiment 47 and units originally left behind at Neuhammer.

In mid-March 1945 a break-out from encirclement in the 'Oppeln–Neisse Pocket' cost further heavy losses, including the divisional commander. By the time they surrendered to the Red Army on 8 May, the survivors had been forced south-west all the way to Melnik north of Prague. As former 'citizens of the USSR' their fate at Soviet hands, like that of captured Latvians, was extremely cruel.

THE ESTONIAN LEGION – SPECIAL INSIGNIA

Collar patches – The Estonian Legion were authorized blank right collar patches; some personnel adopted the SS-runes; but special patches for the division later existed in three forms, at least two of which were widely used. The first, made by the town of Tartu and given to the men of Regiment 45 in February 1944, later spread into other units; this featured an armoured arm holding a sword, with a curved letter 'E' (for Eesti – Estonia) in the crook. The second pattern, designed by the Waffen-SS and issued from June 1944 to replace the privately acquired type, showed a large machine-embroidered curved 'E' with a sword superimposed at a diagonal. This was highly unpopular; and photographs of a third, German-made pattern, reportedly authorized by Himmler in response to complaints and issued while the division was being rebuilt in winter 1944/45, show a machine-embroidered variant of the armoured arm, sword and 'E' emblem.

Arm shields – A number of patterns were used by Estonian personnel, of which three saw widespread use in Waffen-SS units. The style normally worn (on the upper right sleeve) by Estonians serving with the German Army and Luftwaffe showed three diagonal stripes, top right to bottom left, of light blue, black and white. A more elaborately shaped Schuma/Police version bore three golden-yellow lions, and had a yellow border. Both these are known to have been worn on the upper left sleeve by Estonians in the Waffen-SS, including the 'lions' pattern by SS-Panzergrenadier Bataillon *Narwa* of the 5. Division *Wiking*. In mid-1944 an SS-produced pattern was issued for wear on the upper left sleeve.

RUSSIA AND THE UKRAINE

Operation *Barbarossa* brought a huge swathe of Stalin's territory under German occupation. As in the Baltic States, there were many populations disaffected with communist rule, and offered themselves to Nazi service. As we shall see, the SS performed some nimble racial justifications for taking on recruits from amongst the *Untermenschen*, but the opportunity for expansion was too great to pass by. (Had the Germans generally treated the Soviet people in a more enlightened fashion, the outcome of the war on the Eastern Front arguably could have tipped decisively against Stalin.)

The 14. Waffen Grenadier Division der SS (ukrainische Nr.1) demonstrates the sentiments of the new Eastern recruits. Galicia was the administrative title for an area extending from south-east Poland eastwards into the Ukraine, which formed the largest province of the old Austro-Hungarian Empire. The northern part had been seized by Poland in 1921, the remainder being taken by the Soviet Union. On the defeat of Poland in 1939, the Germans ceded the northern part to the Soviets. When the Germans smashed their way into this region in summer 1941 the majority of the population – initially at least – welcomed them as liberators; the Ukrainians were fiercely nationalistic and no lovers of the Russian communist regime.

The former Galicia was absorbed into the so-called Generalgouvernement (General Government), i.e. occupied Poland; but some Germans argued for harnessing Ukrainian

hostility against the Soviets. Many anti-communist security units were raised; and by late 1942 military reverses prompted consideration of more ambitious plans. Sensing another opportunity to expand his SS empire, Himmler began to extol the 'Germanic' virtues of the Galicians, who had been influenced by direct Austrian crown rule since 1772; and in March 1943 he authorized the raising of a volunteer division. This was to be titled and badged strictly as 'Galician' rather than Ukrainian – a fiction which deceived nobody but Hitler. The officers were to be sought among Ukrainian former officers of the Austro-Hungarian and Polish armies, and the NCOs among ex-soldiers of both, with preference for the former.

Fired by the hope that this was a step towards German support for Ukrainian independence, as many as 80,000 volunteers came forward in a matter of weeks; by July a selected 13,000 had been accepted for the new SS division. (The excess were formed into Ordnungspolizei regiments, later used as a pool of replacements for the division.) Drafts of officers and NCOs were despatched to Germany for training, and the division was even authorized a number of priests (of the local Eastern Catholic faith) – something unheard of in German SS units. As the division was formed during summer and autumn 1943 at the Heidelager training area, it seems that the Ukrainian nationalist underground (the UPA), recognizing the growing danger of the Ukraine being retaken by the Soviets, tacitly agreed not to interfere with recruitment, and that a number of them actually joined up.

As with other foreign volunteer formations, however, the nationalistic flavour of the recruiting propaganda was quickly forgotten once the enlistees had joined their units and came under the firm discipline of German officers, and the unpopular SS-Brigadeführer Fritz Freitag discriminated against the officers of Ukrainian origin at every level. Himmler's refusal to allow the word 'Ukrainian' to be even mentioned contributed towards low morale.

In February–March 1944, a battlegroup took part in anti-partisan operations behind the central sector of the Eastern Front. The division moved to the Neuhammer training

LEFT: Ukrainian and Latvian volunteers. 1: Waffen-Grenadier, 14. Waffen Grenadier Division der SS, summer 1944. This fresh recruit to the '1st Galician' (actually, Ukrainian) Division is depicted as if during its rebuilding after being nearly destroyed in the Brody Pocket. On his right collar patch is the rampant lion emblem of Galicia. 2: Waffen-Sturmbannführer, 15. Waffen Grenadier Division der SS, late 1944. This Latvian major wears officers' M1936 style uniform with the peaked service cap; the white-over-black shoulder strap underlay identifies the infantry branch, but white cap piping was regulation for all branches for much of the war. 3: SS-Schütze, 15. Lettische SS-Freiwilligen Division, autumn 1943. This earlier Latvian volunteer wears the M1940 field cap and M1943 tunic. Despite the authorization in March 1943 of the large 'static swastika' collar patch for the Latvian Legion, and thus for the division formed from it (confirmed by an order of June 1944), photographs show the SS-runes in widespread use. 4: Waffen-Untersturmführer, 14. Waffen Grenadier Division der SS, 1944–45. This Ukrainian second lieutenant still wears the Galician arm shield on his upper left sleeve; but on his right collar, instead of the Galician lion or SS-runes, is a rare example of the Ukrainian 'Trident of Vladimir' emblem, now known to have been worn in some instances. (Osprey Publishing © Stephen Andrew)

Here an SS anti-tank unit mans a Pak 40 gun. This 7.5cm weapon could penetrate up to 154mm of armour at 500m range, and it accounted for hundreds of Soviet tanks on the Eastern Front.

area in Silesia in April; and in June, although unready, it was sent to the front under 1. Panzer Armee of Armeegruppe Nordukraine (Army Group North Ukraine). In July the 14. Division found itself around Brody north-east of Lvov, in the path of Operation *Bagration*. The division was forced back almost immediately, and encircled with a number of others in the so-called 'Brody Pocket'. During a break-out attempt on 21–22 July about one man in five managed to escape. The 14. Division survivors were fragmented, some of them later returning via Hungarian territory; others headed for the Carpathian Mountains, and fought on alone behind Soviet lines. Only some 3,000 men returned to Neuhammer as the nucleus for a rebuilt division; but by then 8,000 other Ukrainians were available to join them.

In August 1944, shortly after the rebuilding of the division had commenced at Neuhammer, a Soviet-backed rising in Slovakia threatened the route of withdrawal of 8. Armee from Galicia. A regiment-sized Kampfgruppe was formed from personnel of Waffen-SS training schools and replacement battalions. This force, entitled SS-Panzergrenadier Regiment *Schill*, moved on the centre of the revolt at Neusohl; it was reinforced with a battlegroup formed around III Bataillon, Regiment 29 from the 14. Division. This Kampfgruppe Beyersdorff was only in Slovakia briefly before rejoining the division, which had now transferred to Zilina in Slovakia to continue formation and training. In November 1944 its Ukrainian identity was finally recognized by a change of national suffix in the title.

In late January 1945 the division – 14,000 strong – was ordered to the borders of southern Austria and Slovenia to face Tito's partisans. It almost ceased to exist in late March when Hitler eventually discovered its existence, but he was persuaded to relent. In late April, Himmler agreed to transfer the division to the so-called Ukrainian National Army under General Pavlo Shandruk, but given the chaotic situation in the last two weeks of the war this was little more than a paper exercise. After brief action against Soviet forces, the survivors of the division were more fortunate than many of their fellow Eastern European volunteers. Surrendering to the British near Radstadt on 8 May, Shandruk's troops successfully claimed to be anti-communist Polish 'Galicians' rather than Soviet citizens, and thus escaped being handed over to the Russians.

The nature of war on the Eastern Front made it virtually inevitable that some of the Eastern Waffen-SS formations would be brutalized and undisciplined. Indeed, the reputation of the Waffen-SS, poor even just focusing on its most prestigious divisions,

Most of the Soviet territories produced some degree of recruitment for the Waffen-SS. Here two Waffen-SS men from Turkestan man an MG 42 on the Eastern Front.

ABOVE: Late-war Volksdeutsche and Russian divisions. 1: Waffen-Sturmmann, 24. Waffen Gebirgs (Karstjäger) Division der SS; Austro-Yugoslav border, autumn 1944. This junior NCO, hunting partisans in the mountains, wears the M1942 helmet, basic field-grey M1943 uniform, mountain boots, standard. 2: Grenadier, 30. Waffen Grenadier Division der SS; Rhine front, winter 1944. Nothing identifies this infantry private as a Russian volunteer; but just visible under his greatcoat are the plain black tunic collar patches worn by many foreign SS privates. 3: Waffen-Obersturmführer, Waffen Artillerie Regiment der SS 25; Neuhammer, spring 1945. This Hungarian first lieutenant serving with the artillery unit of the 25. Waffen Grenadier Division der SS *Hunyadi* at the Neuhammer training grounds wears typical officer's field dress, the service cap suggesting that he is not in the firing line. (Osprey Publishing © Stephen Andrew)

plummets to hideous lows when the behaviour of the foreign divisions is factored in. One of the most notorious military rabbles in recent history, 29. Waffen Grenadier Division der SS (russische Nr.1) had its origins in November 1941 at the town of

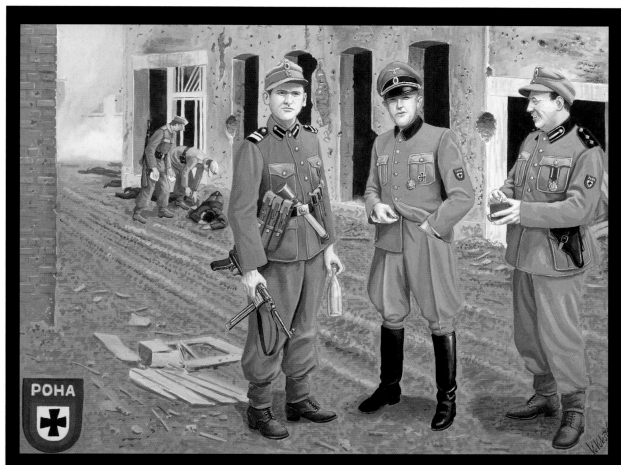

KAMINSKI TROOPS

Few military units in history have gained such appalling reputations for indiscipline cruelty as the troops commanded by Bronislaw Kaminski. From a small mixed band of Red Army deserters, anti-communist white Russian collaborators, Belorussians, Ukrainians and some Poles, he established a 'self defence' force to protect the town of Lokot from Red Army partisans. This unit grew to brigade strength and was ultimately taken over by the Waffen-SS to become the very shortlived 29. Waffen Grenadier Division der SS.

The Kaminski troops wore a hotch-potch mix of whatever uniform items were available, some still wearing Red Army uniform with only an armband to identify them as being in German service. Ultimately, most seemed to wear standard German Army field-grey uniforms, often with the rank insignia specially designed for Russian volunteers, and usually with the unit's own sleeve shield, most of which were very crudely made. (Osprey Publishing © Velimir Vuksic)

Lokot in the Bryansk region of the Ukraine, which was suffering from the depredations of Soviet partisans and Red Army stragglers. In January 1942 the small self-defence militia formed in November came under the command of the deputy mayor, an engineer named Bronislav Kaminski.

Well educated and multi-lingual, Kaminski had attracted the paranoid suspicion of the Soviet authorities, and had emerged from one of the notorious gulags with a fanatical hatred of the communists. The Germans were happy to make use of such men; by March 1942 his militia numbered around 1,600, and in April the Lokot district was granted a limited autonomy. Under Kaminski's leadership the locals rooted out all partisan activity, and farmed their lands so successfully that they were able to provide substantial food supplies to the Germans. Throughout the summer of 1942 Kaminski's militia operated with ruthless zeal alongside German and Hungarian security units, and by the end of the year had expanded to a strength of around 10,000 men.

Czech partisans capture an SS soldier in 1945. Falling into partisan hands was a particularly bad fate for an SS soldier, and usually led to his execution out of hand.

Under the patronage of Reichsleiter Alfred Rosenberg, the Minister for Eastern Territories, in May 1943 Lokot was granted increased autonomy as a Bezirksverwaltung (District Administration). Around this time Kaminski began to lobby for the creation of a Russian Nazi Party, with his military force as its Russkaya Osvoboditelnaya Narodnaya Armiya (RONA; Russian People's Liberation Army). Kaminski lived the life of a feudal warlord while his men looted and killed at will. In the face of a continuing regional threat from anything between 15,000 and 25,000 partisans, he pressed every man he could find into his private army – conscripts, and 'turned' Soviet prisoners and stragglers; the local core now represented only about a quarter of the total. The RONA's atrocities increased, but so did desertion, and a brutal discipline was enforced.

Throughout spring and early summer 1943, RONA troops took part in many anti-partisan sweeps alongside regular German and Hungarian units, as well as another group that was becoming notorious for its barbarity – the Dirlewanger Brigade (see below). By June the RONA was organized as a brigade, with five regiments of around 2,000 men each; and in July the Germans even provided Kaminski with 36 captured Soviet field guns and 24 T-34 tanks. However, following the German defeat at Kursk, in September–October 1943 the RONA was forced to retreat westwards with its protectors, taking with it a huge train of camp followers and livestock. Kaminski countered defeatist murmurings by publicly strangling an unreliable officer.

By October the RONA had withdrawn into Galicia; and it was then that one of its patrons, SS-Gruppenführer Kurt von Gottberg, began to argue for its absorption into the Waffen-SS. Throughout the first half of 1944 the RONA was employed in anti-partisan operations under control of a Kampfgruppe commanded by Gottberg. Its resemblance to a migratory medieval horde made it hard to estimate its fighting strength, but total numbers in its camps are reported as anything up to 27,000 men and women. In July the unit was accepted into the Waffen-SS as SS-Sturmbrigade RONA, and Kaminski himself was commissioned Waffen-Brigadeführer.

In August 1944 perhaps 3,000 RONA men, with five tanks and a couple of 122mm guns, were sent to Warsaw to help put down the Polish Home Army uprising; and it was there that Kaminski's gang reached depths of depravity that offended even the SS. Deployed in the Wola and Ochta districts, they began a drunken orgy of rape, murder and pillage. Supposedly responsible for the deaths of more than 10,000 civilians, they slaughtered patients at the Marie Curie Sklodowska Radium Institute; Kaminski himself apparently participated eagerly in the looting; and two young German servicewomen were reportedly among those raped and murdered.

Kaminski and his senior henchmen were ordered to report to the Lodz HQ of the Höhere SS- und Polizeiführer, SS-Obergruppenführer Erich von dem Bach-Zelewski, for a conference; when they arrived they were given a brisk drumhead court martial,

A Waffen-SS armoured division on the move on the Eastern Front. The vehicles are 10.5cm StuH self-propelled guns; note the extra armour plate bolted to the sides of the vehicle.

and shot. In order to avoid a mutiny Kaminski's death was reported as the result of a partisan ambush; the RONA was withdrawn from Warsaw, and disbanded during September 1944. Some 3,000-plus men who were considered reliable were subsequently transferred to Neuhammer to join General Andrei Vlasov's Russian Liberation Army (ROA), much to the disgust of the latter's General Buniacenko. The rest were put to work digging defences on the Oder front; their fate is unknown.

The second Russian division – 30. Waffen Grenadier Division der SS (russische Nr.2) – has had a far more invisible reputation in the annals of Waffen-SS history. By the time this formation was assembled in July 1944 it was already evident that the Red Army could not be prevented from driving the Wehrmacht out of Russia. Most of the Ukrainian, Belorussian and Russian volunteers or conscripts in German-controlled rear area security units therefore had little to lose by retreating with their masters to escape Soviet vengeance; but many of these auxiliary police still proved highly reluctant to be transformed into battlefield units.

About a dozen of these Schuma battalions were brought together to form a brigade, and during August this was absorbed into the Waffen-SS and designated as a division. Four regiments were originally ordered formed. Many of these units were already grossly understrength, however (one battalion had only 102 men); the formation was further weakened by desertions, and by at least one major mutiny by Ukrainian and Russian personnel of the first two regiments, which were harshly purged.

In September 1944 the division was sent to France for anti-partisan operations; it was felt that service so far from home amid people speaking an alien language would discourage desertions, but this proved optimistic, and there was a steady drain of men who chose to go over to the French maquis despite these obstacles. During late 1944 the division fell back eastwards as the Allies advanced. In October it was reinforced when Regiment 77 was formed, and the division was supposed to provide security for the Rhine crossings. In November personnel saw brief action against General de Lattre's First French Army advancing from the south before retreating to positions on the German/Swiss border. Reduced to fewer than 4,500 men, in January 1945 the 30th was officially downgraded to a brigade (given the national suffix 'White Ruthenian', after a German term for the Carpathian region of the Ukraine). Almost simultaneously it was disbanded, the NCO cadre being posted to other Waffen-SS units and the remainder to General Vlasov's ROA.

THE COSSACKS

Germany had taken full advantage of the hatred of the Moscow regime felt among many of the historically independent Cossack communities. As early as August 1941 the first entire Cossack regiment of the Red Army came over to the Wehrmacht, and others followed, being attached to German units on an ad hoc basis and usually employed for anti-partisan and line of communications security duties. In spring 1943 the German General von Pannwitz assembled a Cossack division, based (with many of their families) at Mielau in Poland. Deployed to Yugoslavia in September 1943, this was later split into two divisions forming XIV Cossack Corps. A mixture of traditional and German Army clothing was worn, with mixed insignia, and armshields identifying the traditional Hosts. At the beginning of 1945 the entire Cossack force was transferred to the Waffen-SS as XV SS-Kosaken Kavallerie Korps, but this was a purely administrative change and the troops continued to wear their old uniforms and insignia.

Terek Cossacks serving in the Waffen-SS. The Cossacks had suffered greatly under Stalin's policies of collectivization and deportation, hence many readily flocked to the German cause.

THE LOW POINT

From the descriptions of the divisions above, it is clear that the Waffen-SS of 1945 was a shadow of its 1941–42 incarnation. The divisions of 1945 were understrength, harried and frequently of poor quality, ripe for being crushed under the powerful boot of victorious allies. If we were to choose one example of how far the Waffen-SS fell from the notion of 'Hitler's Elite', we should look no further than the 36. Waffen Grenadier Division der SS.

This unit was rivalled in brutal depravity only by Kaminski's RONA. Its origins lay in a bizarre suggestion made to Hitler that a unit raised from convicted poachers would have the ideal fieldcraft skills for hunting partisans. He approved the idea, and a small penal company was formed on 15 June 1940 as the 'Oranienberg Poacher Commando', made up of criminal (non-political) prisoners enlisted from various prisons and concentration camps. In September, now about 300 strong, it received

SS Regiment *Dirlewanger* was a horrific force of criminals and deviants, let loose on the population of Warsaw in August 1944. Their commander, Oskar Dirlewanger, had been previously convicted for sexually abusing a young girl, for which he was sent to Welzheim concentration camp.

equipment from the SS-Totenkopfverbände, and was renamed after its commander: 'SS Special Battalion *Dirlewanger*'. Obergruppenführer Oskar Paul Dirlewanger was a degenerate figure, who had been imprisoned for sex offences with a minor, yet nevertheless enjoyed high level protection as a former comrade of recruitment chief SS-Obergruppenführer Gottlob Berger.

In October 1940 the unit was sent to occupied Poland for security duties; reports of atrocities began almost immediately, and continued throughout 1941. Rape and

GETTO OPERATION

The SS and SD were the troops most usually involved in clearing the Jewish ghettos in the East for deportation and 'resettlement' in the concentration camps. These actions usually took place early in the morning, because of the element of surprise, and also because there would be fewer witnesses. In this scene an officer of the Sicherheitsdienst, with the distinctive blank collar patch and SD arm patch, collects the names of the victims of this particular round-up, accompanied by an official of the Gestapo. (Osprey Publishing © Velimir Vuksic)

murder were accompanied by looting, which is probably what drew Dirlewanger's gang to the disapproving attention of the SS legal staff and of SS–Obergruppenführer Krüger, the Höhere SS- und Polizeiführer of the Generalgouvernement. Despite his friends in high places, Dirlewanger's unit – now an 'SS Special Regiment' – was transferred in January 1942 to Belorussia. Immediately upon arrival it began recruiting locally for anti-partisan operations, upon which it was exclusively employed until November 1943, cementing its reputation for barbarity.

Despite its notoriety the unit was expanded to two battalions in August 1942; and Dirlewanger himself was decorated for 'bravery' in May and October. In January 1943 the unit was permitted collar patches and badges of rank (normally forbidden to penal units). The original romantic concept of it being manned by poachers was long forgotten; it accepted riff-raff of all types – German and foreign, military and civilian – and in March 1943 service in the unit was offered as a means of 'redeeming' themselves to virtually all convicted felons. Disorderliness extended to repeated

LEGION FREIES INDIEN / INDISCHES FREIWILLIGEN LEGION

Subhas Chandra Bhose, an Indian nationalist politician who had been imprisoned by the British, made his way to Berlin early in 1941. His offer to raise a volunteer legion from Indian soldiers captured in North Africa was accepted; some 3,000 volunteers were eventually raised, and the Legion was officially formed in December 1942 as (Indisches) Infanterie Regiment 950, with one depot and three line battalions. It was not highly regarded, and was used for garrison duties south of Bordeaux in occupied France until August 1944, when it was withdrawn to Germany and transferred to the Waffen-SS. (The return trip took over two months, and the unit came under repeated attack by French partisans while in transit.) From November 1944 until March 1945 the unit was stationed in Germany; as the war drew to a close the Legion attempted to reach Switzerland, but was captured by Free French and US troops. Handed over to the British, the personnel were shipped back to India and imprisoned. Due to the delicate political climate as Indian independence was negotiated, these men – like those of the Japanese-sponsored 'Indian National Army' also raised by Bhose – were treated leniently. In 1942–44 the unit wore German Army tropical uniform (with turbans for Sikh personnel) and all conventional insignia. A right sleeve armshield bore a natural-coloured leaping tiger motif superimposed on horizontal stripes of saffron/white/green, all below a white panel with 'FREIES INDIEN' in black lettering; this was presumably retained after transfer to the Waffen-SS. A special right hand collar patch displaying a tiger's head was manufactured, and recently discovered photographs confirm that it was definitely worn to some extent. The Germans permitted the introduction of a whole range of decorations by the so-called Committee for Free India; these Azad Hind awards were manufactured by the Austrian firm of Rudolf Souval.

A Waffen-SS Grenadier fighting in Normandy in 1944. Normandy proved ideal defensive terrain for the Germans, owing to the thick hedgerows of the bocage and its winding, claustrophobic country lanes.

shooting incidents between Russian and Lithuanian enlistees, and discipline was enforced by physical brutality, even to officers. Large scale anti-partisan operations sometimes cost the unit significant casualties (some 300 in February–August 1943); a third battalion was then authorized. For a brief period in November–December 1943 the regiment found itself in frontline combat under Army Group Centre, and suffered greatly increased casualties, reducing it to about 260 men. Dirlewanger was then awarded the German Cross in Gold, a decoration second only to the Knight's Cross. His penal regiment was rebuilt in early 1944 with convicts from German military prisons; by February it counted 1,200 men, and in April another 800 replacements were allocated. Anti-partisan battles in Belorussia during May and June were followed by rearguard fighting during the July retreat into Poland following the Red Army's Operation *Bagration*.

In August 1944, like Kaminski's renegade Russians, Dirlewanger's uncontrollable convicts recorded new depths of depravity when they were assigned to help crush the

SONDERKOMMANDO *DIRLEWANGER*

With a reputation even worse than the Kaminski Brigade, the Sonderkommando *Dirlewanger* was one of the most bizarre military units ever to have existed. This unit reached the zenith of barbarism during the suppression of the Warsaw Uprising in August 1944. In this plate, one *Dirlewanger* soldier, identifiable by the distinctive collar patch, gets ready to take aim at a Polish insurgent sniping at the Germans from high up in an opposing building, while his comrade primes a stick grenade ready to lob it through the window of a house occupied by Polish Free Army defenders. A third, armed with a flame-thrower, is ready to use this most effective of weapons in clearing a house occupied by the Poles. (Osprey Publishing © Velimir Vuksic)

Warsaw uprising. They drank, raped and murdered their way through the Old Town, slaughtering fighters and civilians alike without distinction of age or sex. It is reported that a staff officer sent to summon Dirlewanger before the overall operation commander, SS-Obergruppenführer von dem Bach-Zelewski, was driven off at gunpoint. Unlike

RIGHT: Anti-partisan units. 1: SS-Rottenführer, SS Sonderregiment *Dirlewanger*; Belorussia, June 1944. This infamous German penal unit was identified by the collar patch of crossed rifles over a grenade. 2: Waffen-Hauptsturmführer, SS-Sturmbrigade RONA; Warsaw, August 1944. Kaminski's officers wore a mixture of German and Russian items. 3: Schütze, SS-Sturmbrigade RONA; Warsaw, August 1944 (Osprey Publishing © Stephen Andrew)

Kaminski, Dirlewanger was not executed for his atrocities, but received the ultimate accolade – award of the Knight's Cross.

In late August an uprising broke out in Slovakia; in September Berger was named Höhere SS- und Polizeiführer Slovakia, and in mid-October his protégé's unit was transferred there. The *Dirlewanger* regiment (weakened by heavy air attack while en route) saw combat against the Slovak rebels around Biely Potok, Liptovska Osada and Treicy; although successful, the unit reportedly suffered a number of desertions. In November 1944 permission was given for some members to transfer to other Waffen-SS units, and strength was built up to brigade level with further drafts of criminals.

In February 1945, while stationed in Hungary, the unit was redesignated as 36. Waffen Grenadier Division der SS, though in reality it never reached anything like divisional strength. In that month, Dirlewanger returned to Germany for hospital treatment, and was replaced by Fritz Schmedes. The division rapidly crumbled under the impact of the Soviet spring offensive in April 1945, and many men deserted before it was encircled in the Halbe pocket. On about 29 April some elements were captured by the Red Army south-east of Berlin, and were summarily executed. A few may have succeeded in surrendering to US troops. There have been many rumours as to Dirlewanger's personal fate; recent forensic research suggests that he was captured by Polish troops in June 1945 and that, when his identity was discovered, he was beaten to death. Even for those Waffen-SS soldiers without such an execrable reputation as Dirlewanger, the final months of the war were perilous times indeed.

CONCLUSION

LEFT: For many Waffen-SS soldiers, at least those who survived, war service brought pride and comradeship, although the human rights abuses of many elements of the SS meant post-war veterans often hid their past.

Brenda McBryde was born in Britain just ten days before the Armistice ended World War I. During 1938, Brenda started a four-year course of nursing training at the Royal Victoria Infirmary, Newcastle upon Tyne. In April 1943 she qualified as a state registered nurse and then was commissioned into the British Army as a nursing officer in the Queen Alexandra's Imperial Military Nursing Service (Reserve).

During Brenda's service as a nurse in the combat zones of Europe, she frequently had cause to treat German casualties. Some German patients, however, proved to be very different from the rest of their comrades. On one occasion, for example, Brenda treated a barely conscious German trooper who had lost one leg; he was clearly identifiable as a member of the elite Waffen-SS by his silver and black collar runes. As she fed the patient a glass of water, the soldier came to his senses, opened his eyes and instinctively smiled at the individual who was tending to him. Within seconds, however, after his vision had focused on Brenda's uniform, his grateful demeanour suddenly changed. With a convulsive jerk, the SS-trooper spat into her face and screeched, with whatever venom he could muster, a string of obscenities at her. Brenda's commanding officer had witnessed the incident and in a voice hard with anger, he instructed the staff not to treat the SS soldier until all the other newly arrived cases had been dealt with. Fanaticism has traditionally been one of the characteristics we identify with the SS, both the Allgemeine-SS and Waffen-SS. Certainly, as we have seen, the SS were capable of the most trenchant resistance against overwhelming odds, right to the very last days of the war. Furthermore, it took a unique type of person indeed to participate in some of the hideous crimes against humanity that lie at the SS door. In a skewed perspective, Himmler himself acknowledged this in a speech to SS officers at Posen in October 1943:

> I am now referring to the evacuation of the Jews, the eradication of the Jewish people. It's one of those things that is easily said: 'The Jewish people are being eradicated', says every party member, 'this is very obvious, it's in our programme, elimination of the Jews, eradication, we're doing it, hah, a small matter.' [...] But of all those who talk this way, none had observed it, none had endured it. Most of you here know what it means when 100 corpses lie next to each other, when 500 lie there or when 1,000 are lined up. To have endured this and at the same time to have remained a decent person – with exceptions due to human weaknesses – had made us tough. This is a page of glory never mentioned and never to be mentioned. [...] We have the moral right, we had the duty to our people to do it, to kill this people who wanted to kill us.

The logic at work here is obscene, especially the suggestion that those who couldn't stomach mass slaughter were simply prey to 'human weakness'. Himmler made further comments about his attitude towards those of Eastern Europe:

One basic principle must be the absolute rule for the SS men: We must be honest, decent, loyal and comradely to members of our own blood and to nobody else. What happens to a Russian, to a Czech, does not interest me in the slightest. What other nations can offer in the way of good blood of our type, we will take, if necessary, by kidnapping their children and raising them here with us. Whether nations live in prosperity or starve to death interests me only so far as we need them as slaves for our culture; otherwise, it is of no interest to me. Whether 10,000 Russian females fall down from exhaustion while digging an anti-tank ditch interests me only insofar as the anti-tank ditch for Germany is finished.

Ernst Kaltenbrunner, head of the RSHA following Heydrich's assassination, was the most senior SS officer to face war crimes trials. He was convicted of crimes against humanity and executed on 16 October 1946.

Given the expansion of the SS via foreign manpower, explained in detail in the previous chapter, Himmler's statement here can be viewed with considerable irony. Yet the leader

The Nuremberg trials, held between 1945 and 1946, confronted the Nazi and SS hierarchy directly with their crimes. Here we see Göring, Hess, Ribbentrop, Keitel and Jodl listening intently to the proceedings.

of the SS was not necessarily a man of ideological consistency. Even before the Führer's suicide on 30 April 1945, Himmler had secretly met Count Folke Bernadotte of Sweden at Lübeck. At this meeting, Himmler offered to surrender all German armies facing the Western Allies, allowing the latter to advance east to prevent more German territory falling to the Soviets. The Reichsführer hoped that his offer would entice the Western Allies into continuing the war that Germany had waged since 1941 against the Soviet Union – the common enemy of all the states of Europe, Himmler believed. The Western Allies, however, remained committed to accept nothing other than Germany's simultaneous unconditional surrender to the four major Allied powers. Moreover, they recognized Himmler's diplomatic approach as nothing more than a crude attempt to split their alliance with the Soviets, and so rejected his offer on 27 April. When Hitler heard of Himmler's treachery on 28 April, he ordered that his erstwhile 'Loyal Heinrich' be arrested.

Simultaneously, and with Himmler's connivance, SS Colonel-General Karl Wolff, the German military governor of northern Italy, continued the secret negotiations that he had initiated with the Western Allies in February 1945 over the surrender of the German forces deployed in Italy. On 29 April – the day before Hitler's killed himself – in another vain attempt to split the Allied alliance, a representative of General von Vietinghoff signed the instrument of surrender for the German forces located in Italy. By 2 May, some 300,000 German troops in this area had already laid down their arms.

The final German surrender in May 1945 brought with it continuing peril for former SS personnel. On the Eastern Front, those who hadn't been able to escape Soviet capture were typically either executed or worked to death in Soviet labour camps. Those who made it to American or British hands could expect more mercy, although the growing revelations of the Holocaust meant the Allied interrogators remained on the hunt for those directly involved in the worst atrocities.

For the SS leadership, there were various futures. For some, the post-war world brought trial and punishment. In 1947–48, for example, 12 senior SS Einsatzgruppen commanders were put on trial by US authorities in Nuremberg. (These trials were conducted before US military courts, rather than the International Military Tribunal that also operated from the Palace of Justice at Nuremberg). All were convicted, and sentenced to either death by hanging or long terms in imprisonment. Some skilfully deferred their trial through evasion. The most famous of these individuals was Adolf Eichmann, a principal figure in the implementation of the Final Solution. At the end of the war he managed to escape to Argentina (a choice destination for many former SS personnel) and there built a new life for himself under an assumed name. In 1960, however, Israeli Mossad agents managed to identify, kidnap and forcibly deport Eichmann back to Israel, where he went to trial in 1961. Found guilty of crimes against humanity, he was hanged on 31 May 1962. Many SS criminals nevertheless remained beyond reach of the law – the infamous SS Auschwitz doctor Josef Mengele, for example, disappeared into South America and was never seen again. At least the Auschwitz commandant, Rudolf Franz Ferdinand Höss, was captured, and executed on 16 April 1947.

The Reichsführer himself, Heinrich Himmler, escaped trial but not an early death. After a brief attempt at going into hiding, he was captured by British forces and detained. On 23 May 1945, he bit into a cyanide capsule and died within minutes. One of history's greatest mass murderers ultimately escaped retribution, and the opportunity for the world to peer more deeply into his mindset.

BIBLIOGRAPHY

This work is a compilation of several Osprey books all of which are listed in the bibliography below and on the imprint page.

Ailsby, Christopher, *Hell on the Eastern Front: The Waffen-SS War in Russia 1941–1945* (Staplehurst: Spellmount, 1998)

Antil, Peter, *Stalingrad 1942* (Oxford: Osprey, 2007)

Bishop, Chris, *Hitler's Foreign Divisions: Foreign Volunteers in the Waffen-SS, 1940–1945* (London: Amber Books, 2005)

Bishop, Chris, *Essential ID Guide: Waffen-SS Divisions 1939–45* (Stroud: Spellmount, 2007)

Burleigh, Michael, *Germany Turns Eastward* (London: Pan Books, 2002)

Carruthers, Bob (ed.), *Servants of Evil* (London: André Deutsch, 2001)

Davis, Brian, *The German Home Front 1939–45* (Oxford: Osprey, 2007)

Dearn, Alan, *The Hitler Youth 1933–45* (Oxford: Osprey, 2006)

Deighton, Len, *Blitzkrieg: From the Rise of Hitler to the Fall of Dunkirk* (Fakenham: Book Club Associates, 1979)

Estes, Kenneth, *A European Anabasis: Western European Volunteers in the German Army and SS, 1940–1945* (Columbia University Press e-book:)

Evans, Richard J., *The Third Reich in Power 1933–1939: How the Nazis Won Over The Hearts and Minds of a Nation* (London: Penguin Books, 2006)

Flaherty, Thomas (ed.), *The SS* (London: Time-Life, 2004)

Forczyk, Robert, *Rescuing Mussolini: Gran Sasso 1943* (Oxford: Osprey, 2010)

Goldhagen, Daniel, *Hitler's Willing Executioners: Ordinary Germans and the Holocaust* (London: Abacus, 1997)

Graber, G. S., *History of the SS* (London: Robert Hale, 1978)

Grunberger, Richard, *A Social History of the Third Reich* (London: Phoenix, 2005)

Jurado, C. Caballero & Thomas, N., *Germany's Eastern Front Allies (2): Baltic Forces* (Oxford: Osprey, 2002)

Kemp, Anthony, *German Commanders of World War II* (Oxford: Osprey, 1982)

Knopp, Guido, *The SS: A Warning From History* (Stroud: Sutton Publishing, 2002)

Koehl, Robert Lewis, *The SS: A History 1919–45* (Stroud: Tempus Publishing, 2004)

Kogon, Eugen, et al. (eds), *Nazi Mass Murder: A Documentary History of the Use of Poison Gas* (New Haven, CT: Yale University Press, 1993)

Krausnick, Helmut et al., *Anatomy of the SS State* (London: Collins, 1968)

Layton, Geoff, *Germany: The Third Reich 1933–45* (London: Hodder & Stoughton, 2000)

Littlejohn, David, *The SA 1921–45: Hitler's Stormtroopers* (Oxford: Osprey, 1990)

Lucas, James, *Germany Army Handbook 1939–1945* (Stroud: Sutton Publishing, 1998)

Lumsden, Robin, *The Allgemeine-SS* (Oxford: Osprey, 1993)

Mayer, S. L. (ed.), *Signal: Hitler's Wartime Magazine* (London: Bison, 1976)

Ousby, Ian, *Occupation: The Ordeal of France, 1940–1944* (London: Pimlico, 1997)

Pallud, Jean-Paul, *Ardennes 1944: Peiper & Skorzeny* (Oxford: Osprey, 1987)

Quarrie, Bruce, *Waffen-SS Soldier* (Oxford: Osprey, 1993)

Rees, Laurence, *The Nazis: A Warning From History* (London: BBC Worldwide, 2002)

Rhodes, Richard, *Masters of Death: The SS-Einsatzgruppen and the Invention of the Holocaust* (New York, Random House, 2002)

Rikmenspoel, Marc, *Waffen-SS Encyclopedia* (Bedford, PA: Aberjona Press, 2004)

Snyder, Louis L., *Encyclopedia of the Third Reich* (Ware: Wordsworth Edition Limited, 1998)

Trevor-Roper, Hugh, *Hitler's Table Talk 1941–1944* (London: Phoenix Press, 2000)

Trigg, Jonathan, *Hitler's Jihadis: Muslim Volunteers of the Waffen-SS* (Stroud: The History Press, 2008)

Van Hoesel, A. F. G., *Die Jeugd die wij vreesden* (Utrecht: St Gregorinschuis, 1948)

Westwood, D, *German Infantryman (3): Eastern Front 1943–45* (Oxford: Osprey, 2005)

Williamson, Gordon, *The Waffen-SS (1): 1. to 5. Divisions* (Oxford: Osprey, 2003)

Williamson, Gordon, *The Waffen-SS (2): 6. to 10. Divisions* (Oxford: Osprey, 2004)

Williamson, Gordon, *The Waffen-SS (3): 11. to 23. Divisions* (Oxford: Osprey, 2004)

Williamson, Gordon, *The Waffen-SS (4): 24. to 38. Divisions, & Volunteer Legions* (Oxford: Osprey, 2004)

Williamson, Gordon, *German Security and Police Soldier 1939–45* (Oxford: Osprey, 2002)

Williamson, Gordon, *Panzer Crewman 1939–45* (Oxford: Osprey, 2002)

Williamson, Gordon, *Waffen-SS Handbook 1933–1945* (Stroud: Sutton, 2003)

Williamson, Gordon, *World War II German Police Units* (Oxford: Osprey, 2006)

Williamson, Gordon, *German Special Forces of World War II* (Oxford: Osprey, 2009)

Windrow, Martin, *The Waffen-SS* (Oxford: Osprey, 1982)

Yerger, Mark, *Allgemeine-SS – The Commands, Units and Leaders of the General SS* (Atglan, PA: Schiffer Publishing, 1997)

GLOSSARY

Abteilung	Battalion/Detachment
Ahnenerbe	Ancestral Heritage
Allgemeine-SS	General SS
Amtsgruppe	Group Office
Anschluss	Union with Austria, March 1938
Arbeitsgaue	Divisional Work Districts
Armee	Army
Armeegruppe	Army Group
Auftragstaktik	Mission-orientated Tactics
Ausbildung	Training
Bataillon	Battalion
Befelhlshaber der Waffen-SS (BdWSS)	Chief of the Waffen-SS
Bewaffnete-SS	Armed SS
Blitzkrieg	Lightning War
Brigadeführer	Brigade Leader
Chef der Deutschen Polizei im Reichministerium des Innern	Chief of the German Police in the Reich Ministry of the Interior
Deutsche Arbeiterpartei (DAP)	German Workers Party
Deutsche Arbeitsfront (DAF)	German Labour Front
Die Endlösung	'The Final Solution'
Einsatzkommando	Sub-unit of an *Einsatzgruppen*
Einsatzgruppen	'Task Forces' (SD/SS execution squads)
Eisenbahnpolizei	Railway Police
Ersatz	Replacement
Fallschirmjäger	Paratroops
Flieger-HJ	Hitler Youth Paramilitary Aviation Enthusiasts
Fliegerkorps	Air Corps
Freiwilligen	Volunteer

Führer	Leader
Fuß-Standarte	(SS) Foot Regiment
Gau	District
Gauleiter	District Leader
Gebirgs	Mountain
Gebirgsjäger	Mountain light infantry
Geheime Feldpolizei (GFP)	Secret Field Police
Geheime Staatspolizei (Gestapo)	Secret State Police
Gendarmerie	Local/Rural Police
Generalfeldmarschall	Field Marshal
Generalgouvernement	General Government (of Central Poland)
Generalkommissar	Commissar general
Generalleutnant	Lieutenant-General
Generalmajor	Major-General
Generaloberst	Colonel-General
Gruppenführer	Group Leader
Hakenkreuz	'Hook Cross', Swastika
Hauptamt Ordungspolizei	Order Police Headquarters
Hauptamt Persönlicher Stab Reichsführer-SS (Pers. Stab RFSS)	Headquarters Personal Staff RFSS
Hauptamt SS-Gericht	Main SS Legal Office
Hauptamt Volksdeutsche Mittelstelle (VOMI)	Ethnic German Main Assistance Office
Hauptmann	Captain
Heeresgruppe	Army Group
Hitlerjugend (HJ)	Hitler Youth
Höchste SS-und Polizeiführer (HöSSPF)	Supreme SS and Police Leader
Höherer SS-und Polizeiführer (HSSPF)	Higher SS and Police Leader
Inspekteur der Konzentrationslager und SS-Wachverbände	Inspector of Concentration Camps and SS Guard Formations

Inspektion der SS-VT	Inspectorate of SS-VT
Kavallerie	Cavalry
Kreis	Local Council
Kriesgebiete	Area Districts
Kreisleiter	County Leader
Kreispolizeibehörde	City/County Police Authority
Kriminalpolizei (Kripo)	Criminal Police
Kristallnacht	'Night of the Broken Glass'
Lebensborn	'Fount of Life'
Lebensraum	'Living Space'
Nationalsozialistische Deutsche Arbeiterpartei (NSDAP)	National Socialist German Workers Party
Oberabschnitt	Main District
Oberbefehlshaber des Heeres	Commander-in-Chief of the Army
Oberführer	Senior Leader
Obergruppenführer	Senior Group Leader
Oberkommando des Heeres (OKH)	Army High Command
Oberst	Colonel
Oberster SA-Führer	Supreme SA Leader
Oberstgruppenführer	Supreme Group Leader
Obersturmbannführer	Senior Storm Unit Leader
Obersturmfürer	Senior Storm Leader
Ornungspolizei (Orpo)	Order Police
Panzergrenadier	Motorized infantry, armoured infantry
Reichsarbeitsdienst (RAD)	Reich Labour Service
Reichsführer-SS (RFSS)	Reich Leader SS
Reichsgau	Administrative district created in areas annexed by Nazi Germany
Reichskommissar	Reich Commissioner
Reichskommissar für die Festigung des Deutschen Volkstums (RKFDV)	Reich Commissioner for the Strengthening of the German Nation

Reichsleiter	Reich Leader
Reichsministerium für die besetzen Ostgetbiete	Reich Ministry for the Occupied Eastern Territories
Reichssicherheitshauptampt (RSHA)	Reich Main Security Office
Reichswehr	Reich Defence Forces
Reiterstandarte	(SS) Cavalry Regiment
Rotte	(SS) File
Rottenführer	Section Leader
Rückwärtiges Gebiet	Rear Area
Schutzmannschaften der Ordnungspolizei	Detachments of Order Police
Schutzpolizei	Protection Police
Schutzstaffel (SS)	Security Squad/Protection Squadron
schwere Panzerabteilung	Heavy Tank Battalion
Sicherheitsdienst (SD)	Security Service
Sicherheitshauptamt	Main Security Office
Sicherheitspolizei (Sipo)	Security Police
SS-Abschnitt	SS District
SS-Amt	SS Office
SS-Feldgendarmerie	SS Field Police
SS-Führungshauptamt (SS-FHA)	SS Main Operational Office
SS-Hauptamt (SS-HA)	SS Main Office
SS-Kreigsberichter	SS 'War Correspondents'
SS-Oberabschnitt Führer	SS Leader of the Main Districts
SS-Oberführerbereiche	SS Regional Command Areas
SS-Personalhauptamt	SS Personnel Department
SS-Polizei Regiment	SS Police Regiment
SS-Rasse- und Siedlungshauptamt (RuSHA)	SS Race and Settlement Main Office
SS-Totenkopfverbände (SS-TV)	SS Death's Head formation
SS-Truppenübungsplätze	SS troop Training Areas
SS- und Polizeiführer (SSPF)	SS and Police Leader

SS-Verfügungstruppe (SS-VT)	SS Dispositional Troops
SS-Wirtschafts- und Verwaltungshauptamt (WVHA)	SS Economics and Administrative Department
Stabschef	Chief of Staff
Stabshauptamt	Staff Headquarters
Stabswache	Headquarters Guard
Standarte	SS Regiment
Standardtenführer	Regiment Leader
Stoßtrupp	Shock Troops
Studiengesellschaft für Geistesurgeschichte Deutsches Ahnenerbe	The Society for Research into the Spiritual Roots of Germany's Ancestral Heritage
Sturmabteilung (SA)	Assault Detachment/Storm Detachment
Sturmbahn	Storm Unit
Sturmbannführer	Storm Unit Leader
Sturmbataillone	Assault Battalions
Sturmbrigade	Storm Brigade
Technische Nothilfe	Technical Emergency Service
Thule Gesellschaft	Thule Society
Trupp	Platoon
Truppenamt	Troop Office
Untersturmführer	Junior Storm Leader
Volksdeutsche	Ethnic Germans
Volksgerichtshof	People's Court
Volkssturm	People's Militia/Home Army
Waffen-SS	Armed SS
Wehrkreis	Military District
Wehrmacht	(German) Armed Forces
Zug	Platoon

INDEX

References to illustrations are shown in **bold**.